Take charge of
the Future

Embrace the
journey

Andrew
Brunell

 FriesenPress

One Printers Way
Altona, MB R0G 0B0
Canada

www.friesenpress.com

ISBN
978-1-03-915602-9 (Hardcover)
978-1-03-915601-2 (Paperback)
978-1-03-915603-6 (eBook)

1. BUSINESS & ECONOMICS, STRATEGIC PLANNING

Distributed to the trade by The Ingram Book Company

TAKE CHARGE
OF THE FUTURE

*Using the Power of Scenarios to
Drive Strategy and Performance*

Arden Brummell, PhD

ABSTRACT

Take Charge of the Future weaves together a description of the scenarios-to-strategy planning process with a personal journey of learning that provides a wealth of examples and insights for chief executive leaders, board members, planning directors, and practitioners guiding organizations facing increased uncertainty and complexity. The process of creating scenarios and developing strategy provides a powerful vehicle for strategic conversation that builds shared understanding, leads to better informed decision-making, and enhances performance. The book describes how to effectively implement a scenarios-to-strategy process within a strategic management model. Numerous examples illuminate key points and provide snapshots of how the future was viewed at that point in history.

ABOUT THE AUTHOR

Arden Brummell is the managing director of Scenarios to Strategy Inc. with forty years' experience as an academic, planner, and consultant. He has led over one hundred strategic scenario planning projects in Canada, the US, Europe, Africa, and South America. His experience includes work with major international companies, non-profits, and governments. His initial exposure to scenario planning was with Shell Canada and later Royal Dutch Shell in London. Leaving Shell, he established Global Business Network Canada, affiliated with GBN, and later cofounded Scenarios to Strategy Inc., emphasizing the need to systematically link scenarios to strategy. In addition to his work with organizations helping them to think about the future and manage strategically, he is an avid golfer, wine-maker, and wine drinker. He has a PhD from McMaster University in Hamilton, Canada. He is married and lives in Calgary, Canada.

TABLE
OF CONTENTS

INTRODUCTION

In the late 1960s, the planning group within Royal Dutch Shell did an analysis of the global oil market to the year 2000. No one believed it. Pierre Wack, head of Group Planning, decided there had to be another way of developing perspectives on the future. After a global search (nice to have the budget) he came back with an answer: scenarios.

The first Shell scenario work in the early 1970s focused on the rising power of national governments, prospects of nationalization, and potential restrictions on supply. Coupled with that was the steady rise in oil demand. For decades, oil demand had been increasing at 6 percent to 7 percent annually. This was the norm; this was the assumption. But what did it really mean?

A critical question in developing any outlook of the future is to overcome the inertia of the present. How can we get decision makers to open their minds to change? How do we get them to ask the question, what happens if our current assumptions are wrong? Wack created a simple scenario. He projected the growth in demand from 1970 to 1980 on the basis of existing assumptions of future growth. Then he presented the results in a distinct way. If current demand continued to grow at existing rates, then by 1980 the global oil industry would need to open a new refinery every day of the year.

The impact was profound. The Committee of Managing Directors at Royal Dutch Shell immediately realized that was not going to happen. Suddenly, they were open to new ideas. Something had to give. Price, which had hovered near $3 per barrel for years, would be the likely candidate. And, as the results of the oil embargo in 1973 confirmed, price was indeed the item that would give.

There are many lessons from this simple story. Most important is that the value of scenario thinking is to open minds, to create understanding of a broader range of possible future outcomes, and to enhance the ability to adapt. Opening minds increases the ability to adapt to change. This thinking is credited with Shell's response to the 1973 oil embargo. Shell did not predict the details of the embargo, but the scenario work is believed to have opened perspectives such that Shell's response was more measured and forward looking than many of the other oil majors, and ultimately, a key to Shell's expansion from the smallest to one of the largest of the Seven Sisters.[1]

Other insights were to follow. The importance of scenarios as a vehicle for shaping mental models was not fully understood for some years and was probably not articulated until the late 1970s. A second learning was the realization that scenarios focused on uncertainties. In the late 1980s, Kees van der Heijden would clarify the concept of irreducible uncertainties—variables in which the range of uncertainty cannot be reduced by further analysis. Scenarios were not intended to predict the future but to understand and embrace uncertainty and the range of future possible outcomes. Strategically, a range of future outcomes allows the consequences of major decisions to be analyzed across the different scenarios. This was the key connection between scenarios and strategy. Scenarios provided a framework for evaluating the potential consequences of a given strategy across scenarios to test the robustness of the strategy. Much more on this later. But suffice to note that this was the exact opposite of forecasting, which was designed to reduce uncertainty to the most likely outcome. As the refinery story suggests, putting all your eggs in one basket, or forecast, is dangerous.

The next major step in scenario planning was the methodology developed at Global Business Network (GNB), led by Jay Ogilvy and Peter Schwarz. Scenario development in Shell was not a well-documented process. Scenarios were developed by a small number in Group Planning, and individuals learned the approach more or less by osmosis. GBN was the first to develop and publicize a structured methodology to develop scenarios. Peter Schwarz's 1991 book, *The Art of the Long View*, outlined an approach to developing scenarios focused on identifying critical uncertainties. Moreover, the process involved working through a series of steps in a workshop setting. The central logic that scenarios were focused on identifying and understanding uncertainties was crystallized by the methodology created by GBN.

The last major step in the evolution of scenario planning was connecting scenarios to strategy. This is less well defined. The first major step in connecting scenarios to decision-making involved two ideas developed by Kees van der Heijden. One was the seven questions; the other was the management implications workshop. The role of the seven questions was to elicit input from senior managers who did not participate directly in developing the scenarios. The questions provided useful information on management's perspectives, created a direct link to management, and built management support for the scenarios. The management implications workshop, first used with the 1989 Shell scenarios, engaged management teams by asking the simple question: What are the implications of the scenarios for your business? It

---

1   The Seven Sisters was a common reference for the seven major oil companies that dominated the global industry in the 1960s and 1970s. These included Exxon, Chevron, BP, Mobile, Shell, Total, and Texaco.

evoked great conversation, embedded the scenarios in the minds of senior managers, and created a mental mindset open to new ideas and a willingness to act.

While this was a first step in creating strategic thinking, the process was not well structured. In working first with Lee van Horn at Palomar Consulting and then with Greg MacGillivray at Scenarios to Strategy, a structured process to link the creative work of scenarios with the more focused work of strategy development and implementation was developed. The process identifies the implications of the scenarios, strategic thrusts, or focus areas, for the organization, goals, strategies, and actions. The analysis linking the scenarios to strategy can vary depending on the level of senior management involved, the objectives of the project, and the expected role of the facilitators. Describing a process to link scenarios to strategy is a major aspect of this work.

The purpose of this book is to explore the logic and application of scenarios in strategic planning. Scenarios are alternative descriptions of the future. They are stories of how the future could unfold. They may take the form of narratives or bullet points in a PowerPoint presentation. At the very least they describe how a future could unfold and what the eventual outcome will look like. The most important aspect is that the stories—and there must be more than one—diverge, creating a range of future outcomes that challenge our thinking to the limits of our believability.

The key value of scenarios is that they open minds to new possibilities, creating learning. Scenarios are not predictions. The intent is to enlighten, not predict. While forecasts converge, scenarios diverge. In this way, with a range of future possible outcomes, scenarios provide a context for evaluating different strategies across different futures. Instead of strategies for a single future, scenarios explicitly surface and build understanding of strategic risks across a range of futures.

These simple definitions may appear dull when expressed in such dry terms, but if you love exploring new ideas, building challenging narratives, and creating aha! moments of learning and insight, then working with others in developing scenarios and strategies is a truly fulfilling journey. I have led over one hundred strategic scenario projects and have never been bored.

Scenarios are stories. This is my story. I want to pass on my personal learnings from forty years of scenario planning, including a wealth of personal anecdotes, lessons from specific scenario projects, and a description of the methodology. My intent is to use numerous stories from my experience to provide insights into the value and application of scenario planning. The book covers the logic (why), definition (what), and value (what for) of scenarios, details the methodology (how) of scenario development step by step, and outlines an approach to developing strategies from the scenarios to implementation. The connection from scenarios to strategic decisions is the ultimate objective of scenario planning. This can take many forms, but without that link, the value of the exercise is greatly diminished. Examples from real scenario exercises are used extensively to demonstrate key points. Sometimes the stories may be long; that is why this is a book. Finally, I reflect on my experiences and learnings over the decades from my initiation with Shell both in Canada and Group Planning with Royal Dutch Shell, to my work as a consultant, ending with a discussion of major themes and ideas from four decades of thinking and helping others think about the future.

This is a personal book about my journey over four decades of learning in creating scenarios to inform strategy. Each set of scenarios in that journey provides insight on thinking about the future at that time. Each is a now a memory of the future, an earlier title of this book.[2] I wanted to share my journey and pass on any wisdom that I may have gained. I hope you enjoy the read, learn something along the way, and gain insights into your work or life.

Who might enjoy and learn from reading about this journey? All leaders, including chief executives, board members, and senior managers responsible for the strategic management of their organizations need to incorporate thinking about the future into strategic decisions. The scenarios-to-strategy process described in the book provides such a model. A key element of the model is an approach to identifying strategic risk. This should be part of the due diligence of every board member and CEO responsible for the long-term success of their organization. This applies to public, private, non-profit, and government organizations.

A particular focus is on planners responsible for planning processes. As I emphasize in the book, planners should never plan. Their function is to ensure the process works and support managers in creating their plans. As well as designing the process, a key role is to create vehicles for strategic conversation. This is an important ingredient in learning organizations. Want to learn more? Read on.

Practitioners of scenario and strategy development should benefit from the detailed descriptions of how scenarios are developed and how to connect the scenarios to strategy. There are insights on what to do and what not to do with numerous examples to draw on for clarity and insight.

Finally, this book will be of interest to history buffs. *Take Charge of the Future* provides insight on the historical context at the time. What were we experiencing during the oil price collapse in 1986? What were we thinking about the future of the Soviet Union in 1989? What were we thinking about the future of coal in 2005? What were we anticipating about the impacts of climate change in 2010? I was there. I was part of the thinking at the time. I have touched on many of these events. I hope you will find them interesting and insightful as you read this book.

---

2   The term "memories of the future" was first used by Ingvar (1985) who noted that the functions of memory and imagination were located in the same area of the brain. Chermack (2011) notes that scenarios create a "memory" that can serve as an actual experience so that individuals can "make sense of their experience, linking the past to the present to the future." I use the term memories of the future to describe what the perspectives on the future were at that point in time.

PART 1
INTEGRATION AND DIFFERENTIATION

A key objective of the book is to provide an integrated strategic management model that links the building of scenarios to the development of strategies as part of a strategic planning process. The discrete steps in the building of scenarios are well developed. A distinct set of steps in a process linking the scenarios to strategy development is less developed. Chapter 1 defines and outlines the elements in the strategic management model, specifically, what scenarios and strategy are and how they link into strategic management.

Another key objective is to understand the logic of scenarios, how they create value and contribute to decision-making. How do scenarios differ from forecasting? How do they relate to important concepts such as strategic conversations and learning organizations? Chapter 2 explores these connections and differences.

CHAPTER 1
A STRATEGIC
MANAGEMENT MODEL

SCENARIOS

Scenarios are stories describing a range of different futures. Typically, they describe a logical path, over time, leading to a distinct future. They are defined by a number of key characteristics.

1. Multiple: Scenarios always involve more than one description of the future. Each should expose a different logic of how the future could unfold. For example, one scenario might explore the effects of disruptive technologies on an industry. Another might focus on the effects of cyclical markets. Yet a third might focus on rising populism and political factors. The value of scenarios comes from exploring different logics, not varying parameters in a model in which the underlying logic is constant. Further, learning comes from exploring and understanding the differences. One of the most powerful questions—and all learning comes from questions—is: What is the difference between scenario X and scenario Y?

2. Qualitative: Our focus is on qualitative as opposed to quantitative scenarios. This emerges from the fact that scenarios, as we use the term, focus on irreducible uncertainties. The world is complex and uncertain. No amount of analysis can reduce the range of uncertainty or define the distribution of risk for key variables. Hence, these variables cannot be quantified from a statistical perspective. More pragmatically, this focuses our attention on identifying and understanding complex structural change—discontinuities or rapid, abrupt changes—rather than evolutionary change. While evolutionary change may be important in one or more scenarios, a powerful aspect

of scenarios is that they are flexible in exploring disruptions to the current order. Scenarios challenge us to think the unthinkable. Indeed, scenarios are often most valuable when they explicitly ask the question, How could the future look dramatically different from today?

3. Objective: Scenarios can be objective or normative. Our focus is on objective scenarios that strive to describe what could happen and not on what we would like to happen. We are interested in the range of possible futures and not visionary or normative scenarios. Such scenarios have value in specific contexts, but they are not the focus of this work. In their most powerful form, scenarios are believable and compelling stories of how the future could unfold. They are plausible, internally consistent descriptions. Plausibility is a challenging concept. On the one hand we want to push the limits of believability—think the unthinkable. At the same time, if a story becomes science fiction, then no one will pay attention. We need to push the limits of believability to broaden thinking so we can gain new insights—like the refinery-building example from Shell—yet if we go beyond the limit of believability, then we lose credibility and any chance of learning. Good scenarios are plausible and challenging.

4. Focused: Broad scenarios on the future of the world are great to create but are of little strategic value. Focused scenarios, by contrast, are limited in their scope but of great value in strategy development. The process of developing scenarios described in this book begins with the identification of a focal question that highlights the key strategic issue facing the organization. For example, if the issue facing a company is growth, then the focal question might be simply, How does Company X accelerate growth in the next ten years? This identifies both the issue and time horizon. This focuses discussion on factors that will affect growth. It ensures relevance and precludes discussions of, for example, global events that are irrelevant to the key question. We undoubtedly overuse the word "focus," but it is at the heart of scenarios and strategy.

5. Open-ended: Scenarios are outlines of the future. They are not precise. This means that they are never closed. New ideas can be added and the logic expanded. This is powerful because it encourages new audiences to add ideas to the scenarios. Scenario development is a powerful learning experience for those directly involved in the process. Their open-endedness, however, means they can also be a powerful learning experience for those not involved in the process. Of course, scenarios need closure at some point, but their power to engage much wider audiences means they are stories that keep on giving, limited only by the imagination of those using them.

STRATEGY

Scenarios are most valuable when developed within a strategic framework. Scenarios are not an end in themselves but a means to an end: strategy development and implementation. Scenarios are a learning experience, as emphasized by Ramirez and Wilkinson (2016). That is a major aspect of scenarios, but if learning is not transformed into strategies and action, the value is diminished. In short, learning is not enough.

Strategy has numerous definitions. For our purpose, strategy is a plan to achieve a future outcome. This might involve a series of actions to increase market share, enhance key technologies, reduce cost, enhance growth, or improve environmental performance. The key is focus. Allocating resources to a specific strategy to achieve a desired outcome means other possible strategies are not pursued. This is difficult but essential, and all too often ignored.

As an example, I facilitated a meeting of a senior management team to identify key issues that the company needed to address for success in the next year. We narrowed the list to three strategic issues, identified objectives, and assigned responsibilities. One year later I had the opportunity to return, and I raised the question of how they had done in addressing the issues. The answer from a vice-president was, "We didn't address any of them. The president decided to restructure the company in June." Restructuring is a highly visible intervention within control of the company. Management looks decisive. The strategic results are usually more problematic. An act of desperation, perhaps?

In any case, the key point is that developing and executing strategies is very difficult. It requires discipline to focus on what is most important rather than what is easy. It demands innovation and creativity. It demands leadership. Scenarios are a form of strategic thinking that enhances learning and supports creative strategy development. It cannot ensure discipline and leadership, but it is a great starting point for innovative thinking and strategy development.

STRATEGIC PLANNING

Scenario planning is most effective as part of a strategic management process. Figure 1 outlines a simple but powerful strategic management model in which strategic scanning of the external environment provides a basis for strategy development, strategy implementation, and performance management. Over time, changes in the external environment and internal processes lead to feedback that may require adjustments in understanding the external world or internal implementation of the existing strategy.

Figure 1–Strategic Management Model

Integrated Strategic Management

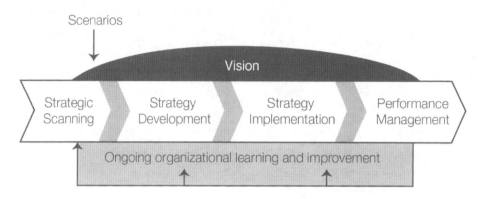

Scenarios are a specific tool in the strategic scanning process. Scanning includes an analysis of the current external environment (social, technological, economic, environmental, and political factors), the current and emerging competitive environment (including actions of competitors and changes in regulation, as appropriate to the organization), as well as perspectives on the future. Altogether this may be referred to as the external environment or business environment.[3] All planning requires perspective on the future, whether implicitly assumed or explicitly articulated. Scenarios specifically articulate a range of perspectives on how the future business environment could unfold.

The scenarios thus provide a context for developing and analyzing a range of potential strategies. The scenarios may stimulate thinking on a number of new strategies or a context for evaluating existing strategies. Scenarios provide the context for asking the question: If Strategy X is pursued, what are the risks and rewards if Scenario A occurs, or Scenario B occurs, or Scenario C occurs, et cetera? Repeat for Strategy Y, Z, et cetera. In this way, the value and robustness of each strategy is analyzed in the face of the uncertainty of the future.

Following strategy development, the analysis should focus on a small number of strategies for implementation. Good strategy is often undermined by poor implementation. As a result, the implementation needs to be monitored and updated. Performance management involves monitoring both the implementation of the strategy and performance of the organization. A common tool for evaluating

---

3   We refer to this as the business environment, but it is not meant to be limited to business. For governments and non-profits, external environment, meaning external to the organization, may be a more appropriate description.

performance is the balanced scorecard, which can be adapted for both managing the strategy implementation and monitoring organization performance.

A key part of the model is the feedback loops to strategy. One learning loop involves changes in performance that require adjustments in implementation of the strategy. This is a management loop designed to adjust the implementation of strategy as conditions change. A second business loop provides feedback on changing external conditions. This feedback may alter the original scenario conditions and expectations or the original analysis in the development of the strategies. While the management loop is an adjustment to existing strategy, the business loop can challenge the overall strategy structure. The latter may require updated scenario thinking.

The focus of this book is on scenarios and strategy development leading to implementation and performance management. The scenario-planning approach emphasizes that scenarios are most effective and valuable as part of a strategic planning process in which scenarios are an initial phase in a larger strategic learning conversation. This process is critical to sound strategic planning. Don Michael (1973)[4] initially articulated the insight that planning is learning. Equally, all learning comes from conversation. Hence, the power of scenarios is their role in strategic conversation—a dominant theme throughout the book.

---

4   We use the format of name and date to reference ideas from other authors. The references are listed at the end of book.

CHAPTER 2
LOGIC OF SCENARIOS

However good our futures research may be, we shall never be able to escape from the ultimate dilemma that our knowledge is about the past, and all our decisions are about the future.
—Ian Morrison

DECISIONS AND EXPECTATIONS

Consider a couple buying their first house. They need to not only choose a specific property but also finance the purchase. In financing, they have a choice between a variable-interest-rate mortgage or a fixed-rate term mortgage. The first varies with the current interest rate. The second is fixed for an extended period. Which should they choose? It depends on their expectations of future interest rates. If they believe that rates will fall, then they should choose the variable rate, wait until rates have bottomed, and then lock into a longer-term fixed-rate mortgage.

On the other hand, if they expect interest rates to rise in the future, then they should take the fixed-rate mortgage and lock in payments. Of course, they do not know if interest rates will rise or fall in the future. They are uncertain. They can, however, evaluate the risks and rewards of different decisions and outcomes. For example, they can evaluate the financial risk if they take a fixed mortgage and rates fall or vice versa. Articulating different future outcomes allows them to evaluate the consequence of different decisions. The future outcome might be beneficial or not, but the decision would have been made understanding the risks involved. That is the key.

What are the lessons from this simple decision process? There are three components to the decision. First, there must be a choice. If there are no options, then the choice is predetermined. Second, there are expectations of how the future will unfold. In this case these are articulated as interest rates either rising or falling. Third, there are future consequences of the decision.

Ultimately, the purpose of scenarios is to improve strategic decisions. In the decision process, scenarios are explicitly focused on future expectations. They are stories of how the future could unfold. They provide an articulated description of a range of future paths so that the consequences of current decisions can be analyzed and evaluated. All too often assumptions about the future are not explicitly articulated and decisions are made without much consideration of what could happen and how different future paths could dramatically alter the consequences or outcomes of the decision. In other words, without a good understanding of future expectations, decisions will be made without fully understanding the strategic risks involved.

UNDERSTANDING THE FUTURE

As the house financing example indicates, the consequences of decisions depend on the future. A simple but profound statement: today is the first day of the rest of my life. The past is important, particularly as it provides insights into how the future might unfold. But the future is everything.

How do we develop understanding of the future and how it could unfold? There are two broad approaches: forecasting and scenarios.

Forecasting

The thrust of forecasting is to predict the future. For example, sophisticated models have been developed for predicting the economy based on quantitatively defined and empirically tested relationships. Supply, demand, and price relationships can be empirically defined based on long-term data analysis. A key number derived from this type of analysis might be, using an oil example, the price elasticity of demand. In other words, if the price of oil goes up, what is the impact on demand? Theory and empirical evidence confirm that a rise in price leads to a fall in demand. The question is how much and how fast. This responsiveness of demand to price is called the price elasticity of demand. There is a similar price elasticity of supply. If the price rises, how much will supply increase?

These are basic relationships in economics. The thrust of the modelling is to refine these types of relationships to make predictions. The underlying philosophy is that if we know enough through empirical analysis and refinement of the parameters determining the relationships, we can reduce variance to zero and make accurate predictions. The thrust is to minimize uncertainty.

Such an approach works well in relatively stable environments, where all key variables can be quantified and interpretation is open to learning. A stable environment means past trends used to calibrate relationships do not fluctuate outside past ranges. For example, rising incomes lead to more demand for cars and trucks. That relationship may be stable for a long period, allowing prediction of auto sales from forecasts of economic growth and individual incomes.

But consider another example. A fall in oil prices leads to a predictable fall in oil supply. In 2014, OPEC[5] orchestrated a dramatic fall in oil prices from approximately $100 a barrel to less than $40 a barrel. This fall in prices should take some time to reduce the supply because, historically, oil supply is price inelastic. In other words, it takes time for companies to stop investing and let oil wells deplete. Similarly, it takes time for supply to respond to a price increase. This relationship has a long history. But things have changed. Hydraulic fracturing, known as fracking, has dramatically altered the structure of supply and demand. The traditional long lags from price change to supply response have been slashed. The time from an oil well being drilled in the US, stimulated with fracking to increase flow, and brought into production has been reduced from years to months. The elasticity of supply (I know these economic terms can be boring but bear with me) has increased markedly. Now, much to the discomfort of OPEC, a small price increase leads to a rapid increase in shale oil production thereby limiting the price increase.[6]

Now a long but revealing story. What does this mean for forecasting? The reality is that in this example, the industry experienced structural change such that past relationships no longer held. Modelling tends to smoothly project the future. It works well if changes are incremental and within the range of variations of the past. Rapid structural change, however, makes modelling extremely difficult. Since rapid structural change is—arguably—the greatest strategic risk an organization can face, forecasting that is unable to identify such risks is a major risk itself.

A second factor is the effect of intangible or unquantifiable variables. Incorporating variables such as technological change, new competition, social values, or political developments is difficult in forecasting. Consider the example of the evolution of social values to the environment and specifically to greenhouse gas emissions in the context of climate change. The villain has become carbon dioxide (CO_2) emissions. This dark cloud, at least for coal and petroleum companies, has been on the horizon for a long time. By the mid 2000s, there was a common consensus that carbon penalties in one form or another were (almost) inevitable. (In scenario jargon this is called

---

5   The Organization of Petroleum Export Countries (OPEC) is a cartel originally of thirteen countries led by Saudi Arabia to manage the price of crude oil by managing the supply. OPEC has traditionally controlled approximately one third of global oil production. More recently OPEC+ has included agreements with Russia in setting quotas for production.

6   More recently, climate change initiatives to restrict oil use have altered the incentive for companies to increase production as prices rise to focus on profitability and return to shareholders. This reduces supply elasticity.

a predetermined variable.) Whether via a carbon tax or cap-and-trade system[7], the result would be a price penalty on carbon emissions.

Seemingly this would be easy to incorporate in quantitative analysis. Coal companies, most impacted by carbon penalties, did analyses to evaluate the competitiveness of coal in power plants versus natural gas or alternatives such as wind or solar. They could evaluate coal's price competitiveness at carbon prices of, say, $30, $50, or $100 per tonne of $CO2$. The economics remained healthy even at seemingly outrageous carbon costs. The result was an industry optimistic that carbon would not hinder plans for new power stations. By the mid 2000s, plans for new coal-fired power plants exceeded one hundred projects in the US. These included plants about to break ground to faint future projects barely defined. The social momentum for restrictions on greenhouse gas (GHG) emissions, however, was growing. The final word came from Wall Street. Financiers said we don't know what the costs are for future carbon liabilities, and we are not going to finance any new coal power plants. All plans ceased immediately and have never been revived. This experience reveals how difficult it is to incorporate social values into quantitative analyses and how uncertainty can emerge from unexpected directions. In short, intangible variables are difficult to model and undermine the ability of forecasting to accurately predict the future.[8]

Finally, a key challenge of forecasting is falling in love with the prediction. Forecasting and scenarios are both intended to be learning exercises. All too often— and this is true of scenarios as well as forecasts—we fall in love with the result. We begin to believe what we have predicted. This was driven home to me in a scenario project I worked on in Shell Canada in the 1980s.

My colleagues and I had developed two scenarios and within the logic of the scenarios generated representative numbers to describe key variables over time. These included numbers on gross domestic product (GDP), exchange rate, inflation, energy demand, et cetera. Were these intelligent estimates plausible, or were they completely misguided and inconsistent? To investigate, we contracted a major economic consulting firm with a sophisticated (3,000-plus equations) econometric model of the Canadian economy to run our scenario numbers through their model. In pushing the envelope, some of our numbers were clearly extreme. For example,

7   A cap-and-trade system allocates greenhouse gas (GHG) emission credits to major emitters such as power utilities, cement plants, and other industrial companies. The overall number of credits is lowered over time forcing companies to reduce their emissions or buy credits from other companies that have a surplus. Selling and buying credits creates a market price on carbon emissions. As credits are successively limited over time, the price of carbon credits will increase if the ability of companies to reduce their emissions is less than the reduction in credits. In this way, unlike a tax set by government, the market for credits sets the price of carbon.

8   This story demonstrates the role of intangible variables in understanding the future. The story may also be an analogy for other industries. Is a similar story of banks restricting access to capital an emerging challenge for the oil and gas industry?

one scenario entertained the idea that the Canada/US exchange rate could fall to 50 cents. Perhaps this was beyond extreme. Sure enough, despite best efforts the model could not come close to replicating a 50-cent Canadian dollar. The question then was: Was our thinking wrong, or was the model calibrated from the past unable to project the possible range of events in the future? In this case, the modelling was an excellent complement to the scenarios because it caused us to rethink the logic of the scenarios and contributed to our learning.

The interesting part of this story, however, was the reaction of one of the modellers. A young economist who had done much of the work was part of the meeting in which the results were discussed. Mostly, he was silent during our discussions in deference to a more senior consultant leading the meeting. The discussion ranged back and forth as we challenged and discussed the results. Finally, as we were discussing some extreme result, the young economist interjected in obvious frustration that we were wrong. He had done the analysis and the scenarios were both wrong. The right answer was: He was so convinced that his model and analysis were so accurate that all this scenario stuff was wrong. He believed wholeheartedly that he knew what was going to happen. He fell in love with his result. There was no room for other results. He forgot that modelling was as much about learning as predicting.

Scenarios

A scenario adopts a different perspective. The underlying philosophy is that the future is highly uncertain and inherently unpredictable. Instead of focusing on reducing uncertainty and developing a single prediction, often a consensus, the emphasis is on identifying and exploring the uncertainties that lead to a range of different futures. The question shifts from what is most likely to what is the range of possible futures. The shift is from convergence to divergence, from single forecast to multiple scenarios, from incremental change to disruptive change, from cyclical change to structural change. Scenarios highlight uncertainty and force consideration of futures that are significantly, even radically different from today and today's expectations. Scenario thinking encourages thinking the unthinkable. Scenario thinking does not try to reduce uncertainty but to embrace it.

As a result, scenarios are most appropriate during periods of turbulence and uncertainty. Figure 2 intentionally portrays the sense of complexity and unpredictability that seems to describe the current global situation. Multiple actors are interacting along a range of dimensions in complex and contradictory ways. The diagram emphasizes change and confusion.

Figure 2—Global Uncertainty

The Future is Complex and Unpredictable

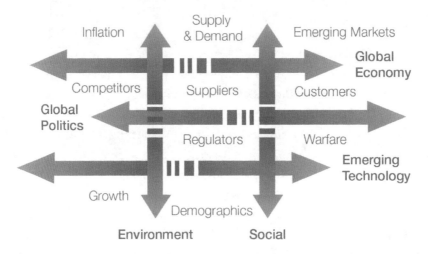

The perspective of rapid change, complexity, and unpredictability has been a dominant theme for the past half–century. Since the 1950s, each decade has been seen, then and in hindsight, as a period of turbulence and instability. The emergence of the Cold War in the 1950s, the Vietnam War and social revolution of the 1960s, the oil embargo and hyperinflation of the 1970s, the arms race in the 1980s, the dot.com boom and Balkan massacres of the 1990s, 911, Afghanistan, Iraq, and devastating wars and hunger, and the Great Recession in the 2000s, followed by Arab Spring, civil war in Syria, the refugee crises in the last decade, and more recently Covid-19, and the Russian invasion of Ukraine are all periods of uncertainty. In short, perception of the world as one of volatility, turbulence, and change is ongoing.

The concept of disruptions is most commonly associated with rapid technological change. Examples are numerous: from steam locomotives to diesel and electric, from film to digital pictures, from telephones to mobile phones, from coal to wind power. While these seem like transitions between stable platforms, they could also be peaks in a process of ongoing change.

Change can take several forms. Change can be seen as continuous or transitional. With transitional change, change is seen as a shift from one relatively stable system to another relatively stable system—jumping from one platform to another. With continuous change, change is seen as ongoing without periods of stability. The rate of change may be variable but there is no concept of a stable end-state. Both can embrace the concept of discontinuities—rapid disruptive changes in the system.

What makes these changes significant is reflected in the impact on business models. Walmart's advanced logistics (and other factors) destroyed the underlying business model of other department stores—but it took a long time. Now Amazon is a threat to all traditional brick-and-mortar establishments. The provision of government services has changed radically with the internet and the explosion of e-government. Income tax returns, for example, are dominated by electronic rather than paper submissions.

Whether continuous or transitional, such changes are structural rather than cyclical. The annual ebb and flow of a river is cyclical. A change in the path of a river is structural. It is the structural changes in a system that are the most difficult to deal with since they require much more challenging and innovative strategic responses. It is not doing more or less of an activity but something different. A scenarios approach can—and should—explicitly explore potential discontinuities and structural change. This is difficult in forecasting.

A further aspect of the challenge in understanding the future is the nature of the variables. As noted previously, many variables are intangible and thus hard to quantify. Technological change, social values, political trends, and environmental sustainability fall into this category. While difficult to incorporate in quantitative models, scenarios are open to discussions of such variables and able to incorporate them into the logic of the scenarios.

The concept of intangibility is further complicated by the need to understand the social context that provides meaning to a situation. There is a growing understanding that events are context dependent. The sovereign Brexiter does not understand the rule-based Eurocrat—or vice versa. They view reality from different contexts. The free-wheeling Texan who is used to wide-open spaces does not understand the social formalities necessary in crowded Tokyo. The cultural context is different. Similarly, trying to understand why someone is walking down a street is unclear until they stop by the mailbox and put in a letter. Context is important. The meaning of an event needs to be placed in the social and cultural context in which it arises. Such context-dependent understanding is difficult in forecasting but critical to scenarios.

A further factor differentiating forecasting and scenario development is time. Predicting tomorrow's weather is much easier than next week's weather. The demand for electricity next year is more reliably predictable than five or ten years ahead. Despite discontinuities and structural changes, systems have continuity and momentum. Large energy systems, for example, change slowly. Hence, predictions are generally much more reliable in the short than the long term.

Finally, a common feature of forecasting and scenario development is learning. With forecasts, the focus is on a single future, albeit with many sensitivities, which tends to undermine an exploration of underlying assumptions and structure. With such questions muted, learning is limited. With scenarios, in contrast, the existence of multiple narratives explicitly raises important questions that foster insights and learning. All understanding is about differences.

Multiple stories immediately highlight the question: How are scenarios A, B, C, and D different from each other? Such questions can lead to important insights. For example, two scenarios ostensibly differentiated by technological differences, may, on reflection, provide insight that the extent and role of technological change depends on social perceptions and acceptance of the value of the technology. Profound? Perhaps not. But the question opens a new perspective on the factors shaping the future. Scenarios explicitly focus on differences. Understanding differences sparks learning.

Scenarios versus Forecasting

To summarize, forecasting and scenarios provide two different perspectives on understanding the future. The forecaster believes the future is predictable, builds consensus around the most likely future, measures success in terms of accuracy of the prediction, and thus focuses on a single, optimal response or strategy. Forecasts focus on reducing uncertainty.

The scenarist, in contrast, believes the future is inherently uncertain and unpredictable, develops a number of scenarios to capture a range of future outcomes, defines success in terms of insights learned, and thus focuses on robust strategies that consider the risks involved. Scenarios embrace uncertainty. These are contrasted in Figure 3.

Figure 3—Two Perspectives on the Future

Two Perspectives on the Future

All decisions are based on expectations

The Scenarist	vs.	The Forecaster
• Future Uncertain		• Future Predictable
• Range of Futures		• Consensus Future
• Insight		• Accuracy
• Robust Strategies		• Optimal Strategy

Both perspectives are valuable in understanding the future. Forecasting is most relevant and valuable in developing future expectations when the situation is relatively stable with well-defined variables over a short time-horizon. Scenarios are most relevant and valuable when the situation is highly uncertain with numerous intangible variables over a long-time frame.

In general (but not exclusively), there is a sense that the range of future possible outcomes increases with time. The divergence of future outcomes, intuitively, is greater with a ten-year outlook than a five-year time horizon. The contrast in the application of forecasting versus scenarios is shown in Figure 4. There is high predictability in the short term. Forecasting is appropriate. Uncertainty increases in the longer term. Scenarios are appropriate. As Peter Schwarz captured brilliantly in the title of his book, scenarios are the art of the long view.

Figure 4–Time Frames: Forecasts Versus Scenarios

Predictability & Uncertainty

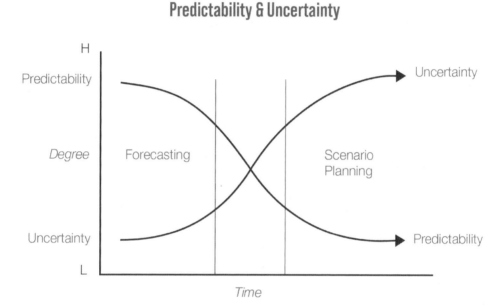

VALUE OF SCENARIOS

The value of scenarios may be divided between the value of the product—the rational—and the value of the process—the intuitive.

The value of the product—the scenario stories—stems from the logic of the scenarios in strategy development. As in the story of the young couple buying a house and deciding on a mortgage, the strategy depends on the choice, future expectations, and ultimately the consequences. Scenarios articulate future expectations. They provide a landscape of the future—a future-scape—on which to develop and test different strategic decisions. The scenarios are valuable in generating and analyzing the new strategies as well as existing or preconceived strategies.

The analysis or testing of strategies across the scenarios provides insight into the outcomes or consequences of pursuing each of the strategies. This analysis surfaces risks and rewards. The question is straightforward: If strategy X is undertaken and the future turns out like scenario A, what are the potential gains or losses? Some strategies may be robust, providing positive gains across all scenarios. Others may show large gains in one scenario but the potential for large losses with other scenarios. This strategy would be higher risk. A risky strategy may still be adopted if the rewards are high. Management selecting that strategy would be making a large bet. The bet, however, would be made knowing some of the risks involved. The worst decision that can be made is one in which the risks are not understood.

The products or outputs of the scenario process are the stories describing how the future could unfold. This rich portrayal of the future provides the logical basis for developing and analyzing different strategies. Scenarios are future expectations that allow choice to be linked to consequences. Rationally, this is valuable, but there is more.

In many cases, the value of scenarios stems more from the process than the product. The process of creating the scenarios brings a group together to share insights and build common understanding. This shared understanding does not mean consensus but an understanding of different logics and perspectives on the present and future. Shared understanding creates alignment in the group, which enhances the ability to make decisions and build commitment to that decision. This is critical in developing and implementing strategies and increases the organization's ability to adapt to changes over time. The intent of scenarios, therefore, is to build shared understanding through opening the minds of managers to different perspectives and stimulating learning about the factors shaping the future. In short, the value of scenario development is to open minds to new ideas, new possibilities, and new paradigms, enabling seeing the world from more than one perspective and encouraging creativity. Ramirez and Wilkinson (2016) emphasize that the value of scenario development is a learning service critical in reframing mental models and opening new perspectives on the present.

This realization emerged along two overlapping trains of thought. One avenue was the importance of learning. Don Michaels (1973) first articulated the insight that planning is learning. The key role of planners was not to plan but to support learning for decision-makers. This theme was more fully expressed in Peter Senge's work (1990) and described by Arie de Geus in his book *The Living Company* (1997).

At the same time, Pierre Wack and Ted Newland, responsible for scenarios in Shell in the 1970s, realized that the power of scenarios is not just in the stories but in the ability to challenge preconceived ideas and open minds to new possibilities. As in the refinery example earlier, the most important result was to open the minds, or mental maps, of Shell managers. Wack (1985a) articulated this opening of minds in his landmark paper, "The Gentle Art of Reperceiving." To emphasize this point, I often, jokingly, introduce my workshops by telling the participants I am there to mess with their minds. The reality is that in sharing and exploring ideas about the future, they open each other's minds. And the realization of insights and learning is the most powerful and valuable aspect of the scenario development process.

STRATEGIC CONVERSATION

The concept of shared understanding and learning as critical for informed decision-making was further developed in two more insights. First, Kees van der Heijden (2005) introduced the concept of strategic conversation. He recognized that opening minds required context. An example: Shell had developed global scenarios that were presented to various senior management teams around the world. After one presentation a refining manager in Singapore said, "How does this help me run my business?" The scenarios had no context or relevance for him. They did not relate to his management issues. From this emerged two innovations. First, van Heijden introduced the seven-questions interview format, designed to engage senior management in a conversation and understand their issues to ensure focus and relevance for the scenarios (Chapter 3). Second, he initiated scenarios to impact workshops designed to follow-up on the scenarios and focus discussions on what was most relevant to managers. It was insufficient to assume managers could identify and act on the implications of the scenarios for their business or mandate. A more formal process was required.

From these insights emerged the broader concept of strategic conversation. Van der Heijden realized that sharing ideas was the essential factor in learning and shared understanding necessary for strategic decision-making. Scenario development was a vehicle for strategic conversation. But, of course, such conversations were not limited to scenarios. Indeed, a conversation at the coffee machine or in the cafeteria could be strategic. From this was the realization that planning was not only learning, but facilitation of strategic conversations. Planners don't plan (although they can); they facilitate strategic conversations to create learning.

What is a strategic conversation? Essentially, it is an exchange of ideas in a social setting. More specifically, strategic conversations have four important properties:

1. They focus on strategic decisions that have significant long-term consequences.

2. They are future-oriented, exploring how the future could unfold differently and affect the consequences of current decisions.

3. They emphasize learning and build shared understanding.

4. They are open, informal, and focused, encouraging reflection and thought.

Open, reflective, and thoughtful defines a style of engagement that is flexible, open to new ideas, and structured to focus on a strategic topic. Quality conversation that allows new ideas to surface is more important than the timing of the agenda. The most productive style of engagement is one that balances structure with flexibility.

Good strategic conversations also embrace the tenets of enquiry as much as advocacy. While most leaders have honed their advocacy skills to reach their senior position, few are as skilled in enquiry. Skilled communicators use enquiry to help others express their ideas more clearly. Enquiry is characterized by asking good questions, not by providing the answers. Good strategic conversations are question-full[9].

Strategic conversations allow participants to build new ideas and perspectives, establish important relationships, and create the necessary alignment to take shared action. Strategic conversations build momentum from shared understanding, to shared decisions, to shared action and, ultimately, shared performance.

CHALLENGE OF COMPLEXITY

The next evolution in understanding the importance of scenario thinking was articulated by Adam Kahane (2004) in a wonderful little book entitled *Solving Tough Problems*. The thrust of his argument was that the world is becoming increasingly complex. The logic is outlined in Figure 5. Globalization and rapid change increase complexity and uncertainty, which affects the nature of the problems we face.

Globalization reflects the expansion of interactions at an increasingly global scale. This includes economic interaction through trade and commerce, which necessarily increases political interactions. There is also an increase in social and psychological interaction. The last century has seen a transformation in travel and communication as tourism has flourished and communication has been divorced from distance, initially with telegrams and telephones and now with the internet and smart phones. This travel and communication explosion has not only increased interaction but also global consciousness (Nelson 1993). There was a time when events in other parts of the world were unknown and thus outside our consciousness. But beyond earthquakes, wars, and famines, we were unaware of other cultures, religions, ideas, and perspectives. They were not part of our knowing. This has changed. The key impact of globalization has been an increase in the scope and scale of relationships so that distant actions and events impinge on and influence our lives, livelihoods, and ideas.

With globalization and rapid change, the world has become more complex. Complexity is fundamentally different from complicated. Calculating all the forces

---

9   Lee van Horn first recognized that since strategic conversations were, indeed, conversations, then improving conversation skills would enhance strategic conversations. He introduced me to the concepts of advocacy and "enquiry as a framework to improve the quality of discussions in meetings and in facilitation."

at work in launching a satellite to the right orbit or trajectory is no doubt difficult and meticulous, but all the calculations are known and can be determined. A launch is complicated; it is not complex.

Complex is when no amount of calculation can solve the problem. The full range of factors or forces may be unknown or their effect may be unknown. Unlike the rocket problem, which is entirely defined by physical forces, complex problems often involve social, economic, or political variables that interact in poorly defined or understood ways. Simplistically, while rocket science is complicated, raising a child, as any parent will tell you, is complex.

Rapid change at a global scale is driving increased complexity and uncertainty. How these affect complexity and uncertainty are summarized in Figure 5. New developments continually challenge our world view. Complexity reflects our limited ability to understand highly interdependent, multi-variable systems. Ecological systems are but one example. The cumulative effects of trace chemical pollutants seeping into a river system are largely unknown because the outcomes depend on many intermediate and interdependent variables. Human systems have similar qualities. Cities, for example, involve complex interactions between subsystems involving land use, energy, transportation, water, and waste, overlain with economic, social, and political systems.

Figure 5—Rising Complexity and Uncertainty

The Future is Complex & Uncertain

Globalization + Rapid Change => Complexity & Uncertainty

Complex Systems
- Many components
- High connectivity
- Open (boundaries)
- Nonlinear Relationships
- Emergent Properties

Uncertainty
- Inherently unpredictable
- Irreducible by analysis
- Distributions of outcomes not known
- Unknown unknowns

Complexity & Uncertainty create new types of problems that require new types of response.

- Systems Thinking
- Shocks and Discontinuities
- Robust Flexible Strategies

Source: Adapted from Thomas Homer-Dixon

Such complexity makes our capacity to intervene problematic. First, the system itself is dynamic, which greatly increases our level of uncertainty. Second, the effects of intervention are uncertain. Efforts to understand the system more fully can reduce the uncertainty, but in many cases, the uncertainty is irreducible. In risk management terms, we simply do not know all the risk factors or the distribution of future events. Making assumptions about probability distributions can be disastrous. The collapse of housing markets in the US set off a chain of events outside the probability distributions embedded in risk models. The failure to understand the effects of fat tails[10] and the dramatic impacts of extreme events contributed to the huge losses incurred by financial institutions in 2008.

The rise in complexity and uncertainty gives rise to what Adam Kahane (2004) has called tough problems. Such problems have three key characteristics:

1. Dynamic Complexity: Causes and effects are separated in time and space (e.g., climate change).

2. Social Complexity: Multiple stakeholders have different interests, perspectives, and priorities (e.g., oil sands development).

3. Generative Complexity: The future is fundamentally unfamiliar and undetermined without analogous models to learn from (e.g., impacts of social media).

Kahane concluded that addressing tough problems requires a systems approach that is broad, integrated, and holistic, an engagement process that involves dialogue and collaboration and creative solutions that go well beyond best practices. In the face of dynamic complex systems and future uncertainty, the challenge is not just to make better decisions, but to develop better decision-making processes that embrace complexity and uncertainty.

The key elements of this new approach to decision-making are shown in Table 1. Complex problems require a different approach than traditional problems. The extraordinary approach requires a broad systems perspective, a recognition of the problem as emergent and different from previous experience, and a process of engagement that actively includes input from multiple stakeholders. Scenarios, Kahane argues, provide a valuable approach to resolving complex problems because

1. They support a holistic, systematic view of the problem;

2. They adopt a proactive, future-focused, innovative approach;

---

10   A fat tail occurs when the probability of a rare outcome—the very low probability events in the tails of a distribution—is higher than assumed. Often a normal distribution is assumed for convenience without contradictory information. If this is wrong, then extreme events—a flood or hurricane—may occur more frequently than assumed. These events have major implications for insurance. This was true in the securitization of sub-prime mortgages that contributed to the 2008 Great Recession.

3. They involve a highly interactive and participatory process that builds shared understanding.

In short, scenarios are increasingly valuable in a world of rapid change and escalating complexity.

Table 1—Two Approaches to Solving Problems

Type of Complexity	Definition	Ordinary Approach—Simple Problems	Extraordinary Approach—Complex Problems	Process Requirement
Dynamic	Cause and effect are far apart	Piece by piece	System as a whole	Systemic
Emergent	Future is unfamiliar and undetermined	Existing solutions	Emerging solution	Generative
Social	Actors' diverse perspectives and interests	Experts and authorities	Stakeholders	Participatory

Source: Adapted from Macklin, Lois (2010), *Case Study Analysis of the Efficacy of Scenario-based Planning as a Public Policy Formulation Tool*, PhD Thesis, University of Calgary, page 2.

CHAPTER SUMMARY

- Strategic decisions depend on an understanding of the choices and expectations of the future as a basis for analyzing consequences.

- Forecasting, using methods to reduce uncertainty and increase accuracy, are most valuable for short-term predictions when systems are relatively stable and variables are quantifiable.

- Scenarios, based on the idea that the future is inherently unpredictable, are most valuable for longer-term analyses when systems are unstable, subject to discontinuities with irreducible uncertainties and intangible variables.

- The value of scenarios stems both from the rational use of the scenarios in strategic decision-making and from the process of creating scenarios, which is designed to challenge conventional mental models by opening minds to new ideas and perspectives.

- Scenario development is one example of a strategic conversation in which the dialogue serves to build important relationships, alignment of ideas, and commitments to undertake shared action.

- A new, complex world landscape requires new decision-making processes that are systemic, engaging, and creative: Scenario-development processes are a valuable approach to such dynamic problems.

Scenario planning and strategy development create opportunities for question-based strategic conversation. Do we understand our environment? Our risks? What is the key strategic issue we are facing? Is our strategy clear? Are we aligned? Breakthroughs in your business will come from asking new and challenging questions. Creating the space for strategic conversation is a powerful approach to decision-making, and ultimately, to making better decisions.

PART 2
SCENARIO DEVELOPMENT

Scenarios deal with two worlds. The world of facts and
the world of perceptions. They explore the facts but
they aim at perceptions inside the heads of decision-makers.
—Pierre Wack

The process of developing scenarios has evolved. From my early experience with
scenarios in Shell, the process was intuitive and top down. The early work of
Pierre Wack and Ted Newland depended heavily on their individual insights and
brilliance. The understanding of the value of scenarios in opening minds was understood. Well-funded research and the active exchange of ideas both within Group
Planning and with leading thinkers outside the company generated quality work
that enhanced respect for scenarios in Shell and externally. The process, however,
remained more intuitive than systematic and dependent on the insights of a small
group of experts.

My first exposure to an alternative process came by chance during an extended
trip to Latin America in 1990. We were visiting the major Shell companies in the
region to present the recently developed global scenarios and engage the management teams in an active discussion of the implications of the scenarios for their
countries and businesses. The trip was successful but an accidental hiccup in our
travel plans occurred when travelling from Chile to Mexico. We had to pass through
Miami. We arrived in Mexico City but our luggage and all our presentation and
workshop materials remained circulating in Miami. With a full day committed, our
hosts wondered if instead of the global scenarios we could develop scenarios of
Mexico. We were totally unprepared. But we tried and blundered our way to creating

scenarios for Mexico from scratch in a day. This experience firmly implanted the power of workshops in my mind. It opened a new perspective on how scenarios could be developed.

While I subsequently experimented with a workshop approach to developing scenarios, consultants at Global Business Network (GBN) were developing a systematic, workshop-based approach to scenario development. When I left Shell and connected with GBN in the mid 1990s I was exposed to this brilliant methodology. The key insight was that the essential idea in scenarios was the concept of uncertainty. Consequently, the key step in developing scenarios is to identify the critical uncertainties that define the range of future outcomes. In effect, GBN codified the intuitive knowledge of scenarios into a step-by-step approach to developing scenarios.

The purpose of Part 2 is to outline the five steps in a workshop-based approach to developing focused scenarios (Figure 6). The approach is based on the GBN model with modifications.

1. Creating Focus – The Focal Question
2. Identifying the Driving Forces
3. Developing Critical Uncertainties
4. Identifying Scenario Characteristics
5. Developing Scenario Paths and Outcomes

Figure 6—Process of Scenario Development

Scenario Development Process

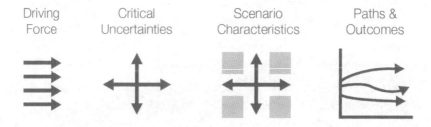

Define Focal Issue, Question, or Decision and Relevant Timeframe

Review Past Events & Discuss Alternative Interpretations

Driving Force | Critical Uncertainties | Scenario Characteristics | Paths & Outcomes

CHAPTER 3
CREATING FOCUS

THE FOCAL QUESTION

The Shell approach to creating global scenarios threads a range of economic, social, political, and technological factors into two scenarios. There is little focus. These broad scenarios, however, provide a framework for more focused nested scenarios For example, the global scenarios provide the logic and context for more specific energy or country scenarios. This is a viable and valuable approach in a large global organization with a robust budget. But even in that context, the value of focused scenarios is increasingly being recognized.

The need to focus emerges from the need for relevance. One problem is how to make the scenarios relevant to senior management, who are the key decision-makers in strategy. Another is to make the scenarios relevant to a more dispersed range of potential users. To solve these problems, Kees van der Heijden introduced two ideas: the seven questions and the scenarios impact workshops. The questions are designed to create focus. The impact workshop is discussed in Part 3 as part of strategy development.

THE INTERVIEW PROCESS

The Seven Questions

The purpose of focusing a scenario project on a critical issue or focal question is to make sure the scenarios are relevant and address real issues. The scenarios need to deal with the most important strategic issues facing the organization. To identify strategic issues an interview framework was developed, which became known within Shell as the seven questions. The seven questions were designed to facilitate an open and engaging conversation on the major factors, forces, and uncertainties affecting the future of the organization. Seven is not a magic number. Occasionally it may be appropriate to add another question specific to that project, but the objective is to generate conversation, not fill out a questionnaire.

Table 2–Generic Interview Questions

Past Changes	What changes over the past ten to fifteen years have had a significant impact on the industry?
Lessons from the Past	What has made your organization successful in the past? What does this organization need to remember? Need to forget?
Current Constraints	What needs to change for your organization to be successful in the future? What are the barriers to change and innovation?
Core Strengths	What are the key capabilities of your organization that distinguish you from your competitors? What do customers value most about your product / services?
Dark Spot	There is a dark spot on the horizon. It is not here yet but could impact the organization in the future. What is it?
Good Future	If you looked back ten years from now and your organization had done very well, what went right? What does a good future look like? What needs to happen for that good future to occur?
Oracle	The future is unknowable, but if you could talk with an oracle who could predict the future, what two questions would you ask?

The questions are intentionally eclectic and provocative (Table 2). For example, the Dark Spot is deliberately truncated—what is it?—to minimize any inherent direction from the question. The interviewee is abruptly left to ponder the question on their own. Similarly, in Lessons from the Past, the question ends with a reversal of thought: what does the organization need to forget? Sometimes the interviewer needs to expand on these abrupt questions. However, the intent is to be provocative and let the questions challenge. These questions and modification of these to adjust to the specific needs of the project have been extremely valuable in eliciting fascinating and surprising answers.

The questions include both internal and external factors. Although the scenarios necessarily focus on the external business environment, the questions include internal questions to ensure discussion on all the issues facing the organization. Current constraints and core strengths, for example, focus on issues internal to the organization. In contrast, Past Changes and the Dark Spot are directed externally. Good Future is a blend with the last component of the question—What needs to happen for the good future to occur?—intentionally directed externally. All too often, without that addition, answers swerve inward. This may tell us about the natural bias in thinking for many executives. Finally, the Oracle question is designed to surface key external uncertainties facing the organization. Answers to this question often foretell the critical uncertainties that will emerge later in the scenario development process.

You can modify these questions, substitute, or add your own questions. Key criteria are to limit the number—seven is almost magical—and to ensure the question encourages discussion. No questions with simple yes or no answers should be included.

The original purpose of the seven questions is to engage senior management in an open conversation to tap their knowledge and perceptions, introduce and clarify understanding of the project, and build support for the final product. The interview is designed as a wide-ranging conversation in which the questions—distributed in advance—provide a framework for the dialogue. Although many executives often develop answers beforehand, this was not expected or encouraged. The intent is to foster spontaneity and new thinking. The objective is not only to solicit answers but to reveal the thinking underlying the answers. In this case, sticking to the outline is not critical; tangents and divergent thinking are encouraged.

The interview also allows conversation on the purpose and scope of the project. (See Box 2). What is the purpose? Who is involved? Are there other participants they would recommend? What is the time frame for completing the project? Would they like updates? The interview, therefore, not only seeks information and insight but builds awareness, support, and curiosity about the final results. Many are also curious about the views of their fellow executives. Most want to be kept informed and want a summary of results of the interviews. In fact, assuring anonymous feedback on the collective thinking of those interviewed is one of the most important aspects of the project, both in building support and raising a critical question: What is the most important strategic issue facing the organization?

Pause for a second. How significant is this question? I will come back to it.

Box 1—The Purpose of Scenarios

An emphasis on clarifying the purpose of the scenarios and who the scenarios are for is strongly promoted by both Chermack (2011) and Ramirez and Wilkinson (2016). Both argue that this early phase merits considerable time and effort for a successful project. Clarifying the purpose is also, as Chermack emphasized, vital for evaluating the success of the project. I have not placed as strong an effort as they suggest, but I strongly agree that clarifying the purpose and expected outcomes is vital. A difference in this approach is that the scenario project, from the outset, is designed to lead to strategies. The process from scenarios to strategies is part of the project from the beginning. Hence, from the outset the purpose of the scenarios is to set the context for strategy development.

The interview process typically generates copious notes that need to be analyzed to identify the common issues across the interviews. Table 3 describes a process to do this. The essential idea is to sort ideas into common themes or buckets and then extract the central idea in the form of a strategic issue. Box 2 clarifies the definition of a strategic issue.

Table 3—Steps in Scenario Interview Analysis

During Interviews	• Begin sorting ideas early
	• Identify common themes in early interviews and test in later interviews
	• Beware of categorizing too early—keep an open mind
	• Look for novelty as interviews progress
	• Use later interviews to confirm your understanding of the ideas
Process to Identify Themes	• Accumulate responses to each question in a single database with no attribution that could identify the interviewee
	• Progress through answers looking for common themes
	• Write down candidate theme and add ideas as you progress through the data creating a cluster of common ideas

Search for Importance	• Test emerging themes against what is important to the organization • Identify those issues that are really strategic—large, irreversible, structural • Is there a critical strategic issue emerging from data (preliminary thinking on focal question)? • Examine differences of opinion to ensure you capture divergent views • Search for importance • Identify internal vs. external issues
Interview Report	• Create summary of the major themes • Summary can be bullet format for presentation purposes or … • Summary can be a written report with a paragraph or two describing each issue • Under no circumstance should any response be attributable to any individual—anonymity and confidentiality must be maintained

Box 2—What is a Strategic Issue?

An issue is an important subject of debate or discussion in which the result is in dispute. This emerges in a broader social context. For example, a sociopolitical issue such as privacy rights emerges in the context of increased information on individuals from electronic devices. A strategic issue, focused on the organization, is defined as an external or internal trend, event, or development that could impact the organization and requires a response. This involves an anticipation of impacts in the future. The increased demand for organizations to provide information on their environmental, social, and governance performance is a strategic issue requiring the organization to respond. The issue is strategic because it may impact the organization's internal operations and external relationships. The impact is the issue for the organization. Climate change, for example, is not an issue: the impact of climate change and climate change regulation is a strategic issue for organizations. Finally, note that an issue is not a problem. Problems have solutions. Issues involve choice and ongoing management. They may be resolved for a period of time, but they are never solved.

As an example, Table 4 gives a summary of issues that were identified in a project on the future of petrochemicals in Alberta. In some cases, issues are fleshed out with each issue comprising a short paragraph to emphasize the challenge posed by the issue. The focal issue that emerged in this example honed in on growth. In the final set of implications following the scenarios, as part of the strategy development process (Part 3), the most important issue to be addressed was integration, which was initially identified in the interviews.

Table 4—Issues Emerging from Interviews—Petrochemical Example (2003)

Feedstock supply	New or unused feedstock sources?
Feedstock market	Relationship gas producers & petrochemical industry buyers?
Value Added	Can petrochemicals move down value chain?
Critical Mass	World scale production, knowledge, expertise?
Integration	Energy and petrochemicals integration for growth?
Technology	Tech developments needed to leverage growth?
Global competition	From low-cost ME production?
Government policy	Role of government in the industry?

There were many lessons from the Alberta petrochemical project. One was the realization of the value of the ideas generated in the interviews. For the process of scenario development, another was the power of dialogue highlighted in Box 3.

Box 3—The Power of Dialogue

In 2003, the Alberta government was concerned about the future of the energy industry and wanted to explore the potential of the petrochemical industry in adding value to oil and gas. The Department of Economic Development invited proposals to develop scenarios on the future of the petrochemical industry. The department had a group of three people with expertise in the petrochemical industry. This meant there was expertise but it was limited. The proposal fell into two approaches. One was provided by a large multinational consulting firm that offered to draw from a large pool of global experts to provide scenarios on the future of petrochemicals in Alberta. The other was my firm's proposal to draw on government, industry, academic, and non-profit think tanks to develop the scenarios using a workshop approach. My approach emphasized doing the work with them rather than doing it for them—the expert-driven approach. The department was leery of this external involvement. Previous efforts to hold discussions with industry representatives frequently ended up, not in dialogue, but ongoing lobbying for specific policies. They felt harangued. We emphasized that discussion of the future had the advantage that multiple views could be accommodated across the different scenarios and no one needed to feel that their ideas were not recognized. In the end, we were selected.

After interviews with a range of external participants (and these were almost all subsequently participants in the workshops), issues were summarized (Table 4) and a focal question defined: How can Alberta grow the petrochemical industry in the future? The time horizon was twenty years. The project was conducted with a mix of internal and external participants, many of whom were senior managers in major petrochemical companies. The conversations were highly participatory and interactive with genuine, thoughtful, and respectful discussions. There was no lobbying.

The scenarios provided a context for identifying the key strategic issues the government and industry needed to address in growing the industry. The critical insight was the opportunity to link the petrochemical industry to the growing oil sands development. The oil sands were clearly destined to be the engine of growth for the province for the next decade or more. The link between oil sands and petrochemicals was the capture of waste gases—called off-gases—from the oil sands and the use of these to create a petrochemical complex in which the off-gases from one facility became the feedstock for another. Bringing a range of producers together to build these links would be difficult. To be the connector and enabler in bringing this together was recognized as an opportunity and valid role for the government to play. The idea was actively pursued in the subsequent years, again through a series of workshops and conferences, and continues today as a basic approach to creating a world-class, integrated petrochemical industry in Alberta.

This was a clear example of scenarios leading to strategy and action. It was also a powerful endorsement of how a workshop approach can bring a range of people together to create a shared understanding of the future. In summing up the project, the sponsors in the Department of Economic

Development remarked that the dialogue between the government and industry was the most important part of the project.

A report summarizing the issues from the interviews is used in three ways.

1. To provide feedback to participants. The summary, anonymous and concise, creates closure with interview participants.

2. To produce input to the scenario development workshop as it summarizes the thinking of the executive (or other key thinkers, experts, or influencers depending on who was interviewed).

3. To identify the focal issue or focal question that will anchor the scenarios.

Occasionally, it is appropriate to provide the raw data from the interviews to the leader of the project (altered to ensure anonymity). This allows the client to review the issues and ensure they are linked to what the interviewees said and not conjured up by the consultant. Further, it provides an opportunity for the client to mine the data and identify new issues, or expand or clarify interpretation of the issues raised in the consultant analysis. Since the interviews are conducted under the commitment of confidentiality and anonymity, both the raw notes and summary must ensure no comments can be associated with any individual.

The interviews originally focused on gaining insight into the thinking of senior managers within an organization. While the process remains the same, the scope of the interviews is often modified to include a range of other experts, influencers, and lateral thinkers. In many projects these interviewees are also participants in the scenario's development workshop. In organizations, there are often key thinkers who are not executives but valuable in contributing unique ideas and perspectives. Such lateral thinkers—referred to as remarkable people in the literature—are a vital addition both to the interviews and the scenario development workshop. There are also often external experts who can enhance both the legitimacy of the results and provide depth and breadth to the discussions. Finally, there are key influencers, either internally or externally, whose opinions are important whether novel or not. While scenarios seek ideas, foster creativity, and build shared understanding, scenario projects are not divorced from politics. Internally, visible support from senior management may be critical for success (Shoemaker, 1995). Support from key power players is needed, particularly in moving from scenarios to strategy to implementation and action. Further, endorsement from an external expert or the CEO can greatly enhance the status of a project to internal decision-makers.

The eclectic approach of the original seven questions has proven to be valuable in a range of projects, not only scenario projects but other strategic projects as well. The basic process usually includes eight to ten interviews but frequently expands to include up to twenty participants. Most ideas are generated in the first six to eight interviews so that additional interviews seldom add much in the way of new ideas. The addition of more interviews is typically driven by political considerations not to exclude important people. One adaptation with more interviews is to feed back issues that have surfaced with the early interviews to the later participants to flesh out and confirm thinking on the issues. In the end, the role of the interviewer is to facilitate the conversation; adaptability is required.

Focal Question

The interviews provide a window into the thinking of decision-makers and influencers. In particular they illuminate the issues that need to be discussed in the scenarios and later in strategy development. One or more issues, or a combination of issues, may stand out. The critical question to be addressed at this point is: Among all the strategic issues raised, what is the single most important issue facing the organization?

Identifying and describing that issue, gaining shared understanding, and building agreement and alignment across senior management (and arguably throughout the organization) is extremely valuable. Achieving focus is the most powerful result of any strategic planning process.

In the scenario process the focal issue is transformed into a question, which provides a reference point for scenario development. In short, the focal question is the question that the scenarios must address to be relevant. It clarifies, for the people in the scenario process, what they are trying to achieve.

The focal question should:
- focus on the organization specifically (not the future of the world),

- highlight a key strategic issue (e.g., growth, profitability, competition position, policy, sustainability, et cetera),

- focus on a single concern (not compound issues).

Focal questions can take different forms. They can focus on a specific decision such as go versus no-go on a major investment. A scenario-to-strategy project with a major US newspaper was triggered by the need to decide whether they should invest in a major upgrade to their printing presses. After exploring the rising effect of the internet, they didn't.

Often the focal question, while specific, is more broadly directed on strategy development for the organization or division, or broader still on the core business or industry. The latter may emphasize changes in the industry such as restructuring, new competition, disruptive technology, or new growth opportunities. The broader perspective is more common if the project is a government department, non-profit, or industry association. Finally, scenarios can be exploratory aimed at learning, team building, or signalling change. For instance, a project with a major post-secondary institution was initiated to signal change to students, staff, and alumni after the appointment of a new president. The project was successful both in signalling that a new president was in charge and in generating new strategic directions for the organization (Brummell and Shaw, 1999).

Examples of focal questions are:

- How can Company X improve its competitive position?

- How can Company Y maximize new growth opportunities?

- What does Non-profit Z need to do to create a sustainable future?

- How can Government Department A improve the quality-of-service in delivering their programs?

- What are the future needs of learners in the education system?

All these have a single focus. A problem can occur if there are competing issues. An example occurred in a project with a railway company. After considerable discussion, a focal question was agreed upon that read: Can AB Rail improve its competitive position and increase growth? The group could not resolve whether short-term cost reduction was more important than long-term growth. The unsatisfactory compromise included both. The subsequent scenario development process was not hindered by the ambiguity of the focal question. At the least it highlighted a very important management challenge. It was not ideal but instructive.

Time Horizon

Scenario projects must define a future time frame. What is the appropriate time horizon for a project? How do you decide? Should it be five years, ten years, or even forty years? It is useful to include the time horizon in the focal question. For instance, picking from an example above, the revised focal question might ask: Looking out to 2030, what are the future needs of learners in the education system? Whether explicitly included in the question or not, this is an important aspect of framing and focusing the project. It is simple to add it to the focal question.

There are several guidelines in determining what the right time frame should be. These are suggestions not prescriptions. Flexibility and intuition are required.

One guideline is to ensure the time frame for the scenarios is longer than the traditional planning period in the organization. If an organization has a five-year plan, then the scenarios must exceed that. A great deal of thinking has likely been expended on the plan, including explicit assumptions on how the future will unfold. To allow participants to think beyond the plan assumption, a longer time frame is needed. While it may be difficult to revise thinking on the five-year horizon, introducing, say, a ten-year horizon allows them to open their minds to new possibilities. It frees them up. They can entertain a range of new possibilities and outcomes.

A second guideline is that the horizon needs a perspective that fits the culture of the organization and dynamics of the industry. Some organizations embrace long-term thinking. This was the culture in Shell (indeed the scenarios may have been instrumental in fostering that culture). This perspective is not common. Many organizations are short-term driven. A ten-year time horizon, for example, would be dismissed. This also depends on the industry. Companies in the technology sector, for example, where change is rapid, have a different time horizon than organizations in sectors with large physical investments where change is slower. Their time horizon would be much shorter.

A third guideline is to focus on the longevity of the investments an organization makes. In banking, for example, loans may have a twenty-year payback. In energy, investments often have very long lives, operating for thirty or forty years. Think of refineries, pipelines, or power generation plants. In technology, investments in both hardware and software have very short lifespans. Investments in human capital, however, which are vital to technology companies, may be important and have a longer time frame.

Finally, a fourth consideration might be the relevant period of uncertainty. In general, the longer the time frame, the greater the uncertainty. Operationally, this means a greater range of future outcomes is possible. Is this always the case? A recent scenario study I worked on included perspectives on the future of electric vehicles in the auto industry. There is considerable uncertainty with respect to the speed and penetration of EVs in replacing traditional gasoline- and diesel-powered vehicles. This is the case in thinking out to 2030. There are factors that could accelerate adoption and factors that could hinder adoption. Now consider a time horizon of 2050. While there are factors that could limit growth of EVs in the shorter term, is there uncertainty that the accumulation of technology over a thirty-year span will significantly enhance the attractiveness of EVs? In short, there may be less uncertainty about the outcome in the long term than in the short term. Subtle aspects like this may be important in deciding on what the appropriate time horizon should be.

Whether two, five, or twenty years, the time horizon for scenarios must exceed the traditional planning period, fit the organizational culture, reflect the investment-decision timeline, and recognize the period of greatest uncertainty. Of these, the investment timing may be the most important for all organizations. After all, the ultimate investment decision is the allocation of human and financial resources within the organization to achieve strategic objectives.

CHAPTER SUMMARY

- To ensure relevance the scenarios need to focus on issues critical to the organization.

- Interviews with key decision-makers, influencers, or experts are a valuable approach to identifying strategic issues, as well as building awareness and support for the project.

- One interview approach is the eclectic seven questions as a guideline to an open conversation.

- Summarizing the interview results into a small number of strategic issues provides a basis for formulating the focal question.

- The focal question reflects the key strategic issue facing the organization. It is the critical issue that the scenarios must address. It acts as an anchor or reference point during the scenario development process, and it needs to be unambiguous and simple, with a specific time horizon.

CHAPTER 4
THE SCENARIO
DEVELOPMENT PROCESS

The whole problem of the world is that fools and fanatics are always
so certain of themselves, but wiser people so full of doubt.
—Bertrand Russell

reating scenarios involves identifying the forces and factors driving change and developing perspectives on a range of possible future outcomes. Typically, this involves a one-and-a-half-day workshop involving up to twenty-five participants. Fewer participants allow more individual input. More participants become unwieldy. [11]

The overarching perspective is that the future is a flow from the past to the present and into the future. Insight into the future can be gained by understanding past and recent developments that have shaped the present. Current events are the seeds of the future. These may be major trends or weak signals. The challenge is to tap the insight of workshop participants on what changes are most important, develop alternative interpretations of these changes, and then project how those changes could play out in shaping the future. All of the ideas and content of the scenarios are generated by the participants.

The workshop process has a number of discrete steps shown previously in Figure 6. The purpose of this chapter is to review each step in the process. It is written from the perspective of a facilitator.

---

11 I have worked with fewer than ten participants and more than fifty. With only a few individuals the brainstorming effect in which people build on the ideas of others can be limited. With too many, the process becomes unwieldy. Breakout groups are large, limiting participation, and reporting back to the plenary is often long and tiresome. Sixteen to twenty is ideal, allowing time for each participant and encouraging interaction.

1. Introduction. Review the purpose, outline, and time frames. Clarify ownership of project.

2. Focal Issue. Review interview results and agree on single focal question.

3. Past Changes. Develop perspective on past changes, trends, and developments. Past changes identify major developments over the past five to ten years that have impacted the industry / external environment and brought it to its current situation. This discussion ensures the scenarios are grounded in reality and start from the current situation. As well, past trends and forces may continue into the future.

4. Driving Forces. Identify the major forces driving change. At this stage, the focus shifts to the future. Participants are asked to identify changes that could occur and impact the focal question. Ideas are captured and subsequently grouped into clusters. The underlying theme in grouping the ideas is identified with a name. These clusters are interpreted as indicators of the major factors and forces impacting the focal issue in the future.

5. Critical Uncertainties. Identify critical uncertainties. These are defined as forces that are both important and uncertain. Participants rate the forces generated with respect to these two dimensions and settle on two critical uncertainties. These are defined as dimensions describing a range of future outcomes to be used in defining scenario logics.

6. Scenario Logics. Develop a logic framework by portraying the two critical uncertainties as orthogonal axes, creating a four-quadrant diagram. Each quadrant represents a different combination of outcomes and hence the initial logic for four distinctly different scenarios.

7. Scenario Characteristics and Storylines. Flesh out the characteristics and storyline for each quadrant in the logic framework. First, brainstorm the characteristics of a future in each quadrant within the logic of the framework. The question is, What could happen in each quadrant? Then develop stories on how that scenario could unfold over time. Characteristics are static. Storylines are dynamic, describing sequences of events through time. The quadrants are literally white spaces that require the insight and creativity of the participants to develop logical and consistent stories of how that future could unfold. The process is a highly interactive and challenging learning experience.

The results, captured at each stage, form the input for writing coherent scenarios. This follows the workshop and is described in Chapter 5.

INTRODUCTION

Do we need to describe how to introduce a workshop? Is there something particularly important to understand in the introduction of a scenarios workshop that is not common to all well-designed workshops? The answer is yes!

The key point is ownership. A critical success factor in developing scenarios is to ensure that the final product is owned by the client or sponsor. If a client refers to the final product as the consultant's scenarios, then the project has failed. Why? If the scenarios are not owned and internalized as the organization's scenarios, the organization will never act on the results. They will be nice but not necessary. They will be interesting but not relevant.

To ensure ownership from the beginning, the client or a senior executive in the organization is asked to open the workshop, including the purpose and importance of the project, before introducing the consultants. A key message at that point is to emphasize that the consultants are responsible for the process, but the participants are responsible for the content of the workshop and the ideas creating scenarios. The participants and the organization, not the facilitator, own the results. This clarifies, from the beginning, the role of the consultants and the ultimate ownership of the project. At the end of the workshop, we—the facilitators—pointedly hand control back to the sponsor for final words. A small point, perhaps, but this can prove vital to the success of the project.

Other aspects of the introduction are straightforward in outlining the purpose of the project, the steps in the workshop, and introductions by the participants. Self-introductions should be short with no discussions. The time to allow participants to bump into each other is in the next step, not in the introductions.

PAST CHANGES

This step identifies the forces that have shaped the past and created the current situation. This exercise is a valuable starting point in ensuring a firm foundation for exploring the future. Identifying past changes allows the group to start from what they know, gain familiarity with each other, learn the process, and identify factors and forces that may continue into the future.

An example from a scenario project on the future of Tanzania, sponsored by Placer Dome in 2003, identified a number of past changes. These included shifts in individual attitudes to the economy, public discontent with corruption, increased awareness of human rights and environmental impacts, shifts in population with urbanization, increased empowerment with a decentralization of bureaucracy, regional integration in East Africa, an improved road system, a shift to a market economy, a liberalized media, the impact of HIV / AIDS, and a shift from a single- to multi-party system. The list was comprehensive and detailed, reflecting the commitment and insights of the participants.

The workshop process involves four steps:

1. independent generation of ideas,

2. collection of ideas,

3. clustering of ideas, and

4. defining driving forces.

As always, the process begins with a question designed to generate ideas. A typical question is: What changes have occurred over the past five to ten years that have affected the current situation? Participants are asked to work independently and write down five to ten changes that answer the question: Why do we ask this so specifically?

Listing answers independently is a very important element in the facilitation process. This incremental method requires participants to write down their ideas independently before group discussion. This minimizes a major problem in brainstorming. If discussion is opened without allowing participants time to reflect, the discussion will be biased by the first idea presented. Minds unduly focus on that initial line of thought. For example, if the topic being discussed is recreation and the first comment is about baseball, everyone thinks about baseball and sports. Recreational activities such as hiking, reading, games, or listening to music are pushed from top of mind. Requiring independent thought avoids the first topic problem, ensures more creative lateral thinking, and means participants are prepared and never caught off guard or embarrassed when asked for ideas. My colleague Greg MacGillivray calls this facilitation method our secret sauce.

After a thinking period of five to ten minutes, the facilitator randomly canvasses participants to share their ideas. Like the first topic problem, avoid the first-person problem by ensuring you do not start with the most senior person in the room. Others may simply fall into line and limit the range of ideas.

Individual ideas are recorded on Post-it notes and randomly pasted on a wall, window, or flip chart. Typically, the collection of ideas includes discussion so that the facilitator and all participants understand the idea as presented and recorded. Facilitation at this point is focused on ensuring clarity by drawing out the meaning of the idea if it is complex or excessively long.[12] Other participants are encouraged

---

12   An important skill in facilitation is helping others express themselves better. This is called enquiry as opposed to advocacy. Prompting questions like: I understood you to mean X, is that what you meant? Or, how is your idea different from the idea expressed by the previous speaker? Or, is the key concept this or this? Enquiry is a vital skill in facilitation, particularly in scenarios workshops.

to help in clarifying ideas and adding related ideas, as is typical in all brainstorming sessions. (See Box 4 for a discussion on brainstorming).

Box 4—A Note on Brainstorming

The workshop approach that I like involves a sequence of brainstorming sessions encouraging creative thinking and generation of ideas. The emphasis is on more and more ideas. This mind opening process is then followed by a structuring process that focuses on closure. Brainstorming is fun, but structuring requires making decisions—a process that is more difficult. Improving the quality of the conversation and hence the quality of the ideas is valuable in any workshop. The facilitator has an important role, both in conducting the facilitation and coaching the participants on good practices. Below is a list of instructions that, if followed, greatly enhance the quality of the conversation in the workshop.

• Suspend assumptions

• Act as colleagues

• Adopt a spirit of enquiry

• Listen deeply with intent

• Probe gently with respect

• Consciously suspend beliefs

• Leave positions at the door

• Seek understanding not points

• Balance advocacy and enquiry

After all the ideas are exhausted, most participants are given a break. Three or four volunteers, however, are invited to sort the individual ideas into groups that share some similarity or theme. The aim is to identify eight to ten clusters with names that reflect the underlying commonality. Examples might be disruptive technology, shifting values, rising environmental concerns, economic growth, increased competition, government policy, global trade. The cluster named disruptive technology, for example, might include specific ideas such as growth in EVs, application of artificial intelligence (AI), advanced materials, tech unicorns, increase R&D by government, and increased e-commerce.

Names that have a dynamic aspect to them are encouraged, such as shifting, rising, or increasing. This reinforces the sense of change inherent in the scenarios. Volunteers are encouraged to keep an open mind and not to lock in to preconceived ideas. The simple approach is to begin by joining two Post-it notes that have an intuitive connection and then add other ideas to create a group. In this way, the structure emerges from the ideas, not a preconceived framework. This is not always possible. Inevitably, participants will begin by selecting all the technology or economic ideas. So be it. The purpose of the task is to structure the ideas into a framework that makes sense.

Following the break, the volunteers present the results of the clustering exercise to the main group. Discussion is encouraged. New names and interpretations are welcomed. The names, capturing the underlying dynamic of each cluster, are important as the clusters are interpreted as the driving forces that have shaped the past leading to the current situation. There should be traceable links connecting the driving forces to the current situation.

In developing driving forces for the future, the same approach is used. Developing the past driving forces is important as an exercise in that it provides a rehearsal for exploring future driving forces. The process of generating ideas independently, clustering ideas, articulating names, and interpreting the underlying themes as driving forces is introduced and the group has learned the process. Repeating the secret sauce is now easier and more effective as the workshop shifts to exploring the future.

DRIVING FORCES

The next task is to identify the forces driving change in the future. The process follows the same steps used to identify the driving forces describing past changes—independently generating ideas, recording and clustering into groups, and naming the driving forces.

Some context may be useful. A framework for thinking about the relationship between an organization and its environment is shown in Figure 7. The organization is depicted as the small circle in the centre. You are not interested in the internal structure, processes, or competencies of the organization[13]. You are interested only in the external influences shaping the future world that the organization is going to have to live in.

The inner ring of the diagram, the transactional environment, identifies actors and factors over which the organization has some influence or control. Influence comes from the transactions between actors—the buying of goods or services from a supplier or negotiations with unions. The extent that an organization has influence

---

13   Internal structure, processes, competencies, and other factors need to be considered in developing and implementing strategies. They are not relevant in developing scenarios.

or some control in this space is typically described in economics as market power. In a monopoly situation, for example, the organization has tremendous power in securing favourable terms from suppliers and exercising control of prices of its products or services.

Figure 7—Forces and Factors

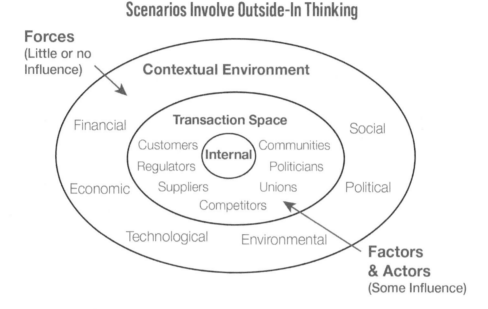

Railways and utilities are examples of companies that have considerable market power since in their area of service there is no direct competition; there is only one rail line or power line or gas line to each customer. Companies with strong network effects also have high levels of market power. Tech companies such Google, Facebook, and Microsoft fall into this category. To prevent the abuse of such power, regulation and enforcement by regulators is required. In an oligopoly situation, power is shared among a small number of competitors, while in a competitive market there are a large number of competitors with little influence individually in directing this space. Farming, retailing, and many professions would be examples.[14]

The outer ring, the contextual environment, describes a space over which organizations have virtually no control. (Even governments accept that there are some areas where they do not have control.) Economic growth, for example, is largely

---

14 An interesting aspect of this framework is its implication for strategy. It would seem to be a favourable strategy for any company to try to expand its influence outward in the transactional space. This should lead to more power and higher profitability. This is one of the logics in integrating either forward or backward in the supply chain. It gives more control over transactions. Similarly, Amazon's strategy to dominate e-commerce seems to be designed to expand control in the transaction space.

beyond the influence of any single company. Financial markets, social values, political trends, technological developments, and environmental concerns are all outside the influence of even very large organizations. In these examples, organizations are environment takers not environment makers. This is particularly true when considering a global context. The focus in developing scenarios is to identify and understand the forces driving change in the contextual environment. This is the space where the greatest uncertainties arise.

Generating Ideas

The process for identifying factors and forces driving future changes mimics the method used in identifying past changes. A question you can use is: What changes could occur over the next twenty years that could impact the focal question? Then ask participants to identify ten to fifteen changes that could occur and, working independently, write them down. No effort is made to distinguish factors and forces as this would add an unnecessary complication to the thinking. However, a sharp distinction should be emphasized that ideas are changes that could occur and not what participants would like to occur.

Participants are given ten to fifteen minutes to list their ideas. They are reminded to push their thinking to the limit and think the unthinkable. Identifying weak signals is encouraged. You want participants to be as creative as possible and explore the outer limits of believability. When the group has clearly run out of ideas, each participant is asked in random order to provide one or two ideas to be recorded on Post-it notes. Constraining each person to one or two ideas limits the ability of a single person to dominate the conversation. Everyone has a second or third opportunity to present their ideas before the discussion ends.

Collecting Ideas

A group of twenty can generate as many as one hundred or more distinct ideas. A key task is to record each idea succinctly and accurately. Some dialogue is required between the participant and the facilitator to ensure the recorded idea is concise—it is only a Post-it note—and clearly captures the idea intended. Visibly displaying and often repeating the words written down ensures accuracy and maintains ownership. The ideas must never be seen to be the facilitator's ideas.[15]

---

15   A facilitator often has ideas that may be valuable. One way to introduce ideas is to pose a question. Directing the question to the group, the facilitator might pose a question: Have you considered whether X could influence Y? Or, from the telecom industry: Competition emerged from an unlikely source. Could this happen in the energy business? My approach was to introduce an idea via a question. If accepted, it was added. If not, I would raise it once more. If still rejected, I buried it. It is always important to recognize that the group knows their business better than you do.

Clustering Ideas

Next, three or four volunteers, ideally with some diversity in experience, position, or perspective sort the ideas into ten to twelve clusters reflecting some underlying commonality or theme. They then discuss and create names that capture the underlying theme of the cluster of ideas. As before, action words are encouraged to reinforce the sense of dynamism involved in forces driving change. Facilitators should oversee the process, but not control it. If clusters are too large with too many ideas, for example, the facilitators can help split the ideas into more groups. Differences between these groups may be subtle but important. They can also often advise on the names, but ultimately the volunteers' decisions must prevail.

Defining Driving Forces

The volunteers then present the results back to the entire group. This reinforces that these ideas are generated and owned by the participants and not manipulated by the consultants. Typically, a lively discussion ensues, often leading to important changes in the interpretation and naming of the clusters. This is healthy. It is remarkable that if the group has used this process to develop past changes, the level of learning is noticeable. More ideas are generated, clusters are tighter, and interpretations are scrutinized more rigorously.

At this point it is important to stress what has been accomplished. The ten to twelve forces emerging from the ideas of change can be interpreted as a framework for understanding the future environment for this organization. Each force is a dimension of change. This means that any description of the future should reference each of the ten to twelve dimensions. For example, if shifting social values is a driving force, then a description of that force must be included in any scenario describing the future. In some scenarios this may be a major force captured in the logic of the scenario. In others, it may play a minor role in driving the logic of the scenario. Nevertheless, in all scenarios a reference to shifting social values should be included. The key principle is that all of the forces should be described in the final story, whether central to the logic or not.

CRITICAL UNCERTAINTIES

This step defines two critical uncertainties that will form the logical framework supporting the development of four scenarios.[16] The development of the critical uncertainties and subsequent development of the vertical and horizontal axes for the logic framework is the most difficult and arguably the most important aspect of the scenario development process. The psychological dynamic of the workshop is shown in Figure 8.

The initial steps in defining the focus and driving forces are relatively stress free. The emphasis is on expanding ideas rather than narrowing choices. In the diagram, the degree of complexity, uncertainty, anxiety, and frustration—the stress level—is low but rising. Developing the critical uncertainties, however, raises the level of stress, peaking with the selection of the axes that are used to formulate the underlying logic or framework for each quadrant of the four-box matrix. The level of stress then falls as the group shifts back to idea generation and creativity in fleshing out the characteristics and storylines. The process is challenging for the facilitators and for the participants, but the rewards are worth it.

Figure 8—Zones of Terror

Scenario Creation & the Zones of Terror

Source: Global Business Network

---

16 We are focusing on a deductive approach in which critical uncertainties are defined and used to generate the logic framework for the scenarios from a top-down perspective. An inductive approach involves developing the scenarios from a range of ideas in bottom-up process. This is analogous to an empirical exploration aimed at making sense of data rather than analyzing data from a theoretical framework. See Chermack (2011) for a more detailed description.

Uncertain versus Predetermined

The intent of scenarios is to explore the range of future possible outcomes. Starting from the current situation, you want to think through how distinctly different futures could unfold. How do you do this? Some things you are confident you can predict. Others, with a wide range of possible outcomes, are uncertain. It is these uncertainties that you need to focus on in creating a range of scenarios that are different in logic while exploring the outer boundaries of possible future outcomes.

Uncertainty is an abstract concept. In mathematics there is a distinction between risk and uncertainty. Risk describes a situation in which the distribution of outcomes is known. A normal distribution is assumed in many statistical analyses. For example, there may be considerable statistical information on house prices in a given market, which allows a relationship between price changes and interest rates to be established. Then the probability of a given rise or fall as interest rates change can be estimated. A mortgage lender can calculate interest-rate risk and use that in approving or rejecting a mortgage.[17]

Uncertainty, unlike risk, is a situation in which the distribution of outcomes is completely unknown. In some cases, additional information or analysis can reduce the uncertainty, but in many cases, as described by Kees van der Heijden, the uncertainty is irreducible. In other words, there is no additional information that can reduce the inherent uncertainty in the situation. Changes in social values, environmental concerns, political trends, technological disruptions, and economic restructuring are examples of irreducible uncertainties. It is not that you cannot think of a range of possibilities. It is that the probabilities of different outcomes are unknown. You can imagine shifts in social values, but you cannot describe the distribution of possible outcomes. This is an irreducible uncertainty.

Uncertainty can be defined as the range of future outcomes for a given variable. Consider Figure 9. Some variables have a high level of certainty. In other words, they are predictable within a limited range. Population is one example. Projections of population growth have a history of accuracy within a narrow range of outcomes. As shown in the left part of the diagram, from a common starting point, projections through time follow similar paths and diverge minimally. In the language of scenarios, these are defined as pre-determined variables. [18]

---

17 Assumptions in the distribution of outcomes can have serious consequences. A major factor in the great recession of 2008 was a miscalculation of security risk. The distribution tails were much larger than assumed, meaning the risk of extreme events was higher than assumed. As a result, the extreme conditions underlying mortgage securities were unexpected and proved catastrophic.

18 Identifying a variable as predetermined is vital. If you believe a future outcome is almost inevitable, then you must make sure you plan for it. In the excitement of scenarios, the value of predetermined outcomes for planning should not be ignored.

In contrast, some variables are highly uncertain. They have a wide range of future possibilities. This is shown on the right side of the diagram. The paths diverge over time until the end points create a wide gap in future outcomes. An example is technology. There may be little uncertainty that technological change will be rapid. The uncertainty emerges from the impacts of technology. Will future technological change, reinforce, or disrupt your current business model? An example is electric cars. For auto makers, converting to electric motors reinforces their existing business model: mass assembly and marketing of automobiles.[19] For petroleum refiners and marketers, a shift to EVs would be highly disruptive in undermining their existing business model. In this example, there is a wide range of future outcomes with significant impacts. This is defined as uncertainty. In part, the uncertainty depends on the specific definition of the uncertainty, but in general, the operational way of defining uncertainty is to identify the range of possible outcomes for a given variable.

Figure 9—Defining Uncertainty

Defining Uncertainty

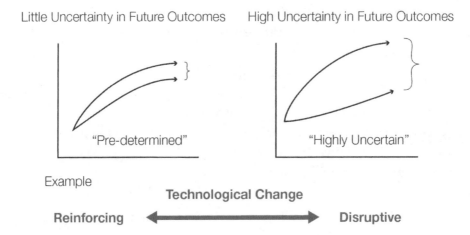

What are Critical Uncertainties?

The distinction between an uncertainty and a critical uncertainty is in both the range of uncertainty and its importance. Some variables may be uncertain but not very important in the context of future outcomes relative to the focal question. Critical uncertainties are defined as driving forces that are both important and uncertain. The

---

19 There is some disruption to auto manufacturers in that the motor and power train is significantly different and skill requirements for workers are distinctly different, but the basic business model remains the same.

Venn diagram shown in Figure 10 clarifies the definition of a critical uncertainty as the intersection of importance and uncertainty. A critical uncertainty is both.

How do you identify critical uncertainties in a practical way?

Rank the driving forces in terms of their importance.

Define what the uncertainty is for each important driving force.

Rank the important driving forces in terms of their degree of uncertainty.

Importance

First, ask participants to focus on the set of driving forces identified by the group. You focus on these forces because they are relevant as a framework for thinking about the future in the context of our focal question. Next, ask participants to reflect on which driving forces are most important. All are important to some degree or they would not have emerged. But some are more important than others. Give each participant three votes and ask them to write down their choices independently. Participants are not allowed to put all their votes on one driving force; they must distribute them across forces. Some discussion or lobbying is allowed, but the intent is not to have a lengthy debate at this point. Then call the vote. This leads to a ranking of the driving forces. A few will receive a large number of votes, others only one or two. This generates a ranking of forces by importance.

Figure 10—Identifying Critical Uncertainties

Critical Uncertainties

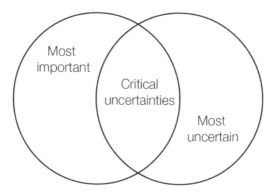

... Critical uncertainties are those that are both most important
<u>and</u> most uncertain

Uncertainty

After ranking the driving forces in terms of importance, the task is to rank the driving forces in terms of uncertainty. Select one of the most important driving forces identified by the group and ask participants to write down two different future outcomes that they think could occur. Encourage them to think of polar extremes. As an example, for a driving force named economic growth, future outcomes might include high-versus-low investment, traditional-versus-new industry, entrepreneurial versus big business, export-driven versus domestic, and / or demand or market-driven versus policy-driven. Each provides a variation on what the key uncertainty is in economic growth. Draw a line and list the opposites as they are introduced, creating a list of descriptors at each end. This reinforces the concept that uncertainty is reflected in the differences between the polar opposites identified as possible outcomes along that variable. The intent at this point is not to settle on or reduce the subtleties to an essential difference but to ensure the group has an initial understanding of the nature and extent of the uncertainty associated with that driving force. Later, a clear and succinct description of the uncertainty is required for those forces identified as most uncertain.

The exercise is repeated for the three or four most important driving forces. In each case the question is whether participants can articulate two distinct future possible outcomes. House prices accelerate or collapse. That indicates uncertainty. If they can quickly describe one outcome but struggle to define a second, different outcome, then there is probably little uncertainty. One must be careful, however. Rapid technological change may be inevitable. There is no slow in technological change. But while the pace of change is not uncertain, the impact, reinforcing or disruptive, may be highly uncertain. That was the case in a study of the future of electric vehicles. The shift to EVs seemed inevitable in the long term, but the timing and extent of penetration of EVs in the market, in the short term, is highly uncertain.

Identifying Critical Uncertainties

Having had an initial discussion of the uncertainty of each of the most important driving forces, the next step is to identify two critical uncertainties. This involves voting to narrow the choices and then discussion as needed to select two critical uncertainties—forces with a high impact (importance) and distinctly different outcomes (uncertainty). In voting, each participant is asked to pick the two forces they feel are most uncertain and write them down. Then proceed through each driving force and ask, via a show of hands, who voted for each. Having asked them to write down their choices beforehand, there is no bias in the order of voting. There is always a tendency for participants to be influenced by others. For example, without preselected choices, individuals will often change their vote if they see others voting for a particular driving force. This is another example of using the secret sauce to minimize bias in the process.

The voting usually narrows the critical-uncertainty candidates quite quickly to two or three. Voting alone, however, does not determine the critical uncertainties. A further step is needed to test the potential critical uncertainties to ensure they provide a valuable framework for developing the scenarios. Specifically, are they independent and do they provide a framework for developing challenging scenarios?

The process of developing scenarios is described the case study below. The example is summarized from a project focused on the future of environmental policy and decision-making processes in Alberta, sponsored by the Alberta Ecotrust Foundation.

SCENARIO DEVELOPMENT: CASE STUDY

In 2012, the Alberta Ecotrust Foundation sponsored a scenario project to broaden thinking and build shared understanding of the complex, interacting forces and key uncertainties shaping the future of environmental policy and decision-making processes in Alberta. The underlying concept was that better decisions required better decision-making processes. The intent of the scenario project, (including a complementary systems-mapping exercise)[20] was to develop foresight capacity among environmental non-governmental organizations (NGOs) in influencing government policy in Alberta. The project was unique, both in the integration of scenarios and systems mapping and in the focus of the scenarios on a process of decision-making. Typically, scenarios are focused on an industry, sector, or country, not a process. This was unique. The focal question was: How does Alberta create effective environmental policy and decision-making processes to improve societal outcomes over the next ten years?

In the scenario-development workshop, approximately twenty-five participants, from academia, environmental NGOs, government, and industry, identified past and future changes and driving forces (Figure 11) before embarking on the process of defining critical uncertainties.

20 Systems Mapping is a methodology that describes a current system in terms of nodes, connections, and influences. Scenarios provide a framework for identifying future challenges that can impact the current system, thereby identifying changes required in the current system to meet those challenges. This is further discussed in Chapter 9.

Figure 11—Driving Forces Example

Driving Forces — Environmental Policy & Decision-Making Processes

In developing critical uncertainties, the first task is to rank the forces by importance. In discussion, the two driving forces, public action and role of stakeholders, were seen as closely related and combined before voting on importance. The five selected as most important were:

1. Public Action / Role of Stakeholders,

2. Economics,

3. System Management and Tools,

4. External Pressures,

5. Social Values.

They all had very similar votes.

The second task is to develop initial thinking on what the underlying uncertainty is with respect to each of the important driving forces. The objective is to build shared understanding of the range of uncertainty for each of the most important driving forces. In this example, the five less important forces were ignored. The result of brainstorming to identify polar outcomes on three of the driving forces is shown below.

Table 5—Brainstorming to Identify Uncertainty

Social Values

Private	←————→	**Public**
Polarized		Cohesive
Me/Now		Us/For Future
Rural		Urban
Anti-Government		
Low Environment		Pro-Government

Economics

Weak	←————→	**Strong**
Bust		Boom
Low gov't revenues		High gov't revenues
Low energy price		High energy price
Fear		Hope

Public Action/Engagement of Stakeholders

Divided	←————→	**Collaborative**
Well resourced		Unresourced
In flux		Stable
Burnt out		Engaged
Disenfranchised		Valued
Hierarchy		Networks
Old Channels		New Channels
Local		Global
Uninformed		Informed
Autonomous		Cooperative
Special Interest		Public Interest
Concentrated Power		Diffused Power

The brainstorming provides a preliminary understanding of the uncertainty underlying each of the five most important driving forces. This informs the voting on the most uncertain driving forces. In this example, voting identified two critical uncertainties: economy and public engagement. These formed the axes for the scenario framework, shown in Figure 12. The diagram shows the critical uncertainties as vertical and horizontal (orthogonal) axes defined both by their name, e.g., economy and stakeholder engagement, and by the polar end points. Each quadrant is a different combination of the polar extremes. This gives each quadrant a basic logic. The upper-right quadrant defines a scenario with high growth and collaborative stakeholder engagement. The framework creates the basic logic for developing the scenarios.

The axes appeared to meet the criterion of independence, but there was a need to ensure that the axes would create a framework leading to interesting, important, and challenging scenarios. Participants were asked to think about each quadrant and brainstorm potential characteristics that would describe that world. After ideas were written down, a list was generated for each quadrant relatively quickly with little concern for consistency. In some cases, initial ideas may be logically inconsistent but this was not the focus at this point. The intent is to get an initial perspective on what the scenario might look like and whether it is feasible—could it happen—and challenging. Some of the initial characteristics for each quadrant are shown in Figure 13. The initial conclusion was that the axes were independent and the framework offered the potential for scenarios that would be plausible and challenging in our thinking on the future of policy decision-making in Alberta.

Ultimately two critical uncertainties were specifically defined as:

Economy. Will Alberta's economy experience rapid development, strong economic growth, and rising government revenues or slow development, low economic growth, and stagnant government revenues?[21]

Stakeholder Engagement. Will interaction among stakeholders (including the public, government, NGOs, Indigenous communities, industry, and others) lead to high levels of collaboration, a focus on public interests, utilize rich social networks, and support distributed power? Or will relationships among stakeholders lead to polarized positions, an emphasis on private interests, and hierarchical structures with power concentrated in the hands of a few?

---

21 Initially the economy dimension was defined by the simple end points of high and low growth as shown in Figure 13. This was used in the testing phase. The definition was subsequently refined to the more detailed description in Figure 14.

Figure 12–Basic Logic of the Matrix

Alberta Ecotrust – Basic Logic

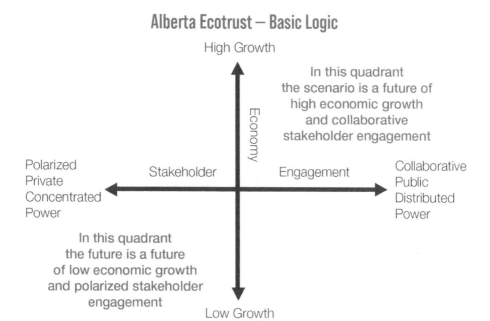

At this point it is useful to step back from the detailed and mechanical process to ask a key question: What are the two critical uncertainties facing the policy and decision-making process in Alberta? Specifically, are we confident these two critical uncertainties are truly the most critical ones? In discussing the work of the work-shop with an outsider, could you confidently tell them that the two most important uncertainties affecting policy and decision-making processes were the economy and stakeholder engagement? Faithfully answering that question is extremely valuable and insightful regardless of the final scenarios. Like identifying the critical issue facing an organization (the focal question), identifying the critical uncertainties is another valuable learning resulting from the scenario development process.

Subsequently, a full set of characteristics for each quadrant was developed, sto-rylines were created and names attached. Figure 13 shows the initial brainstorming of characteristics used to ensure the axes were not correlated and that the scenarios would be challenging. Figure 14 shows the final descriptions of the critical uncer-tainties and ultimate names of the scenarios in each quadrant. (These steps are dis-cussed in the following sections.)

Figure 13—Identifying Scenario Characteristics

Alberta Ecotrust — Initial Characteristics

- Big business, small government
- High growth & investment
- Economy dominant
- Environment seen as externality
- Lack of social cohesion
- Democratic deficit
- Social media influential
- Litigation and conflict

High Growth

- Increased resources and capacity
- Increased land pressure
- Increased knowledge & information
- Environment valued
- Agreement on tradeoffs
- Public – private balance
- Integrated decision-making
- Increased GHG emissions

Economy

Polarized
Private
Concentrated
Power

Stakeholder   Engagement

Collaborative
Public
Distributed
Power

- Low oil prices & slow growth
- Cabinet / elite decision-making
- Simple approval processes
- Conflicts allowed to fester
- Low public focus on environment
- Apathy for many
- Aboriginal activism
- Siege mentality

Low Growth

- External environmental pressures
- Low oil prices, growth & investment
- Social innovation in collaboration
- Oil company collaboration
- Capacity building
- Consensus decision-making
- Downloading of responsibility
- Government takes process seriously

Figure 14—Final Scenario Framework with Names

Alberta Ecotrust — Scenario Framework

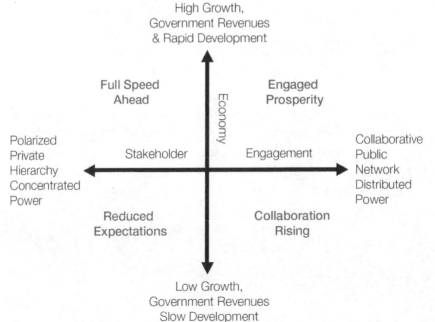

High Growth,
Government Revenues
& Rapid Development

Full Speed
Ahead

Engaged
Prosperity

Economy

Polarized
Private
Hierarchy
Concentrated
Power

Stakeholder   Engagement

Collaborative
Public
Network
Distributed
Power

Reduced
Expectations

Collaboration
Rising

Low Growth,
Government Revenues
Slow Development

SCENARIO LOGICS

In the logic of developing scenarios, critical uncertainties are understood as embracing a range or continuum of outcomes that can be portrayed as a dimension from one extreme to the other. These dimensions create four distinct quadrants or combinations of the two critical uncertainties (some would say, a typical two-by-two matrix loved by all consultants). Constructing the matrix and creating the scenario logic framework should be relatively straightforward: define each axis as one of the two critical uncertainties. The task, however, is seldom that simple. There are two constraints: independence and challenge.

Independent Axes

One constraint is to ensure the axes are independent, which means they are not correlated. Figure 15 shows the difference between independent orthogonal axes (left graphic) and correlated ones (right graphic).

Figure 15—Independent Axes

Constructing the Matrix – Independant Axes

The critical uncertainties must be independent
Independent axes are geometrically orthogonal (i.e., right angles)
The left shows independent axes
The right shows axes that are correlated

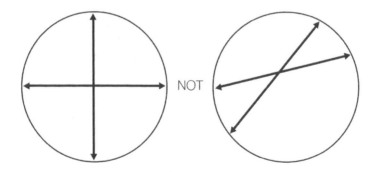

In the latter, the four quadrants are effectively reduced to two. Consider the Alberta Ecotrust example described above. Two important dimensions that could be candidates for critical uncertainties forming the axes of the matrix were social values and public action / engagement of stakeholders. Note descriptions of the axes and end points. Social values range from private, polarized, and me to public, cohesive, and engaged. Public action / role of stakeholders ranges from divided, autonomous, and special interest to collaborative, engaged, and public interest. The similarity of descriptions is the first sign that the two potential axes have similar thrusts and might be correlated. Reflection on the meaning of the dimensions also raises concerns. It becomes difficult to envisage a world in which social values are public, cohesive, and engaged and public engagement is divided, autonomous, and dominated by special interests. A world that is public, cohesive, and engaged seems to go well with public actions that are collaborative and engaged in the public interest. These axes would not yield scenarios that are distinct and challenging.

In general, axes tend to be broadly economic, social, or political, and occasionally technological. Axes focused on environmental issues are essentially a variation of a social concern. Two economic, two social, or two political dimensions will not work. Economic / social or economic / political combinations work well. A social / political pairing can work but needs to be carefully defined since social trends and values often have political expressions. Technology axes tend to work well in most cases, but, again, care in the specific definition is required. For example, if the definition of the uncertainty in technology relates to whether its impacts are reinforcing or disruptive, then it may not fit with an economic uncertainty focused on the structure of the economy. Technology would seem to be a major cause of the restructuring of the economy. The shift from a manufacturing-dominated economy to a service and information-dominated economy is an example of restructuring.

A key role for an experienced scenario facilitator is to point out such pitfalls and ensure the axes in the scenario framework are independent and not correlated. Choosing the axes does not only depend on the experience of the facilitator, but also on a process of testing the axes. Testing involves experimenting with different combinations of axes. This reveals problems with correlation and whether the emerging scenarios are insightful and challenging.

Testing to Ensure Challenging Scenarios

How do we ensure the scenarios are challenging? Do the scenarios push the thinking of the organization? Do they surface a range of new outcomes that the organization needs to consider? Will they broaden the thinking and raise new possibilities for the organization? Do they raise tensions and conflicts that the organization must address? These questions cannot be fully determined at this point, but in getting to the matrix we can test the emerging scenarios for their novelty, insight, and challenge.

The approach to developing the axes is to test-drive them. How do you do that? First, you need to select two candidates from the list of potential critical uncertainties. Sometimes, the voting generates two clear critical uncertainties. Other times there might be three potential candidates. In either case, the process is the same.

Second, having selected two candidate dimensions, you use two levels of questions to test the fitness of the axes. One set of questions focuses on identifying specific characteristics. A second emphasizes broad first impressions.

Having selected two candidate dimensions, you can ask participants to reflect on the combination represented in each quadrant, upper right, lower left, et cetera, and to list four or five characteristics describing that future world. For example, what does a world characterized by high economic growth and collaborative public engagement look like? What characteristics would you use to describe that world? In the real case, from our case study (Alberta Ecotrust), responses included increased resources, increased knowledge and information, agreements on trade-offs, integrated decision-making, balance of public/private, high compliance, and increased greenhouse gas (GHG) emissions (Figure 13). The beginnings of an interesting and challenging scenario began to emerge. Note that although initial thinking might have been a little euphoric, not all was sunshine. Increased GHG emissions clearly recognized that growth and collaboration were great future prospects, but that they come with challenges. Indeed, to be compelling, all good scenario narratives need some level of conflict. Like a good novel, there needs to be some tension to be believable and to be challenging.

A second set of questions approaches the potential scenarios at a higher level. The intent is to elevate the discussion to more general trends and directions. Specifically, what are the broad first impressions? Typical questions might include:

1. Considering possible outcomes in each quadrant, e.g., upper right, lower lefts, et cetera. Is that combination of outcomes plausible? Could that happen?

2. Is there a major thrust or direction that could be interesting to explore and challenging for the organization? Does that combination of outcomes challenge the focal question?

3. Are the futures in each quadrant distinctly different?

These questions open a conversation at a high level on the validity of the critical uncertainties in generating four distinct, plausible, and challenging scenarios. The discussion will unerringly highlight whether the axes are independent as well as whether they are plausible, challenging, and different.

A note of caution. It is not unusual for one quadrant to challenge the test of plausibility. In testing the logic framework, one should not accept or reject the framework too quickly. The perspective that a quadrant is not feasible usually signals correlation; the axes are not independent. A counter example is provided in Box 5. It describes a project on the future of higher education (i.e., post-secondary college and university) in which the initial scenario framework provoked scepticism that the scenario in one quadrant was not possible. The scepticism proved to be wrong. Understanding how a scenario in that quadrant could occur proved to be particularly instructive with valuable insights into the forces shaping the future of higher education that is completely different from traditional post-secondary schools in Canada.

The process is repeated for each quadrant and a decision is made either to test another combination of axes or to proceed with that combination. In the case study, the two axes, economy and stakeholder engagement, were adopted to form the scenario logic. The next steps were to flesh out the characteristics for each quadrant, explore storylines to reflect the dynamic of the story over time, and agree on names. How do we do that?

Box 5—Unexpected Insights from a Rogue Quadrant

In an interesting study on the future of higher education (university and college) in the early 2000s in Alberta, a challenge occurred in testing the axes. The emergent critical uncertainties, shown in Figure 16, were competition (open or limited) and delivery (public or private). Three of the scenarios quickly emerge—Competitive Edge, Prozactivity, and Controlled Growth.

Figure 16—Future of Higher Education

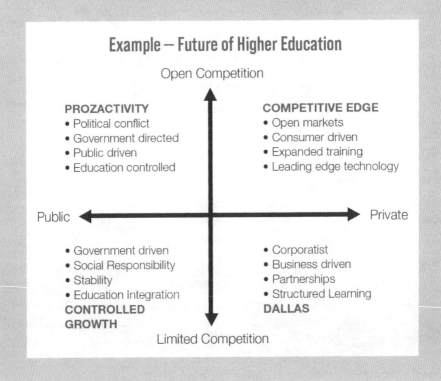

Example – Future of Higher Education

Open Competition

PROZACTIVITY
- Political conflict
- Government directed
- Public driven
- Education controlled

COMPETITIVE EDGE
- Open markets
- Consumer driven
- Expanded training
- Leading edge technology

Public ← → Private

- Government driven
- Social Responsibility
- Stability
- Education Integration
CONTROLLED GROWTH

- Corporatist
- Business driven
- Partnerships
- Structured Learning
DALLAS

Limited Competition

Competitive Edge is a world of increased competition and more private delivery, an easy combination to imagine. Prozactivity (what a great name) highlights the disturbing prospect, at least for some, of a public system with increased competition. Controlled growth reinforces the status quo of a publicly dominated system searching for managed efficiency. The fourth quadrant seemed to pose a difficulty. How could you have a move to a private system and limited competition? Weren't they incompatible? The challenge was to reconcile the initial incompatibility.

The answer came from the question: What is the purpose of a merger or acquisition in the business world? Is the purpose of an acquisition to take over a competitor and reduce competition? Is that the logic of this scenario? The idea that consolidation emerges from competition led the group to realize that their initial thinking was too narrow. They then equated this unbridled competition leading to less competition as synonymous with the TV show *Dallas*, a series that ran in the 1970s and featured Texas oil millionaires. Despite discouraging the use of movie or TV names for scenarios, this proved to be a very good choice whose meaning was instantly recognized. The moral of the story: don't be too quick to discard an axis that appears to create implausible outcomes. Whenever dramatic, unexpected events occur people say, who could have guessed that could happen? A comment like that confesses a failure of imagination that resulted in the organization's inability to anticipate major changes.

CHARACTERISTICS AND STORYLINES

The axes defining the framework represent scaffolding for building scenarios. The task is to flesh out the scenarios by expanding on the characteristics for each quadrant of the matrix and creating a story of how each scenario unfolds over time.

Characteristics are descriptions of the scenario. They can be part of the dynamic or the outcome. A dynamic might be strong economic growth or environment valued. An outcome usually describes an end state such as increased resources or increased GHG emissions. Continuing with the Alberta Ecotrust example, the question asked to generate characteristics was, What changes could occur if economic growth is high and stakeholder engagement is collaborative and public with power distributed? Participants generate ideas supplementing the initial characteristics to flesh out descriptions of the scenario embedded in each quadrant.

While characteristics serve to define an end point, storylines describe the path from today to the future. They link events over time consistent with the logic and theme of the scenario. Like a novel, they begin to tell the plot or sequence of events over time. Ultimately, a plot is not a story. A story includes the logic inherent in the sequence of events. The story tells why one event causes or follows from another. [22]

The objective is to fill out the scenarios with characteristics and generate initial storylines. In the workshop, this stage typically involves dividing participants into two groups to generate the characteristics, storylines, and names. The purpose of dividing into groups is to encourage more individual participation and interaction, as well as efficiency. In a smaller group, each individual has more opportunity to participate and articulate ideas. The process is more inclusive and productive in encouraging an exchange of ideas with greater depth of thinking.

The plenary group can be divided into breakout groups by preselecting individuals to ensure diversity. Alternatively, individuals can be assigned randomly during the session. There are clear advantages in having a range of personalities and viewpoints in each group, but manipulating the process excessively can appear heavy handed. Self-selection can be an alternative where each individual chooses the group they prefer. This is often unbalanced so the facilitator or sponsor can intervene and assign a few people surreptitiously, ensuring diversity without seeming to manipulate the outcome.

The tasks assigned to each breakout group are to identify characteristics, create storylines, and select names in each of two quadrants. The quadrants allocated are intentionally the diagonal quadrants in the matrix. Why? The intent is to maximize the differences in the two scenarios that each group is developing. One group works on quadrant one (upper right) and quadrant three (lower left). The other group works on quadrants two and four. A major challenge in developing scenarios is to ensure the scenarios are distinctly different. You do not want the scenarios to converge toward a common centre with similar logics and outcomes. Assigning diagonal quadrants ensures that each group is working on two extremely different scenarios, scenarios that differ on both dimensions.

This problem becomes more acute if the decision is made to create four breakout groups, one for each quadrant. With a very large group this is an option.[23] It supports greater participation but risks the problem of convergence. Many participants may have a specific idea on how the future will unfold. They may have a strong perspective that, for example, big business is powerful and corrupt requiring government intervention for a good outcome. (I am exaggerating for effect.) The difficulty is that they will attempt to shoehorn that idea into whichever group they are in, whether the ideas fit the logic of the scenario or not. They are not being intentionally disruptive;

22 The term "scenario" was originally used in the movie industry to outline the logic of the narrative. It did not include dialogue or details of sets or lighting, only the logic of the story. In politics and economics, the term was popularized by Herman Kahn in the 1960s to describe alternative global futures.

23 The problem may occur whether the session involves an independent facilitator or is self-facilitated by participants using a clear set of instructions.

with four groups they only have one scenario to embed their thinking in. At least with two scenarios to develop, the individual can insert that strongly held idea into the scenario that is logically more appropriate.

The psychological challenge of preconceived ideas sounds sinister but is merely a reflection of reality. To surface this issue and encourage an open mind, I introduce the idea of the willing suspension of disbelief. An example is in watching a movie. You may become emotionally involved while watching a movie. You feel the pain, sorrow, or fear portrayed. You empathize with it. But you know that this is not real. It is just a movie. The disclaimer that no animals were hurt confirms that the story portrayed is not real. Yet the emotion is real. What you have done is set aside your disbeliefs. That is what we ask in the scenario process. Set aside your disbeliefs and open your thinking to new ideas. Consciously try to see events from different perspectives. Is the glass half full or half empty? Two different perspectives of the same fact. Such differences can influence decisions. If half empty, plan to buy another bottle of whisky. If half full, you might save it for another day. For scenario thinking, push the boundaries.

For breakout groups, the process involves three steps: characteristics, storylines, and names.

Characteristics

The generation of characteristics proceeds with a series of questions. Thinking about quadrant one, for example, how would you describe that world in 2030 (the time horizon)? What are the characteristics of that future? How could the world change?

As always, participants are asked to reflect and write down ten or more ideas on the characteristics of the future framed by the quadrant selected. As participants work independently and write down ideas, you can supplement the initial question with further questions to stimulate more and more divergent thinking. For example, you might remind them of the list of driving forces and encourage them to think about how each driving force might play out in that quadrant. Or you might encourage them to think of characteristics that describe the dynamic or thrust of the scenario and not just the final outcome. And then you might push them to think the unthinkable.

Generating ideas is always fruitful. The fact that they have rehearsed the process and created a number of ideas in testing the framework in the plenary facilitates the process in the breakout groups. As well, the much smaller group is conducive to increased participation. As before, the process involves randomly soliciting ideas from participants and recording the ideas expeditiously with minimal conversation or judgement. Adding ideas in a brainstorming forum is encouraged, along with clarification, but deeper discussion of whether an idea is appropriate or valid for that scenario is discouraged. The intent is to get all the idea recorded before opening discussion on logic and relevance.

Having recorded ideas, the discussion turns to logic. What are the themes that are emerging? Is this a scenario about economics, social values, technology, competition, policy, or what? The intent is to raise the level of thinking from the specific characteristics to a higher level of abstraction. You are trying to understand how each scenario could occur. One useful prompt is to ask participants to put themselves, or a customer, or a competitor in the scenario and ask what they would do. What would motivate them in this future world?

One challenge is to surface and deal with inherent conflict across characteristics. Opening these for discussion is necessary in exposing the underlying logic. Why did one person, for example, see increased immigration in a scenario while another person sees increased social divisions leading to restrictions on immigration in the same scenario? Clarifying these differences between seemingly conflicting ideas can be very revealing in exposing the underlying logic of the scenario that is emerging. Ultimately, such conflicts will need to be addressed in the final narratives. So, use them at this point in the process to clarify thinking and the logic of the scenario.

Storylines

Having generated a list of characteristics, not all of which are logically consistent, and a few basic themes to describe the thrust of the scenario, the next task is to begin to flesh out storylines. How do we do that? The steps involved are summarized in Figure 17.

Figure 17—Creating Storylines

Storylines – Creating Strings of Snippets

The purpose is to describe how the scenario unfolds over time. We are looking for sequences of events that demonstrate the overall logic of the scenario.

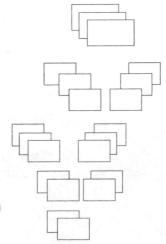

1. Each person writes down a sequence of 3 or 4 developments or events which reflect the logic of the scenario. Record these on post-it notes. These are called snippets.

2. Display all the sequences which have a common theme into longer sequences.

3. Arrange the story snippets into time periods.

    Short Term

      Medium Term

        Long Term

4. Use the snippets as a rich source of information for writing the scenarios.

To begin, ask each participant, working independently, to write down an event or development that could occur consistent with the logic of the scenario.[24] Then ask, If that happened, what would happen next? Then what would happen? The intent is to generate a sequence of snippets creating a logical string of developments over time. Such a sequence is called a vignette. Similar sequences from different people can be combined and events assigned rough time frames (short, medium, or long). A summarized set of events, not well connected but divided into time frames, is shown in Figure 17 from our Alberta Ecotrust case study.

Figure 18–Storyline Development

Storyline Development
Ideas Generated for Full Speed Ahead

2013-2015	2016-2018	2019-2023
• Policy and regs for energy implemented • Balance public/private interests • Single regulator - land use downgraded • Limited investment in gov't capacity • Plans lack specificity • Municipalities, watershed groups etc – rising frustration • Entrenched interests – property rights trump public interests and planning on private lands • High food prices • Gateway and XL approved	• Applies energy model regs to agriculture etc (present gov't gets re-elected) • Regional plans ineffective • Frustration/interests bought off • New political power – smaller gov't, scope of gov't, private goods, market actors • Cities gain political influence • Destroys collaboration • Technology improves efficiency of energy extraction with environmental mitigation objectives	• More GHG emissions • More sprawl • Deteriorating environmental situation • Environmental outcomes are worse in a predicable way • Improvements in pockets

24   In some scenarios a trigger event or development may be required. A useful prompting question in such a case is: What is necessary for this scenario to occur? Realizing that for a scenario to occur depends on specific circumstances is valuable insight and particularly useful when designing signposts.

Developing detailed and logical storylines can be difficult, particularly at the end of a long workshop when participants may be getting tired. (Mental work is surprisingly tiring!) While the logic shown in Figure 18 is sound, the reality is that a good result is a list of developments sorted by time with at least some clear connections across events. Nevertheless, this adds another perspective from participants on the characteristics and logic of the scenarios and a valuable set of specific developments that can be woven into the scenario stories.

Box 6—A Note on Inductive Versus Deductive Scenarios

There are two broad methods of developing scenarios.[25] One is deductive; the other, inductive. A deductive approach begins with a theory or theoretical hypothesis, uses logical reasoning to deduce results, and then seeks observations to support or refute the theory. Our approach is deductive. It proceeds in a top-down process from identifying driving forces to critical uncertainties to the two-dimension logic framework to describing characteristics and paths. Each step follows a deductive logical order.

An inductive approach begins with examples of observations that you analyze and build into a theory. It works from the bottom up. Developing sequences of snippets is one approach. Participants are asked to brainstorm sequences of events or developments that could occur. The sequences are combined to generate not only the beginning of scenario stories but emergent themes. Examining differences across the nascent scenarios, inductively surfaces the underlying key uncertainties. With these insights further refinement of the scenarios ensures the development of a wide range of stories.

A process similar to this was used to develop the well-known Mont Fleur scenarios in the early 1990s that shaped political developments in South Africa, post-apartheid (Kahane, 2001, 2012). An inductive approach is rich in content and encourages a high level of interaction, participation, and creative thinking but is time-consuming. The process is open-ended. It is difficult to design and manage a workshop, for example, with expected time lines. Premature closing of a conversation can destroy the entire process. Allowing time for reflection so ideas can ferment is difficult. Deductive approaches involve a discrete set of steps that can be managed in a reasonable time frame, which makes them more attractive as an approach in most organizational settings.

---

25 For a more comprehensive discussion see Chermack (2011).

Names

The third workshop task is to generate a name for each scenario. Names should be insightful in capturing a major theme of the scenarios, short—two to three words— and memorable. Personally, I like names that emphasize dynamics or change. One graphic scenario name that emerged in a project I conducted for an energy company was "Black Tide Rising." This vividly captured the idea of a rising supply of oil in the world. The names in the Alberta Ecotrust case study ("Collaboration Rising," "Reduced Expectations," "Full Speed Ahead," and "Engaged Prosperity") follow the criteria of being short, dynamic, and memorable while capturing a major theme. See Box 7 for examples of great names.

In soliciting names for scenarios there are two pitfalls: time and trivia. Selecting a good name can be time-consuming.[26] No name satisfies everyone. A procession of names can be a nightmare. Frustration rising is a name for this process. To avoid this possibility, you can restrict the process using the coercion of democracy by voting. First, each participant generates a single name. Second, vote on the names. Give each person two votes so they don't just vote for their own suggestion. Finally, select the top two (assuming two get a similar number of votes) and vote on those two names. You have the luxury of changing names later, although care must be taken.[27] This process is expedient in getting names for the scenarios in a short period. Surprisingly, the names generated are often appropriate and remain attached to the final written scenarios

The second pitfall involves names that are provocative, silly, or obscure. Near the end of the workshop, focus can be lacking. Probably the most common challenge is the suggestion of adopting names of books or titles of movies. *Blade Runner* is undoubtedly the leading movie name proposed for scenarios. Book titles have included *Paradise Lost, Catcher in the Rye*, and *1984*, to name a few.[28] The difficulty with titles as names is that while the meaning is clear to some, it can be obscure to many. How many people know, remember, or relate to *Blade Runner*? Is it the original version or the more recent one? For some it is insightful, for others it is a mystery. As a result, try to steer the names away from books or movies.

---

26 One scenario exercise at Shell in the late 1980s took more than two months and literally hundreds of hours to finally agree on names. Excellent names emerged but few organizations have the luxury of devoting such resources to creating scenario names.

27 Changing the names later might be necessary but should be approached with caution. If all the names are radically changed, the process may appear manipulated and undermine the integrity and support for the entire project.

28 An interesting observation is that Americans and Canadians frequently propose movie names for scenarios while the British lean more to book titles. In the same way, British actors, when reviewing a part, ask how many lines they would have, while American actors ask how many scenes they would have. An insight into cultural differences, perhaps? Neither work well for scenario names.

Finally, in some cases, names need to be politically correct. You would all like to be unrestricted in selecting names, but if the scenarios will ultimately be widely distributed, and especially those that will be public, some restraint is necessary. "Screw the Rich" might sound great to some, but if exposed to public scrutiny could undermine the entire purpose of the project. Focusing on a provocative name may lead readers to reject the entire set of scenarios. Public sector organizations usually release documents and reports, and provocative titles on scenarios could lead to embarrassing publicity. No organization wants that. While self-censorship may be necessary, replacing a politically incorrect name should be viewed as a challenge to be more creative.

Box 7–Great Scenario Names

Selecting scenario names is difficult but often great names emerge. Three examples reflect projects from Ralston Purina, The *Los Angeles Times,* and McGraw Hill. The future of the pet products industry (1998) focused on industry structure and the impact of technology. The scenario names captured creatively the scenario differences in the four quadrants. "Jurassic Park" focused on consolidation and tech-driven new products. Although a movie name, it captured the revival of lumbering giants through new technology. "Bou*tech" reflected fragmented structure and new products. "Petwork Quilt" portrayed the fragmented structure and few new products, while "Land of the Agile Retail Giants" captured the rise in power of large retailers relative to product manufacturers. These were enticing names that highlighted the underlying logic of each scenario.

A *Los Angeles Times* project (1999) on the future of newspaper publishing generated four great names. "Surf City" described a future in which a plethora of news companies provided customize content to consumers. It denoted a wild and free publishing world. "Son of a Niche" described a future combining consolidation in publishing and a focus on individualized content. "McFuture," in contrast, was a world of consolidation of channels, high barriers to entry, and traditional content, i.e., the same for everyone and low cost. Finally, "Capture the Portal" was a future in which control of the portal—the website—was critical. All great names reflecting the logic and capturing the imagination.

The future of educational publishing was the focus of a project by McGraw Hill (2000). "Land of Giants" reflected a consolidated industry and student-centred learning. In contrast, "Ivory Tower" was consolidation and traditional teacher-centred learning. "Skill Seekers" described a fragmented industry and student-centred learning. "Mavericks" was a future with a fragmented industry and teacher-centred learning.

Many others could be quoted. The key point is that scenario names can and should be short, memorable, relevant to the audience, and insightful in capturing a critical theme of the scenario.

CHAPTER SUMMARY

- The scenario development process involves a series of discrete steps (Figures 6 and 19).

- Conducted in a workshop setting, the steps are initiated by a sequence of questions designed to create highly participatory, interactive, and inclusive conversations.

- Responses to questions use the incremental method, requiring participants to write down ideas independently before discussion.

- The most important and most difficult part of the process is defining the critical uncertainties. These emerge as the answer to the question: What are the two most important uncertainties facing the industry or sector in the future?

- The ideas and information generated in the scenario development workshop provide the basis for writing the scenarios.

- The process is summarized in Figure 19 (previously shown as Figure 6).

Figure 19—Process of Scenario Development

Scenario Development Process

Define Focal Issue, Question, or Decision and Relevant Timeframe

Review Past Events & Discuss Alternative Interpretations

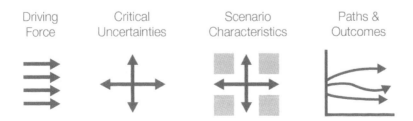

| Driving Force | Critical Uncertainties | Scenario Characteristics | Paths & Outcomes |

CHAPTER 5
CREATING SCENARIOS

The wealth of information generated in the scenario-development workshop provides the raw material for creating scenarios. Although the landscape is rich in ideas describing characteristics, initial logics, and storylines, the ideas are often incoherent or incomplete. Gaps are common. The paths, while directive, are more trails with faint branches and logical conflicts than clear highways. The raw data needs to be transformed into coherent stories describing different paths into the future. The challenge is to fill in and make sense of the landscape and clarify the directions and paths that create logical and consistent stories. In short, the scenario writer needs to be proactive in creating the stories. The writer needs to ensure the logic and ideas generated by participants are honoured and reflected in the scenarios, but also needs to enhance the basic logic to create compelling, coherent, and challenging scenarios. It is not a simple translation.

POWER OF STORIES

There is debate about whether written stories are necessary. One argument is that many organizations are more suited to visual presentations using viewgraphs and bullet-point statements to communicate. There is considerable truth in this. Organizational cultures vary. For example, an organization that has a strong engineering culture often shows a preference for bullet descriptions. They are short, precise, and definitive. Engineers also like axes and lean strongly to visual displays. Reading long stories is seldom part of the culture. If that is the case, why not write scenarios in bullets and not prose? Should not the scenarios be shaped to reflect the culture and learning style dominant in an organization?[29]

There are two counterarguments. Bullet statements have limitations, while stories have significant attractions. The challenge with bullets is that they are too definitive. Their apparent precision means that they are accepted as correct without challenge. They are too unequivocal. They do not encourage dialogue and debate. The purpose of scenarios, however, is to stimulate thinking and challenge conventional perspectives and ideas. The very nature of only writing scenarios in bullet form is contrary to the spirit of the exercise.

In contrast, written narratives are a powerful way of communicating. They are an ancient and enduring way of making and communicating meaning. They underpin many professions, including law, education, politics, writing, philosophy, history, and journalism. They are also important in business. Stories are valuable in simplifying complex issues, engaging individuals at a cognitive level, and weaving together ideas to create fresh perspectives. Stories are also memorable. Writing stories, in short, is a valuable way of communicating that encourages engagement and dialogue.

The power of stories in creating meaning does not imply that presentations and other creative ways of conveying ideas are inappropriate. Different people learn differently. Why not use multiple styles? Why not use bullets, stories, and presentations to communicate the scenarios? Written stories engage the reader. Bullets work well for some audiences. Presentations are a way of life in all organizations. I encourage all forms of communication. First, let's focus on writing narratives. Then I'll review summary tables and presentations, which are dominated by bullets.

CREATING STORIES

The challenge is to write engaging, challenging stories that describe four distinctly different futures. The four-quadrant logic framework gives the overall direction of the story. The characteristics and storylines provide the raw data for the scenarios. There is no specific formula for developing the stories. A practical approach to developing scenarios with a format for presenting the scenario stories is provided below.

---

29   While companies with an engineering or accounting culture embrace visual axes and bullets, the opposite is true for people-focused organizations. I have worked with lawyers. They can digest fifty-page briefs without batting an eye, but struggle to understand figures and diagrams. Another group I have worked with is police. Their training is focused on understanding and interpreting behaviour. They can work with diagrams but bring discipline and deep experience in observing behaviour. All great to work with, each with different perspectives. Whether people choose disciplines that reflect their perspective or people in different disciplines are trained differently is an interesting question. For scenarios, you need to adapt to the culture.

Structure and Style

The simple template includes an overview and main story. The overview is approximately one-half page in length, designed to give the reader a quick summary of the scenario. The overview highlights the main theme of the scenario and key characteristics in a logical sequence. The simplest style for the overview is to write it in the present tense. As well as introducing the scenario, the overviews of the four scenarios can be extracted and used to create an executive summary for the final document if that is appropriate. (See an example of a written scenario in this format in the appendix.)

The main story expands on the overview with more detailed descriptions and examples to flesh out a comprehensive and coherent story. Typically, the main story is two and a half to three pages, although it is often difficult to keep it that brief. As the old saying goes, if I had more time, I would make it shorter. Draft the overview first, write the story, and then revise both. The alternative is equally valid: write the overview last.

What verb tense should you use in writing the main story? I recommend the third person past tense. In this way the story is told from an observer looking back from the future. Why? A story written in the past tense makes it more real and believable. It seems that the events have happened. Occasionally, the present tense will work. You never use the future tense. Saying something will happen always raises doubt. You want the reader immersed in the story without questioning every statement. I have used first person—"I was there"—and even dialogue—but using the third person and past tense works well.

The structure includes an initial bridging paragraph, a main body with subheadings describing development over time, and a last paragraph to highlight the final outcomes. The subheadings allow the reader to follow the flow of thinking more easily. The initial bridging paragraph is designed to link a current development with the thrust of the story. This often involves an interpretation of current or recent events that leads into the scenario story, for example, "After the Great Recession, product demand was . . ."; "The takeover of the high-tech company signalled . . ."; or "The rising environmental concern over climate change challenged policy assumptions of . . ." In these examples, the first signals that demand is a key theme. In the second, consolidation or industry structure is a key theme. In the third, the impact of climate-change effects on policy is surfaced as a major theme. Connecting the known past to the uncertain future is not only a useful way to get started; it lends credibility to the story. Readers can immediately relate to the known developments and see the story as an extension of that flow of ideas. In addition, using the same past events for different scenarios but interpreting the past events differently signals immediately differences in perspective between the scenarios. For example, a fall in the market might be interpreted as a result of government intervention in one scenario and interpreted as the result of falling demand in the other. Immediately, one scenario would be signalling that government policy was a major driving force, while the other would be signalling that market demand was a major driving force.

Following the bridging paragraph, writing the story requires building the logic through time. The storylines developed in the workshop are the starting point. They are seldom fully fleshed out in terms of logic or consistency. After all, they were created on the fly by a number of individuals. One approach to developing the logic and stories is to define the topics that need to be addressed. Recall that the driving forces represent a framework for describing the future. Reviewing each driving force and mapping out how each would play out in each quadrant is a valuable step in understanding the thrust and logic of each scenario. Add other specific factors, such as technology, demand, policy, customers, competitors, et cetera, and you are beginning to get a distinct portrait of each scenario. The logic can then be enriched by posing a series of questions in your mind, for example: What motivates consumers in this scenario? What is driving government policy? What is the driving force behind social change? From this exploration a deeper understanding of each scenario and how they differ should emerge.

This approach may be sufficient to begin writing the story. Another tool is the logic map or logical sequence of cause and effect. A story includes a plot, which is the sequence of events. A story includes the logic of the sequence of events. You need to describe how the key forces and events lead to the final outcomes. My logic maps are messy initially but become more focused as I work with them. Figure 20 provides an example of a logic map used in developing the scenario Full Speed Ahead, one of the Alberta Ecotrust Foundation scenarios.

The logic map clarifies the story over time. In the Full Speed Ahead example, the three initial thrusts are economic development, Alberta environmental stakeholders, and international anti-oil sands activism. These create pressures and conflicts between economic-growth advocates and environmental activists and stakeholders that cannot be reconciled. Policy is inadequate and pressure mounts on the government to respond. Policies supporting development and industry and property rights clash with policies supporting environmental protection, recognition of environmental services, and efforts to force consideration of environmental externalities. In this scenario, government decision-making leads to a focus on simpler technical solutions, compliance, and compromise with power diffused to regions making action difficult and piecemeal.

The final paragraph, often with a subheading showing the time-horizon date, such as 2040, summarizes the changes that have occurred. As in the example, the changes include trade-offs, centralized power, and a search for technical solutions.

Figure 20—Example of a Logic Map

Example of a Logic Map – Full Speed Ahead

Policy & decision processes inadequate to deal with environment & social pressures

Role of the Writer

The workshop provides the raw material for the scenarios. The role of the writer is to turn that into a finished product. The raw material may not be consistent. There may be errors or mistakes. Ideas in the workshop were generated rapidly without time for reflection or revision. People's views of the scenarios while working in the workshop can differ significantly. The writer's task is to make sense of the ideas and concepts and create a coherent and logical description of the scenario. The assignment is to honour the ideas that emerged from the workshop while creating a logical and meaningful story. This can be a difficult balancing act.

Communicating Scenarios

The written narratives are the centrepiece for communicating the scenario thinking. In the written document, I start with a brief review of the scenario development process. The review highlights the focal question, driving forces, and critical uncertainties. The four-quadrant diagram with the critical uncertainties and scenario names provides a smooth connection to the scenario stories. At this point I add a four-quadrant table summarizing the main characteristics and logic of each scenario. The four summary descriptions juxtaposed on a single page allow the reader to identify differences between scenarios as well as providing a concise overview of the scenarios prior to immersing the reader in the written narratives. (See an example of the table in the appendix.)

Following the written portion—the scenario stories—I end the report with a summary of major scenario characteristics. This table is valuable in clarifying differences across scenarios for each driving force. The mix of bullets in the overview, scenario stories, and a bullet summary table at the end accommodates different learning styles and follows the old communication strategy: tell them what you are going to tell them, tell them, and then tell them what you told them. This is a tried-and-true principle in all communication departments.

This format allows for different combinations of material to be used for different purposes and audiences. For example, an executive summary can be created by combining the focal question, driving forces and scenario framework diagrams with the one-page bullet summary and the scenario overviews. Presto, a four-page executive summary. Similarly, a basic presentation includes the focal question, driving forces, and scenario framework diagrams with four viewgraphs populated with the bullets from the summary tables in the document. Of course, good presentations will flesh out the basics with added material and diagrams to engage the audience in creative ways. Research on key variables can greatly enhance the quality and relevance of the scenarios (Chermack, 2011). Videos have often been used to supplement presentations and engage participants in workshops.

In the appendix, the Full Speed Ahead scenario from the Alberta Ecotrust scenarios highlighted in the logic map (Figure 20) is an example of a summary table, overview, and elements of written scenarios. This is primarily for practitioners and those wanting a more explicit example of the scenario template described here.

The Good, the Bad and the Unlikely

The central concept in scenarios is that the future is uncertain. This means that there is no known distribution of future outcomes. The purpose of the scenarios is to explore the range of possible future outcomes in the context of the focal question. This provides perspectives on the future as a basis for developing strategies.

Inevitably, two interpretations creep into the discussion. One is an effort to assign probabilities to the scenarios. Another is to assign value to the scenarios in terms of good or bad scenarios. Both concepts are misguided. Why?

Assigning likelihoods or probabilities undermines the basic premise of scenarios that the future is uncertain. Specifically, likely scenarios attract attention; unlikely scenarios are ignored. If something cannot happen, then why search for implications?

If something is likely, then we should focus on the implications of that scenario. This narrowing of focus raises the same concerns expressed in our discussion of forecasts versus scenarios. Basing strategies on a single future is dangerous. The danger is further compounded if the likely scenario is a positive scenario (at least on the surface), which is often the case. Then there is little challenge to conventional thinking, and the power of scenarios to surface risks is reduced. This is the opposite of what we are trying to accomplish with scenarios. Engaging in discussions of likelihood or probabilities distorts the basic underlying concept of scenarios and hinders the learning component of the exercise. Discussion of probabilities is not a good idea with scenarios.

Discussion of good and bad scenarios is similarly unproductive. In our approach, at least one of the scenarios is negative. What does this mean? In scenarios, life is not good or bad, only more of the same or different. Typically, an organization has an official future that is implicit in their thinking and planning (Schwartz, 2000). The five-year plan often articulates or reflects that dominant perspective on the future. The official future usually underpins the existing business model, which works in a world of growing markets and rising demand (or economic growth and rising tax revenues for governments). The official future is usually very optimistic. Such a scenario is important; it is often plausible and reflects common thinking. But it is dangerous in developing strategy and making decisions on a single view. It does not lend itself to surfacing and addressing new risks.

Negative stories are typically associated with potential changes that would affect the existing business model. Such stories are often downplayed as unlikely and not taken seriously. Potential insights are then lost. At some point, the scenario has been deemed plausible and should be understood to gain insights into how the future could unfold and what that could mean for the organization. As a result, when developing strategy, you need to ask participants to set aside their disbeliefs, consider all scenarios equally likely, and not prejudge them as good or bad. As Arie de Geus at Shell eloquently and pointedly summarized, the question is not, could it happen, but what would you do if it did happen?

Negative scenarios are always productive in generating insights in two ways. First, they challenge our thinking. For example, consider the higher education rogue scenario ultimately named Dallas shown in Figure 16. That scenario reflected a world in which there was a shift toward private organizations and less competition. The initial response by participants was that this was a contradiction. Private meant more competition, didn't it? The effort to understand how this combination of outcomes could occur resulted in the insight that dominant universities with prominent reputations and expertise, such as Harvard or Oxford, or a company with enormous marketing clout, such as the University of Phoenix or Microsoft, could overwhelm competitors in the development and delivery of courses through licensing to other institutions or providing courses online to large student populations. The realization was that mergers and acquisitions in the private sector were designed to limit competition, not encourage it. Similar developments were possible in the public universe of higher education. For a major public institution in Canada, this was a challenge. Without exploring this negative scenario, valuable insights would have been lost.

Second, if leaders, executives, and managers refuse to consider negative scenarios, they are failing to meet their responsibility to think about and understand how the organization could respond to potential threats. They are abdicating their due diligence as leaders of the organization. Insights are lost both in what could happen and what it means. There is insight to be gained both in how the scenario could occur and the implications to the organization. This is how a black swan event occurs (Taleb, 2007). This is an event in which knowledge was available beforehand to understand and anticipate potential developments but was understood only after the event. A black swan event is a surprise—often with severe impacts—that could have been anticipated. Scenarios are intended to take the surprise out of black swans.

The essential message is, treat each scenario as plausible and equally likely and discourage broad generalizations of good or bad scenarios.

Context and Culture

Scenarios that have negative futures (I hate the term but we must face reality) have huge learning potential. Realizing that potential may be difficult. This depends on the culture and context of the organization. Public institutions that may be required to release their reports to the public are inevitably sensitive to how those scenarios will be interpreted and used. There is a threat that a negative scenario will be taken out of context, leading to bad publicity. This means, for example, that names need to be selected carefully if they will or could become public. A private company has a different context. The scenarios are strategic assets that are not designed to become public.

This public / private context can be further complicated by the culture of the organization. Work with a very large health organization provided a vivid example of how challenges to context and culture can derail a project. The project proceeded well through interviews and generation of issues. Some credibility was lost when the major public and political issue of patient wait times for operations was not articulated—a failure of the interviews. Nevertheless, development of the scenarios using the deductive approach generated four plausible and challenging scenarios—at least in the consultants' view.

As these emerged, however, tensions surfaced. There were two difficulties. First, three of the four scenarios were viewed as negative. Learning from these scenarios on what could hinder or prevent their vision of the ideal health system was a non-starter.

The client feared that these scenarios would become public and politically embarrassing to the public health care system and the government.

Second, as discussions progressed, we—the consultants—realized they did not want scenarios describing what could happen but wanted scenarios describing how to get to their vision. There was a joint failure to define the problem correctly. The underlying reality was that they believed they could create their own future. There was no realization of external uncertainties affecting the system. For example, are some chronic diseases a result of lifestyle choices? If so, should individuals be held responsible? Or does it matter? All people deserve care regardless of cause and responsibility. Such differences in societal perspectives and values would, seemingly, have a significant impact on how the health care system was structured and operated. This was not part of their thinking.

A third issue was credibility. The scenario team was viewed by some of the participants as outsiders to the system and regarded with suspicion. Harsh perhaps, but a real barrier to opening ideas on the future of health care. In the end, scenarios were never written. The project was a failure. It may have opened our minds but it did not open theirs.

In retrospect, the important role of context and culture was reinforced. More generally, organizations differ in their capacity to generate and utilize scenarios. Even relatively large and sophisticated government departments can lack the capacity to understand, internalize, and utilize scenarios to direct strategy and policy.[30]

OBJECTIVE, NORMATIVE, AND TRANSFORMATIVE SCENARIOS

Our approach focuses on objective rather than normative or transformative scenarios. The question in objective scenarios is: What could happen? The question in normative scenarios is: What do we want to happen? The latter, in our view, undermines the principle that the future is inherently uncertain and unpredictable. It may raise questions, often ethical, of what should happen and how that could occur. A richer question is trying to identify what needs to happen for a desired future to occur. It is a narrow approach to exploring the future that does not surface driving forces and uncertainties, and in turn, does not surface risks.

Normative scenarios are often descriptions of paths to a visionary future. They describe a desired endpoint and story of how to get there. The health-care example is a case in point. They had a clearly articulated vision they wanted to achieve. They wanted a description of how to get there. In this context there is a role for scenario

---

30   Lois Macklin (2008) highlighted this constraint in evaluating a scenario project conducted by the Canadian government. An excellent scenario project was ineffective in stimulating change because there was limited capacity in staff, experience, and commitment within the department to follow through.

thinking. The question that should have been asked was: Are there different paths to the vision? This would have generated a different conversation surfacing the key variable and leverage points leading to different paths and ultimately converging on a single, albeit complex, future. As in all learning, the critical starting point is an insightful question.

A variation on these are transformative scenarios as typified by the Mont Fleur scenarios credited with transforming understanding on the future of South Africa after apartheid (Kahane, 2012). In that example, the scenario process created an understanding and commitment to action by participants that ultimately influenced the course of society. In this way, transformative scenarios are similar to normative scenarios in identifying a desired future and what is needed to achieve that future — not necessarily in detail but in directional terms. These are typically large, ambitious projects in which the scenario process is designed to stimulate and direct change for the community, region, or country. The underlying principle is that the participants can ultimately influence the future.

In developing strategic scenarios, the emphasis is on objective rather than normative or transformative approaches. This is based on the perspective that the future is uncertain and beyond the control of a single organization. The organization, therefore, needs to adapt to the future; it cannot create it on its own. Nevertheless, there is a role for strategic scenarios to inform the vision and provide a basis for developing strategies to bridge the gap between the present and the desired future. More on that later.

Decision Scenarios

Scenarios are most effective as part of a strategic management process. In describing alternative futures, scenarios create expectations necessary in understanding the consequences of strategic decisions. This approach is emphasized at the outset by the development of the focal question. An insightful focal question is a vital part of the process. In some instances, the focus is even more specifically defined around an impending decision.

Decision scenarios are tightly connected to an impending decision. In working with the *Los Angeles Times*, the trigger for their strategic scenario project was a pending decision to invest hundreds of millions to buy a new printing press. Ultimately, recognizing the potential impact of the internet, they chose not to invest.

Similarly, a major pet-food manufacturer was trying to understand the impact of bovine spongiform encephalopathy (BSE), commonly called mad cow disease, on their supply chain. The US government was conducting a review and had established a timeline for adopting new regulations. The company wanted to understand the implications of the new regulations. In this case, there were three options: status quo, moderate restrictions, or severe restrictions on supply material inputs. The critical factor in pet food is protein. So, restrictions on the use of beef renderings, for example, would create a hole in the current supply of ingredients.

The project involved examining what would happen after each decision. The team played out the results of each option to learn what could occur and where the risks were. The project was very successful in preparing the company for whichever decision was made. Their understanding of the range of possible outcomes meant they were prepared when the new regulations were released. Equally significant, however, was the realization of potential supply limitations regardless of the decision. They realized that they needed to move away from certain protein sources under any circumstances. This was a revelation and major strategic result.

Figure 21 shows how different levels of uncertainty and complexity relate to different applications of scenarios. If key variables are predetermined, then the challenge is to vary known parameters to explore the future. Forecasting is appropriate in that situation. If the challenge is to understand how different alternatives could play out, as in the BSE pet food case, then there is more uncertainty from external factors. Decision scenarios are appropriate. As the external environment becomes more uncertain and complex, application of focused scenarios becomes appropriate. This is the area where most strategic scenario work occurs. Preliminary scenario work is now emerging as the complexity of large systems becomes more relevant. This is described as dynamic ambiguity defined by multiple interacting systems. This is often the context of transformative scenarios. The impact of

Covid-19 on global supply chains highlighted the challenge in understanding such a large and complex system. Global energy systems are similarly complex and uncertain. These are examples of dynamic ambiguity. [31]

---

[31] My colleague Greg McGillivray is exploring this systems world. He characterizes pre-2000 as the era of strategic management focused on organizations. He argues that post-2000 we have moved into an era that is characterized as complex with a focus on emergent systems. Scenarios as a learning tool are likely to play an important role in this larger, complex view, but how that might play out is not clear.

Figure 21—Levels of Uncertainty

Levels of Uncertainty

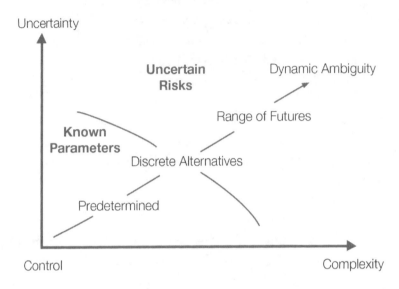

Scenario Signposts

The process of developing scenarios and the stories that are articulated create a framework for understanding ongoing events. Signposts provide a method of systematically capturing that benefit. Environmental scanning provides a broad form of monitoring external change. Signposts provide a focused approach to monitoring external change. The emphasis is on external developments that signal which scenario may be emerging. If the scenarios are rich and relevant, then all signals of change will fit into the scenario framework. If signals begin to emerge that do not relate to the scenarios, this is a sign that new scenarios are required. Insightful scenarios are typically relevant for an extended period of time, usually many years.

Signposts or early indicators are signs of change in the external environment that point to one or another of the scenarios. They are little signs of big change. The objective is to anticipate changes or impending discontinuities so that the organization can act early and gain competitive or strategic advantage, or not be blindsided by unexpected events.

Figure 22—Coal Industry Example

Coal Industry Scenario Framework (2005)

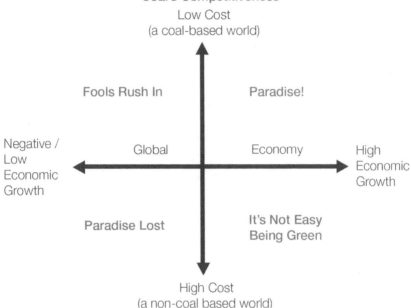

Signposts may be a specific event (e.g., election outcome, trade decision, or new technology application) or a variable (e.g., growth rate, price, market share, sales, electricity demand, et cetera) whose value over time points to one scenario or another. Good signposts clearly differentiate one scenario path from another. Ideal signposts point to a single scenario, but often a signpost will differentiate one pair of scenarios from another pair (upper quadrants from the lower ones, or left quadrants from the right). The signposts below were developed to differentiate across four scenarios originally developed for a coal company. The four scenarios: Paradise!, Fools Rush In, Paradise Lost, and It's Not Easy Being Green are shown in the scenario framework in Figure 21. Table 6 defines the signpost and the implications for the different scenarios.

Within the scenario framework, signposts emerge from the critical uncertainties, driving forces, and logic of the scenarios. The critical uncertainties are vital in determining which scenario is emerging. In the coal scenarios, a critical uncertainty is the global economy. Will the economy grow fast or slow? One signpost will be to watch GDP growth rates, a direct measure of critical uncertainty; however, in this example, US industrial growth rates, GDP, or industrial production, may be a lagging indicator rather than a leading one. Another signpost might be oil and gas prices, fuel use in power generation, or carbon regulations. The specific signpost and its value as an early indicator will depend on the organization and the scenarios.

Table 6—Example of Selected Signposts from Coal Industry circa 2006

Signposts	Description	Scenario Implication
Economic Growth (US Industrial Production)	• Strong growth industrial production • Weak growth industrial production	• **Paradise! / It's Not Easy** • **Fools Rush In** • **Paradise Lost**
Oil & Gas Prices (Future Price Strip—affects coal's competitiveness)	• High prices • Moderate prices (natural. gas + environmental concerns) • Low prices / volatile	• **Fools Rush In (coal boost)** • **Paradise!** (innovation / Integrated Gasification Combined Cycle (IGCC) • **It's Not Easy Being Green** • **Paradise Lost** (natural gas prices hurt coal competitiveness)
Fuel Use in New Generation Capacity	• Low-cost coal dominant • Low capital cost for natural gas • Strong generation capacity growth • "dirty coal" penalized	• **Fools Rush In** • **Paradise Lost** • **Paradise!** • **It's Not Easy Being Green**
LNG Expansion (Number of plants permitted and commissioned)	• Many plants in US permitted & under construction • One or two permitted in US over next few years • Ongoing difficulties / delays	• **It's Not Easy Being Green** • **Paradise!** • **Paradise Lost** • **Fools Rush In**
Regulations on Carbon (e.g., taxes, emissions trading)	• Major new restrictions • Relaxation of Regulations	• **It's Not Easy / Paradise Lost** • **Paradise!** • **Fools Rush In**

New Technology	• Numerous IGCC investments	• **Paradise!**
	• Expansions focus on improved conventional designs	• **Fools Rush In**
		• **It's Not Easy Being Green**
	• Focus on renewables	• **Paradise Lost**
	• Fight to preserve old coal plants	
Behaviour of Utilities	• Conservative / cost-based contracts / reactive	• **It's Not Easy / Paradise Lost**
	• Hedging / market-based contracts / proactive	• **Paradise! / Fools Rush In**

If the first look for key signposts is in the critical uncertainties, the second is in the driving forces. As this example from the coal industry shows, the range of future developments for each driving force may be outlined and associated with each scenario.

There are also unique developments that may signal a specific scenario. The developments define the unique logic of that scenario. The question posed is: What events in the short term are needed for the emergence of scenario X in the long term? If a specific event occurs, then this is a key signal for a specific scenario. Perhaps a financial crisis is needed to create the impetus for change described in a scenario. Perhaps a steady rise in demand is needed for a scenario to occur. Alternatively, the signal could be less of an event and more of a turning point. For example, the falling cost and rising efficiency of batteries, when reaching a certain competitive point, could be the signal for a rapid change and restructuring of the auto market.

Developing Signposts

The process of developing signposts is straightforward. Assemble a small group to brainstorm signposts. A group multiplies creativity as more participants interact and generate more ideas. Ensure familiarity with the scenarios and their logic and then explore three questions:

1. What events or developments would indicate change along the axes of the critical uncertainties?

2. Considering the driving forces, what events or developments would signal changes in those forces?

3. Considering each scenario, what events or developments are necessary for that scenario to occur?

Capture the ideas, consolidate similar ideas, and then prioritize. Signposts should be well defined so that they can be monitored, leading (not lagging) indicators, relevant, and clearly connected to the scenarios. In the coal example, US industrial production is more precise and therefore better defined than global GDP. Each has been identified as an early indicator, but liquefied natural gas (LNG) expansion may be more of a lagging, and thereby confirming, indicator than leading indicator. Carefully connect each signpost to the scenarios by showing how changes in the signpost indicate which scenario is emerging. Prioritizing the list of signposts should be part of the workshop. No more than ten should be included or the effort to monitor will be undermined. It is also a sign of sloppy thinking. Completing the logic of each signpost, however, may need careful thought by an individual or small team to complete after the workshop.

Monitoring Process

Developing signposts is valuable in deepening a group's understanding of the scenarios, the forces driving change, and how the scenarios could unfold. Signposts also create a dashboard for monitoring external change relevant to the organization and its strategic issues. All of this can evaporate without a commitment to regularly monitor and review the signposts. One approach is to ask everyone involved to keep their eyes open for change, reporting back when they identify change. This is doomed to failure.

A reporting process requires assigning responsibilities to specific individuals or departments, a clear reporting mechanism, and a deadline for feedback. The reporting mechanism need not be complicated. A sufficient process may only require a senior executive to include a signpost update as an agenda item at routine strategy meetings. This does two things. First, reporting the output from monitoring to senior management ensures the activity is important and relevant to management. Second, it assigns responsibility on a regular basis for the activity. This will be reinforced if changes do occur and management acts on the changes. Then the relevance of the process will be entrenched in the organization psyche.

CHAPTER SUMMARY

- The challenge in creating scenarios is to develop logical and consistent stories from the rich but often inconsistent ideas from the scenario-development workshop.

- The scenario writer must be proactive in creating compelling, coherent, and challenging stories, while honouring the ideas generated by participants in the workshop.

- Written narratives represent a powerful way of communicating that invites readers to engage with the story.

- Supplementing narratives with bullet points in tables and presentations allows people with different learning styles to absorb and understand the scenarios.

- All driving forces should be touched on in each scenario with emphasis varying across scenarios.

- A useful tool in developing the plot is to create a logic map outlining the cause-and-effect linkages in the story.

- It is best not to describe scenarios as good or bad or to assign probabilities as that undermines the potential learnings from seemingly low probability or negative scenarios.

- Context and culture can affect the learning value of scenarios: organizations subject to public disclosure may find negative scenarios difficult to deal with under threat of public misinformation.

- Inward-looking cultures can reduce the capacity to generate and utilize scenarios.

- The focus is on objective scenarios emphasizing the question: What could happen?

- Scenarios are most effective when they are focused on a specific focal question or strategic decision.

- Signposts are early indicators of change designed to systematically monitor future events so that the organization can respond quickly to sudden changes.

REFLECTIONS ON THE SCENARIO DEVELOPMENT PROCESS

As we shift from scenarios to strategy, some observations on the scenario development process overall are worth reinforcing.

Scenarios:
- focus on learning and opening minds through strategic conversations;

- benefit from the direct participation of decision-makers and a diversity of views, including from external participants, stakeholders, and remarkable people with unconventional views and experiences;

- reveal as much or more about the present as the future;

- have multiple applications and purposes: leadership, creativity, alignment, context, and strategy;

- create a framework to analyze the future consequences of current decisions; and

- provide a vehicle for surfacing strategic risks.

PART 3
STRATEGY DEVELOPMENT

Strategic Planning does not deal with future decisions,
but with the futurity of present decisions
—Peter Drucker

The objective of scenarios is to describe a range of future paths and outcomes. The scenarios represent the shared understanding of how the external environment of an organization could evolve in the future. They articulate a set of future expectations required to evaluate the consequences of the strategic choices currently facing the organization.

The objective of strategy is to provide direction to the organization. One definition of strategy is a high-level plan to achieve a set of goals under conditions of uncertainty. This is similar to Henry Mintzberg's (1998) definition of strategy as plan defined as a directed course of action to achieve an intended set of goals. Another perspective from Mintzberg describes strategy as position in which an organization tries to position itself with a brand or product or service determined primarily by factors outside the firm. Michael Porter (1980), in contrast, defined strategy as the broad formula for how a business is going to compete, what its goals should be, and what policies will be needed to carry out those goals. More succinctly, he defined strategy as a combination of the ends (goals) for which the firm is striving and the means (policies) by which it is seeking to get there. Later, Porter (1986) emphasized strategy based on the activities that a firm chooses to do to differentiate itself from rivals. He discouraged the view of strategy as an organization merely positioning itself in a market because, in his view, it does not lead to a path of sustainable strategy.

These definitions have a number of elements in common. First, strategies are designed to achieve specific goals. Second, they should include a plan of actions intended to achieve the goals. Third, strategy is about essential actions the organization can take to achieve its goals, but in the context of the external environment. Fourth, strategies always involve choice among alternative courses of action and focus. In short, strategy is the definition of goals and development of robust plans (means and activities) to achieve those intended goals (focus) in the face of external uncertainty. Above all, strategy means focus. Strategy defines not only what you do but what you don't do. In many organizations, the latter is as important as the former.

A sharp distinction in our process, reflected in these definitions, is the shift from scenarios focused exclusively on the external environment to strategy focused on the organization. The organization should never be included in the description of the scenarios. With the shift to strategy development, the implications of the scenarios for the organization become the focus.

The value of scenarios in strategy development derives from both the product and the process. The process of scenario development involves active engagement through a series of strategic conversations that create a shared understanding of how the future external environment could evolve. This shared understanding creates a common commitment and alignment that is vital in strategy development and ultimately implementation. Specifically, shared understanding creates alignment in thinking that supports decision-making and, crucially, commitment to executing decisions.

Alignment means going in the same direction with space for innovation and creativity. A military command structure is based on rigid alignment: obey orders. While vital in war, most organizations seek alignment in direction but without rigidity in execution. The very nature of scenarios emphasizing multiple perspectives inherently discourages rigidity and promotes flexibility and adaptation. Successful execution in implementing strategy is enhanced when everyone is on the same page.

The product of scenario development is the set of written stories with their logic and characteristics. Their full value is realized when the scenarios are part of a larger strategic planning process. The scenarios articulate future expectations necessary to understand and analyze the implications of strategic choices. Scenarios provide the context for examining the future consequences of current decisions. In this role, scenarios as a product are most valuable within a strategic management process.

In a similar vein, the value of strategy development reflects both the process and the product. The product is a strategic plan that identifies and guides decisions directing the future of the organization. The plan, discussed in more detail in Chapter 6, is a coordinated approach to achieving the strategic goals identified in the strategy development process. The process, like the scenario development, involves a series of strategic conversations that build shared understanding, alignment, and commitment.

Active engagement is critical in this process. While participation may be an intellectual exercise in which the individual is divorced from the results, with engagement the individual has an emotional connection to the results (see Box 8). Within an organization, engagement in the strategy development process is vital in gaining commitment for successful implementation of the strategic plan.

Box 8—Participation versus Engagement

Participation can be an intellectual exercise. Engagement is an emotional exercise. What is the difference and why is it important? Consider the modern organization and the nature of employees. The level of education has been rising for many decades. Such employees do not respond to command-and-control directives. Instead, they act only if they understand the purpose of the directives from managers and increasingly expect to be included in contributing to the thinking underlying the course of action. They want and expect to be involved. In scenario development, the focus is on the external environment. For many participants this may be largely an intellectual exercise. They can set aside their disbeliefs and participate in thinking about possible futures. Challenging and exciting but not necessarily internalized.

In strategy development, you are striving for a deeper level of engagement that is both intellectual and emotional. This often happens in part because the focus has shifted from the nebulous external world to the company. The company, by definition, is us. Strategic decisions will affect us. A strategic development process that goes beyond intellectual participation to emotional involvement means that shared understanding, alignment, and commitment are strengthened and, more importantly, a strong platform is established for successful implementation, which is the next step in the strategic management model.

The strategic management model forming the basis of our approach, first described and presented as Figure 1 in Chapter 1, is reproduced here as Figure 23. Scenarios are part of strategic scanning of the external environment. Part 3 shifts from scenarios to strategy development. Strategy implementation and performance management are discussed in Part 4.

Two aspects of this model merit emphasis. First, the model describes a process of strategic management rather than a strategic plan. The output of strategy development is a set of strategies forming a plan. Strategic management involves an ongoing conscious process of managing the implementation, which includes monitoring performance so that the implementation can be adjusted with feedback over time (first feedback arrow) and the overall performance of the organization in the context of external change (second and third feedback arrows). The feedback loops, in the ongoing organizational learning and improvement box, recognize the need to review the implementation of the strategies, the strategies themselves, and the ongoing evolution of the external environment. While a strategic plan is initially static, strategic management is dynamic.

Figure 23—Strategic Management Model

Integrated Strategic Management

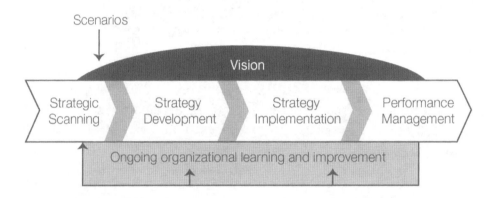

Second, there is a strong recognition of the need for vision. Vision in this context has two meanings. First, a vision for an organization should describe both what it wants to become, an internal description, and a desired future end state, often an external description of performance and position. We are using the term vision to include leadership. The basis of scenarios is that foresight is vital for the ongoing success and performance of an organization. Equally important is the leadership of the organization to utilize that foresight and mobilize the employees and management of the organization to achieve the desired future outcome. Foresight is of no value without leadership. And leadership without foresight is not leadership.

In Chapter 6, the focus is on the process from scenarios to strategies. Descriptions of the steps in the process are followed by three real-world examples. In Chapter 7 the focus is on the product in the form of a strategic plan. This includes a discussion of strategic intent, which includes vision, mission, and values, a description of the major elements composing a strategic plan, and how strategic planning fits into the annual planning cycle. In Chapter 8 a different approach to developing strategy is introduced based on The Business Idea. This is a complementary approach to developing strategies from scenarios.

CHAPTER 6
SCENARIOS TO STRATEGY

Anticipating the future in a volatile environment calls for more than systematic analysis; it also demands creativity, insight and intuition. Scenarios combine these elements into a foundation for robust strategies. The test of a good scenario is not whether it portrays the future accurately but whether it enables an organization to learn and adapt.
—Peter Schwartz

OVERVIEW

The process for developing strategies from scenarios is outlined in the roadmap shown in Figure 24. It is complicated but worth a minute to familiarize yourself with the steps in the process.

Figure 24—Roadmap—Scenarios-to-Strategies Process

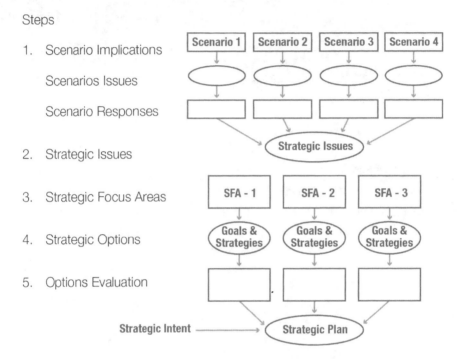

The process involves five steps. Briefly, the purpose of each step is:

Step 1—Scenario Implications: To identify, for each scenario, implications (challenges, opportunities, and risks), summarize these into major issues, and generate potential responses to each issue for the organization.

Step 2—Strategic Issues: To identify the key strategic issues across the scenarios.

Step 3—Strategic Focus Areas: To identify areas where the organization needs focused attention, clear direction, and articulated goals and strategies. This is the critical element of the process.

Step 4—Strategic Options: To define goals and develop strategies to achieve those goals within each focus area.

Step 5—Strategic Options Evaluation: To analyze the risks and rewards of each strategic option with sufficient detail that a strategic decision can be made to pursue that option or not.

Ultimately, the process of strategy development leads to a strategic plan. This is the product that provides a comprehensive description of the strategies the organization wants to pursue. As well as the strategies developed, a strategic plan typically includes a set of overarching concepts, including the organization's vision, mission, and values. More recently, other concepts have become important, including purpose and the "why?" of the organization. These new concepts reflect the ongoing societal expectation of organizations from business to non-profits to governments. Collectively, I refer to these elements as strategic intent. They serve to define organizational aspirations and expectations of behaviour. I discuss the elements of a strategic plan in Chapter 7.

The foundation for developing strategies from scenarios is to identify the implications of the scenarios for the organization. Our approach involves designing a workshop that engages participants in exploring the implications of the scenarios through brainstorming and active conversation. This approach emphasizes the use of workshops in creating spaces for strategic conversation that encourage participation and engagement. (I know I am getting repetitive but engagement and shared understanding are vital to success.)

Typically, a one-day scenarios-to-implications workshop involves all or most of the participants who were engaged in developing the scenarios.[32] The purpose of the workshop is to identify the implications of the scenarios for the organization, summarize the implications into issues and potential strategic responses, and identify and initiate analysis of strategic focus areas. The extent and depth of the discussions depends on the ambitions of the designers and stamina of the participants.

Before plunging into scenario implications, it is useful to review and refresh understanding of the scenarios. As a result, the opening session reviews the scenarios and encourages feedback. The scenarios are still a work in progress, and this is the first time that participants have had an opportunity to review the written scenarios together.

Implications

The first step in the scenarios to strategy process is to generate ideas on implications for each scenario. Divide the participants into two groups. One group is assigned scenarios from quadrants one and three; the other quadrants two and four. Implications are defined as challenges to overcome, opportunities to pursue, and risks to manage. Highlight that these depend on individual perspectives. One person's challenge is another person's opportunity.

The key question posed is: In considering Scenario X, what are the challenges, opportunities, and risks to the organization? Following the incremental approach, ask each participant to write down ideas independently. After ten to fifteen minutes, when it is evident that participants are not writing down new ideas, start asking a randomly selected individual to describe a challenge, opportunity, or risk that they

---

32 Additional participants may be added at this point. It is important that new participants do not try to open old discussions on the scenarios. Newcomers need to be encouraged to limit their comments to points of clarity and not the basic logic of the scenarios that have already been agreed to.

have written down. Ideas are recorded by a facilitator. Brainstorming rules apply. Give all participants an opportunity to present their ideas. When participants are drained of ideas, the next step is to open a general discussion on the challenges, opportunities, and risks that have been presented. Allow time for the group to understand and digest the range of ideas. In a number of cases, specific implications may need clarification. At some point it is necessary to remove duplication by combining ideas that are similar and shifting the conversation toward which challenges, opportunities, and risks seem most important. It is not necessary to formally prioritize importance but to encourage a coalescing of common or related ideas into groups.

The process continues for each scenario. The objective is to summarize the range of ideas into issues. Participants are asked to reflect across challenges, opportunities, and risks to identify the major issues that the organization would have to address if that scenario occurred. After writing down answers, ideas are recorded and discussion opened. This is a major shift in understanding from the individual implications to much more general issues. The step, however, does not appear difficult to most people, and the process is very seldom bogged down by the need to carefully define terms from challenges and risks to issues. Discussion on the meaning and definition of each issue is important. The list of issues can then be prioritized, typically using a voting process, generating three to five major issues for each scenario.

The process then shifts from prioritizing the issues to exploring the potential responses. The question posed is: What strategic responses could the organization pursue to address the issue in this scenario? Independent responses are recorded, discussed, and prioritized. This is a valuable step in initiating thinking about future developments and potential strategies for the organization. We are explicitly moving from what could happen to what would we do if it did happen. Ultimately that is the purpose of the entire exercise.

The breakout groups then reconvene and present their results to the plenary on major implications, strategic issues, and potential responses. This generates considerable discussion often focused on clarifying exactly what the issue is. Is it a revenue issue or human-resource issue or competitive issue or …? Clearly defining the issue is an extremely important part of any issue analysis. Spending time on ensuring the underlying issue is articulated clearly is often one of the most insightful parts of the discussion.

Strategic Issues

The second step in the process is to identifying issues across the scenarios. First, the discussion focuses on combining similar issues that emerged from different scenarios. Second, is to begin to prioritize the list of issues. After grouping, clarification of definitions, and discussion of which issues may be more important and why, take a vote to identify the four or five most important strategic issues emerging from the scenarios.

Box 9—Issues in Strategic Management

Creating a summary list of strategic issues is valuable for two reasons. First, summarizing the scenario implications into a small set of strategic issues is a useful step toward defining strategic focus areas, which is the next step in the scenarios-to-strategy process. Second, for many organizations, particularly associations, government departments, and non-profit organizations, issues are often the focus of their work. An industry association, for example, typically functions on the basis of identifying and lobbying the association's position on specific issues. Identifying the most important strategic issues facing the industry and thus the association in the future is a valuable result. Moreover, and this applies to NGOs as well, there is little capacity to develop and implement longer-term strategies. An association has limited capacity to implement independently a strategy outside of the action of the members of the association. Government departments also often operate through issues (or "files" in the language of government). Nevertheless, a key part of their mandate is to identify and prepare policy positions on emerging issues.

Business organizations may also use strategic issues in their planning. Identifying two or three major issues to be addressed in a given time frame, for example over the next year, can be an effective management tool. It is less comprehensive than the strategy approach recommended here, but it does provide strategic focus if implemented. If a company is facing, say, a financial, environmental, or a competitive issue, assigning that to a senior executive or manager to resolve over the next year gives action on that issue tremendous momentum. It should be part of the performance management process and may complement a more comprehensive strategic plan. Issues can function as priorities, which we touch on later, within the overall strategic plan. A key difference between a business and an association, NGO, or government department is the capacity to design and implement a strategic plan. The company has control of its resources and management to implement a plan. This is seldom the case with associations, NGOs, and government bureaucracies. Associations are driven by their members; NGOs seldom have the capacity to design or implement long-term plans; and government bureaucracies are dominated by politics.

At this point, an observation worth noting is the enthusiasm that surfaces in these discussions, despite their complexity. The range and depth of ideas and thinking is often remarkable. Despite the lengthy process, there is usually a high level of input and dialogue. This level of engagement is, in part, because participants are finally focusing on what the organization can do. The scenario development process involves lengthy discussions about the future with discussion of the organization muted. With a shift to strategy, that ban is lifted and a renewed burst of energy is released.

Strategic Focus Areas

The third step in the process is to identify three or four strategic focus areas. What is a strategic focus area? Focus areas are broad areas of strategic importance requiring clear direction. Initially, we used the term "strategic thrust" to signal the step from issues to a broader conceptual level. The idea of strategic thrust was to capture a sense of the dynamic of where the organization was going. What were the key strategic directions the organization could pursue for success in the future? The term proved problematic as it was intuitively difficult for some people to understand. Instead, the term "strategic focus areas" captured the concept more simply. In effect, what major areas does the organization need to focus on for future success? Or where does the organization need explicit strategies? This concept seems to work more effectively.

To generate ideas, participants are asked to identify independently three or four strategic focus areas that the organization needs to focus on to achieve success. The definition is vague but seems to elicit responses with little need for detailed clarification. This is an example of the messy nature of strategy development. (The process may be messy but the result should not be.) It is not a perfunctory fill-in-the-blanks exercise. At some point a deeper understanding needs to emerge. There needs to be an insight that exceeds the simple addition of ideas into something more profound. For some this is an aha moment. For others it is an intellectual challenge. This is often satisfying but difficult to program. As Peter Schwartz might say, this is a moment when there is more art than science.

The result is the generation of a number of ideas on strategic focus areas. Free-ranging discussion can quickly narrow the list to a small set of candidates for further exploration. In the coal industry example from 2005, four strategic focus areas were: domestic growth, international growth, transportation infrastructure, and new technology. These were broad strategic focus areas in which choosing one would clearly define a major strategic direction for the company. In this case it is evident that not all directions could be pursued at once (or that implementation might need to be prioritized). In another example, a utility company developed a list that included customer relations and brand management, financial capability, and system reliability.

The key point is that strategic focus areas are broad yet focus the strategic discussion. In the end, the organization will be able to state that they are focusing on A, B, and C.

An important caveat is necessary. In defining strategic focus areas, the emphasis must be on strategic. Strategic refers to directional focus that differentiates an organization from competitors, NGOs, associations, or departments. This is different from areas of management that are critical for operations. In the utility example, a critical area for operations is safety. This is an area of no compromise. While this is critical for successful operation of the company and requires ongoing management attention and resources, it is not strategic. It did not define a new direction or position or enhance the performance of the company in the future. It is a basic operational requirement necessary for any utility to stay in business. All utility companies need to operate with a very high standard of safety. Broad areas of the organization, particularly health, safety, and environment require ongoing levels of performance necessary for the organization to operate and exist. They are critical and necessary but seldom strategic. [33] A rough check on whether a focus area is strategic is to ask: What areas need ongoing operational excellence? What areas need clear strategies for future success? For instance, for restaurants cleanliness is a minimum requirement to do business; it is a cost of admission. It is not strategic since all restaurants must meet this requirement. Reputation, quality of food, and ambience, however, are strategic in differentiating that restaurant from competitors.

Strategic Options

The fourth step in the process is to develop strategic options. This requires developing goals and strategies to achieve the goals in each strategic focus area. There may be multiple goals and multiple strategies in each area. The options may refer to different goals or strategies within a focus area or strategic options between focus areas. Sounds complicated but it's not.

A strategic option consists of a goal and a strategy to achieve the goal. There is debate about the difference between a goal and an objective. For me, a goal is more narrowly defined and specific. It includes a specific time frame and means of monitoring progress toward the goal. An objective is more open ended and directional without a specific time frame. For example, an objective might be for a company to increase market share. A goal would specify an increase in market share of 5 percent in three years.

Whether a strategic option is associated with a goal or an objective is largely semantics. In part it depends on the organization, which may have its own established

---

33 In some industries, environmental performance has become strategic as companies strive to differentiate themselves on environmental grounds. This may be based on moral grounds but may also be strategic in attracting high quality employees, responding to shareholders and attracting capital.

lexicon. Identifying a goal forces a more precise definition of the desired outcome and encourages a more explicit consideration of how, in reality, the goal can be achieved. In either case, a desired outcome in the form of a goal or an objective is necessary in defining a strategic option.

The second component of a strategic option is a strategy. A strategy entails the actions required to achieve the goal. It starts to sound like consultant jargon but defining the goal and describing the strategy are critical for evaluating the strategic option.

A successful implications workshop should end with identification of strategic focus areas and initial discussion of goals. In some cases, there may be inklings of strategies. The depth of discussion and confidence in the validity of the focus areas and goals depends on the time available. There is time to revise as you move toward defining and evaluating strategic options. How do you do that?

You take the High Road and I'll take the Low Road

There are a number of variations on how to flesh out and analyze strategic options. Following are descriptions of two broad approaches that differ in style and level of detail in the outcomes but follow the same basic process. One uses an active facilitation approach to develop detailed strategic action plans. The other uses an independent work team approach with less detailed action plans. One drives for plans that can be implemented directly. The other aims for sufficient detail to allow management to make choices between options for further analysis and development. One takes the high road and one takes the low road. Eventually, both lead to the same destination.

The facilitated approach emphasizes detailed descriptions of action plans in defining strategies. This process involves a facilitated workshop to first refine the definition of the strategic focus areas and goals generated in the implications workshop and, second, evaluate the strategies for feasibility and risk. In this scenarios-to-strategy workshop, breakout groups review and refine the initial goals and strategies, including well defined action plans. The strategies can be a relatively detailed series of actions designed to achieve the strategic goal. The level of detail depends on the level of knowledge in the group.

The breakout groups then present their idea to the group as a whole for discussion and input. This conversation helps to clarify and refine the ideas. Participants then reconvene in small groups to begin a process of evaluating the emerging strategic options for feasibility and risk. A strategic option template (Box 10) is used to direct and focus the conversation. Completing the template means that all critical elements needed to identify resources and risks are considered. This evaluation template is a valuable tool used in both approaches.

After a thorough analysis of the proposed strategies, the results are presented back to the plenary for discussion. The result is a set of strategies with clearly defined goals and plans that can be directly incorporated into a strategic plan. Ultimately decisions on which strategies will or will not be pursued and in what order of priority will be made by senior management. The process has generated the key building blocks for a strategic plan.

The alternative approach is to give the development of strategic options to work teams for each strategic focus area. A team might include five or six participants knowledgeable in a specific area, although they are encouraged to reach out for further expertise as needed. Their task is to work through the strategic options evaluation framework, present their results, and make recommendations to the senior management team. Requiring a recommendation makes the process a little more personal. A subtle addition is to assign a senior manager to lead the team. This further focuses attention and raises commitment. No one should ever embarrass a vice-president.

The purpose of the strategic option evaluation form is twofold. First, it is intended to provide a comprehensive framework for evaluating a strategic option. Some questions may be more relevant or important to one organization or another. The questions can be modified. Second, the questions lay out a thinking process and sequence for presentation. Essentially, answering each question creates a potential viewgraph. It is valuable if each group and each strategic option is presented in a common format.

In theory, each strategic focus area could have more than one strategic option with different goals and multiple strategies for each goal. In this team approach, however, the intent is to create advocates for the strategic focus area. They define the goal and preferred strategy to achieve that goal. They should consider alternative goals and strategies but, in their evaluation, they should agree on a single strategic option. As in the workshop approach, the ultimate decision rests with the senior management team.

What are the pros and cons of these two approaches? The workshop approach is very efficient in the use of time and resources in driving the results, engages more people directly with the potential to generate more ideas, and allows greater peer review with people involved in the scenario and strategy development process. The team approach allows more time for reflection, gathering of additional information and ideas, and can create a higher level of commitment as the team becomes an advocate for the strategy. There is no inherent advantage in the two approaches. The steps in the process are essentially the same. In part, which approach may work better depends on the culture and complexity of the organization. The steps are highlighted in the examples in the following section.

Box 10—Strategic Option Evaluation Framework[34]

The purpose of the strategic option evaluation framework is to assist in the development and analysis of specific strategies to inform decision-making. The framework provides a series of questions for teams to work through in an organized manner so that there is a full understanding of the implications—advantages and disadvantages—of pursuing a specific strategic option. The questions cover five main topics: 1) definition, objectives, and fit; 2) requirements to implement the strategy; 3) evaluation of risks and rewards; 4) adaptations to improve the strategy; and 5) performance measures to define the requirements for managing the implementation of the strategies.

The questions are not exhaustive. Some overlap. Other important questions may, indeed are likely, to emerge in the course of the analysis as teams examine the strategic option and develop innovative approaches and ideas in implementing the strategy.

12 Questions for Evaluating and Improving Strategies

1. Definition—In one sentence, what is the strategy?

2. Objectives—What are the key objectives of the strategy? What are the desired outcomes?

3. Strategic Fit—Does the strategy align with the vision, mission, and values of the organization?

4. Issues—What strategic issues does this strategy address?

5. Competitive Advantage—Does this strategy create a distinct competitive advantage for the organization?

6. Implementation—What specific actions need to occur to implement the strategy, by whom, and in what time frame?

7. Barriers—What are the barriers to implementation that need to be addressed? How will those barriers be addressed?

8. Resources—What internal resources are needed to implement the strategy? Where can you get the needed resources?

---

34 This framework includes modifications from the 10-Facet Framework developed by Scenarios to Strategy Inc. from the original set of questions.

9. External Relations—How will the strategy affect external stakeholders? What support is needed from them to successfully implement the strategy? How will you get their support?

10. Risks and Rewards—What are the major rewards in pursuing this strategy? What are the risks? How do the risks vary across the scenarios? Is the strategy robust across the scenarios? (See Box 12 on Wind Tunnelling.)

11. Adaptation—How could you improve the strategy to make it more robust? What are the strengths and weaknesses? How could you enhance the strengths and reduce the weaknesses?

12. Performance—What performance measures need to be developed to implement the strategy? (Think of the acronym (SMART—Specific, Measurable, Achievable, Responsible & Timing.)

Recommendation: In summary, what is your recommendation to the management team? Be specific about who, what, when, and how in implementing the strategy.

THREE EXAMPLES OF STRATEGY DEVELOPMENT

The process of developing strategies from scenarios has evolved through experiences with a range of projects and clients. The central concept is the idea of strategic focus areas. This seems so simple but took time to crystallize. Three examples highlight different ways to develop and implement strategies from scenarios. They also introduce other variations in the process from scenarios to strategy.

Example 1: Northern Alberta Institute of Technology (NAIT)

In 1999 a new president, Dr. Sam Shaw, was installed to lead the Northern Alberta Institute of Technology (NAIT). He immediately recognized the need to review the strategic plan and create a vision for the institution. At the same time, he wanted to signal new leadership. This was an opportunity for change. He decided to undertake a scenario-planning exercise. The project was very successful at signalling change—a key goal—stimulating new ideas, and initiating an inclusive strategy development process (See Brummell & Shaw, 1999).

How did this happen? A large number of department heads, instructors, and administrators were actively engaged in the project. The scenario development process was instrumental in building shared understanding and generating an insightful and challenging set of scenarios. The scenario framework identifying the critical uncertainties and names (shown in Figure 16 in Box 5, Chapter 5 as part of discussions on higher education).

In this project, the scenarios were used as a springboard to develop a vision for the institution. At the same time, they provided the basis for identifying strategic issues and potential responses. Indirectly we—facilitators and leadership team—identified a number of strategic focus areas, although we did not use that term or have that focus at the time. The way these results were used to implement strategy was instructive.

One of the key insights from the scenarios and implication work was the vital importance of the institution's relationships with local and regional businesses. The overwhelming majority of programs at NAIT involve hands-on learning. Most programs are designed to lead to apprenticeships and technical qualifications. Many involve cooperative programs in which students have extended work experiences with local businesses. This combination of formal learning in the classroom with real-world work experience means that graduates are work-ready the moment they graduate.

A major challenge with a technical institute is to ensure students are able to get experience with the latest technology. It is almost impossible for institutions like NAIT to invest sufficiently to stay up to date with the latest equipment. The cooperative program means that students are exposed to the latest technology being used by companies in their field. Students, teachers, the institution, and businesses, all benefit. The company gets a willing worker during apprenticeship with the prospect of hiring that student on graduation. The student gets real-world work experience using the latest technology, and NAIT fulfills its commitment to the highest quality training.

This vital relationship, however, has often been neglected. Typically, relationships did not develop between the institution and the external company, but between individual instructors and individuals in the external companies. These were personal relationships. While these relationships were encouraged, they were dependent on individuals. Some instructors were good at building and maintaining such relationships; others were not. Even those with excellent relationships faced a range of other pressures so that they lacked the time to maintain these external relationships. More importantly there was very little recognition or explicit support for these activities. In short, this was a strategic area with no clear strategy to maintain or enhance this vital activity.

How could NAIT develop strategies to support the relationship with external companies? This was both a strategic and tactical issue. The process Sam Shaw initiated put specific focus on this issue. In a large multi-department institution, it is a challenge to implement top-down strategies. Success depends on bringing departments into the process by soliciting input on how to implement change. In this case, the planning process highlighted the importance of relationships with external companies and asked each department to identify all their external relationships and develop plans to strengthen those relationships. This ensured focus while requiring them to create their own plans. As well as building commitment and alignment, there was considerable learning across departments, as ideas for sustaining relationships were shared. Inevitably, asking someone is more powerful than telling someone.

This example highlighted two important insights. First, identifying strategic focus areas as a way of organizing and directing the development of important strategies for an organization is a valuable approach. Second, engaging stakeholders in a strategy-development process to build alignment and commitment for that strategy is powerful, in part, because it builds commitment to implement the strategy.

Example 2: A Major US Coal Company

In the mid 2000s a major US coal company faced conflicting prospects. One was the growth prospect from rising demand for electricity and thus coal-fired power plants. The other was the increasing risk from growing environmental concerns about climate change and the potential imposition of penalties on CO2 emissions. In this uncertain environment the company decided to develop scenarios to explore the opportunities and risks and refine their strategic plans. The firm's senior executives understood that the attractive growth opportunities were tempered by the risk of punitive regulations that might be imposed on carbon emissions in response to climate change concerns. These concerns were rising. What form could penalties take? How severe could they be? How could regulatory penalties affect the demand for coal? The focal issue was not about carbon penalties, however, but growth opportunities. How could the company grow profitably in a changing energy world?

The scenario development process led to four scenarios, which are instructive in hindsight. They capture the thinking at the time and are worth reviewing in the context of what eventually happened. While scenarios are not designed to predict, they are intended to broaden perspectives and surface the unexpected. In this case they failed. The limits from these scenarios are presented in Box 13. Following this interlude, we return to the distinct strategy development process in this example.

Box 11—Coal Scenarios 2005—Insights from the Past

The scenarios framework shown in Figure 25 is based on two critical uncertainties. One focuses on the potential for economic growth that drives the demand for electricity. Second is the competitiveness of coal versus other fuels in the market for power production. The outlook was rosy. Projections of power demand were bullish. Coal was cost competitive with other fuels. Nuclear power was hampered by construction cost overruns and safety concerns. Natural gas was extremely expensive, and projections emphasized future gas shortages. Renewables were only viable with large subsidies and were not dispatchable (i.e., they are produced intermittently when the wind blows and the sun shines, requiring coal or gas backup capacity). Dirty but cheap seemed like a reasonable trade-off.

Coupled with this analysis was the investment going into coal. Figure 26 shows the coal-fired power plants under construction, advanced development, early development, or proposed in 2005.

Figure 25—Coal Scenario Framework

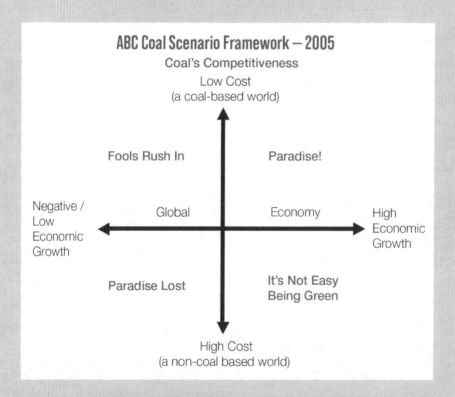

The scenarios challenged that bright future by recognizing the potential impact of environmental concerns. Paradise! was driven by technology and economy. Strong growth would drive demand and combined cycle technology would raise efficiency and lower CO_2 emissions. Fools Rush In, was characterized by a weak economy and stagnant demand.

Security and cost concerns gave coal a strong competitive edge, sustaining demand. Paradise Lost explored a future in which weak economic growth undermined power demand and politics determined regulation. Conservation by force meant high carbon penalties with a shift to gas. It's Not Easy Being Green focused on rising environmental concerns during a period of strong economic growth. High energy prices and government initiatives would affect demand for dirty coal. In both Paradise Lost and It's Not Easy Being Green, the main mechanism was seen as a CO_2 trading system. In the latter, however, there would be a greater penetration of renewables supported by direct government subsidies.

In the analysis, the prospects for coal were reinforced by considering the cost per tonne of CO_2 emissions. Even with high penalties of $50 per tonne (in 2005), coal remained competitive with natural gas, which was projected to exceed $10 per thousand cubic feet for the foreseeable future.

What happened? Two unexpected events overtook the thinking in the scenarios. First, the scenarios understood the impact of carbon penalties would be a cost of doing business. Even high penalties meant that coal could remain competitive. Coal producers would simply pay to emit CO_2. This view changed. Financial investors became concerned that the risks from climate change policies could be very high. More important, they could not quantify the risks. Wall Street pulled the plug on new coal investments and none of the almost 200 power plants planned in the US could attract funding.[35]

---

35 In some ways this is ironic given that Wall Street felt comfortable with the risk of securitized mortgage funds that triggered the financial collapse and Great Recession of 2008.

Figure 26—Proposed Coal-Based Power Plants

New coal-based power plants – 2005

Status of New Coal-Based Plants
- Under Construction
- Advanced Development
- Early Development
- Proposed

Expected Coal Consumption
(at 80% utilization, in 000's tons)
- 4,000 – 10,000
- 1,000 – 3,999
- 200 – 999

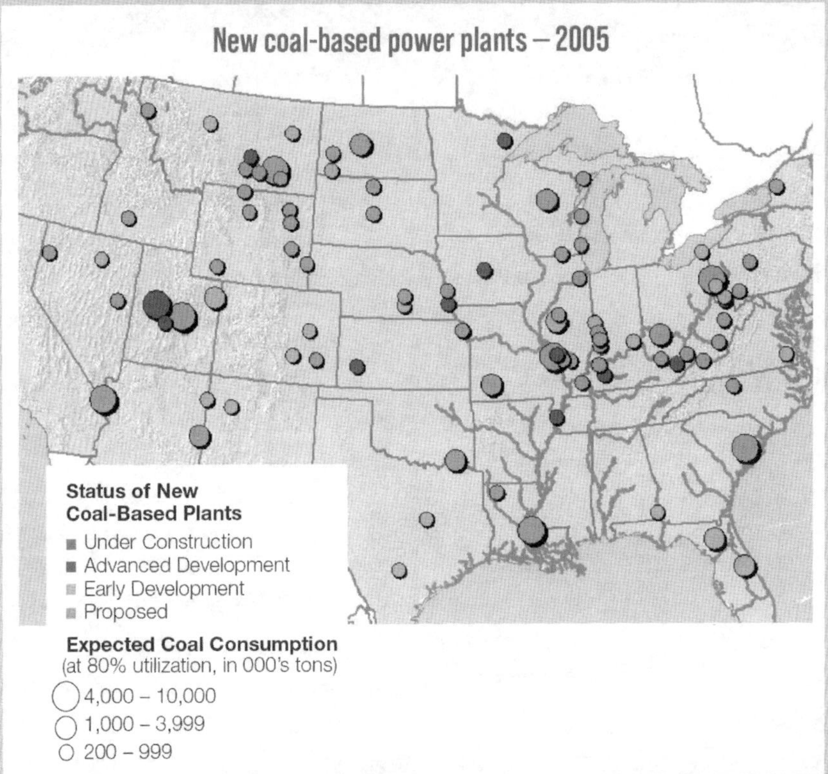

Second, assumptions about natural gas were, literally, fractured. With hydraulic fracturing, production of natural gas surged and prices fell. Independent of carbon penalties, the cost of electricity production from natural gas fell below that of coal. Coal lost its competitive edge. The market, not regulation, undermined the coal industry in the US.

The purpose of scenarios is to expose these events, to think the unthinkable. Why did we not see these potential events in 2005? To some degree we were successful in raising the risks associated with rising climate change concerns and potential regulatory penalties. What we failed to identify was how those environmental risks would play out with the abrupt collapse of financing. The threat turned out not to be just a straightforward cost of doing business. Nor did we—the coal company executives and us as facilitators—foresee the radical change in the natural gas supply. Economics might have given us a clue. High gas prices should stimulate supply, but we relied on technical expertise which said the gas did not exist. This is a cautionary tale. The process worked, but we were not radical enough in our thinking. Use scenarios to embrace the unthinkable and think the unbelievable.

For ABC Coal the process of developing strategies followed a different path than our standard structured model. This approach focused on defining strategic options at the outset. The process involved 5 steps:

1. Generate potential strategic options for each scenario.

2. Consolidate the list of strategic options across scenarios.

3. Identify strategic risks for selected options across scenarios (known as "wind tunnelling"; see Box 12).

4. Use structured criticism to reduce risk and enhance value of each strategic option.

5. Select three to four options for in-depth work team analysis.

Generating Options

After a brief review of implications, the process plunged directly into generating potential strategic options. The question posed was: If scenario X occurred, what strategies could ABC Coal pursue? This question effectively requires the participant to think through the scenario, identify implications, and generate potential responses in a single pass. Although this is complex, it generates a robust set of responses. At least it did in this case. Separate groups used this question to generate a range of potential strategic options within each scenario. Each option included a definition and objectives. In light of their growth opportunities, which was the focal question, the list of options was reduced to two or three for presentation back to the group.

Consolidating Options

The potential options generated for each scenario were reviewed to consolidate ideas into four or five potential options across scenarios. To facilitate this process, a set of decision criteria were developed. These criteria focused on growth, performance, and risk. For example, did the strategic option increase the size of the company, increase market share, or enhance capabilities? Or did the option raise the return on investment (ROI), profit per ton, or relationships with customers? And did the option raise or reduce risks? These questions provided a framework for sorting strategic options at a preliminary stage. The result was to reduce the scenario-generated strategic options to a set of broad strategies for risk evaluation across the scenarios.

Strategic Risks

Each of the potential strategic options was defined in enough detail, including objectives, to be meaningfully understood in discussions, but was only an outline of what a final strategic option would entail. In this format, the focus shifted to identifying risk and reward. The process is known in scenario jargon as wind tunnelling—like testing a prototype airplane in a wind tunnel to see how it flies. The process is defined in detail in Box 12. In short, if strategic option one was undertaken and scenario X occurred, what would be the risks and rewards? This is repeated for each strategic option and each scenario leading to a matrix of pros and cons for each strategic option across the scenarios. (In turn, the risks and rewards can be subjectively quantified as shown in Box 12). In the end the intent is to identify which strategic options are risky or robust across the scenarios and which strategic options offer high versus low rewards. High risk does not preclude adopting a strategic option if the rewards are high. Then it is a matter of management judgement. Similarly, if a strategic option is robust, it is not automatically adopted. It may offer low rewards for the investment required.

Structured Criticism

In this example, the emerging strategic options were subjected to a process called structured criticism. Briefly, this involves identifying the strengths and weaknesses and developing adaptations on the strategy to mitigate the weaknesses and enhance the strengths. (Step 11 in the Strategic Option Evaluation Framework, Box 10). The intent is to engage all participants in the workshop in improving and clarifying the strategic option.

Work Teams

The process generated four strategic focus areas with relatively well developed initial strategic options. The four focus areas were:

- domestic growth (organic or acquisitions),

- international growth (acquisitions),

- expand into transportation / terminals / trading,

- new technologies (coal to liquids).[36]

---

36 As a footnote to this project, initially, consideration of new technologies was not a priority. The following year, however, the company undertook an in-depth analysis of the viability of coal-to-liquids technology in general, and particularly to develop remote coal deposits that lacked transportation infrastructure. Though promising, the final review decided that the economics did not justify the technological and market risks.

Teams of five to six people were assigned to each area, headed by a vice-president with instructions to analyze strategic options and present their results to the senior management team at the next meeting. The strategic-option evaluation framework was developed and used as the common template for each team to analyze the strategic option(s), advocate for a specific option, and make a recommendation to the management team.

The work teams had the advantage of building on the extensive thinking generated in the scenario-to-strategy workshops and drawing on other expertise and research in the company. Four weeks later the teams presented their results to management. It was a spirited and lively affair.

Noted elements of this process were the accelerated shift from scenarios directly to strategic options, the extensive workshop time devoted to consolidating, fleshing out, and modifying the options, the use of decision criteria, the assessment of strategic risk using wind tunnelling, and finally the assignment of final strategic-option development to small work teams.

This process differed somewhat from the structured approach, notably in the short circuit from scenarios to options. The overall sequence, however, is similar. The key point that emerged was the central role of strategic focus areas as a vital bridge in strategy development.

Box 12—Wind Tunnelling

Wind tunnelling is a high-level subjective evaluation of different strategic options designed to surface the strategic risks and rewards associated with each option. Specifically, it is an analysis process to identify sources of upside potential, downside risks, and possible actions to build leverage and surface additional sources of uncertainty. For a new or existing strategic option, analogous to real wind-tunnel testing aerodynamics, the question asked is: How will this strategy fly in each scenario? The scenarios provide a framework to test strategies. The process ensures articulation of existing and proposed strategies and objectives. It forces consideration of the consequences of current and prospective strategies and it explicitly focuses on risks and rewards. Again, it is another vehicle for strategic conversation.

The process uses the matrix shown in Figure 27. Each cell represents a different combination of a strategic option and a scenario. Consider cell 1A. The question is: If strategic Option 1 was implemented and Scenario A occurred, what would be the risks and rewards? What would be the pros and cons of adopting that strategic option? The thought process involves thinking through the scenario and the option to come to a conclusion on positive and negative outcomes. The answer may be captured by articulating a list of pros and cons. This may be followed by a subjective quantification in the form of pluses (++) or minuses (- -) to indicate the net reward versus risk. In this five-point scale, two plus signs (++) indicate that that strategy in that scenario would be very positive or yield high reward. A double negative (- -) indicates that the strategy, if that scenario occurred, would be very negative or entail high risk.

As an example, consider our coal company. Strategic Option 1 might be to expand coal mining production. Scenario A might be a future in which there is strong demand for electricity, natural gas prices are high, and emission penalties are modest. Coal would be competitive and profitable, making an investment in expanded mining capacity a high reward (++). However, Scenario D might be a future in which natural gas prices are low, electricity demand is weak, and high carbon emission penalties are imposed. This would make an investment in increased coal production unprofitable (- -). The other scenarios generate risks and rewards between these extremes. The end result is a recognition that investing in increased coal mining production is risky. Management may or may not decide to take the risk, but they will make that decision knowing the risks involved.

Figure 27—Wind Tunnelling Matrix

Wind Tunnelling Matrix

	Scenario A	Scenario B	Scenario C	Scenario D
Strategic Option 1	++	+	0	--
Strategic Option 2		If Strategy 2 is implemented, and the future is Scenario A, what are the pros and cons, strengths and vulnerabilities of that strategy?		
Strategic Option 3				
Strategic Option 4	+	++	+	0

Completing the full matrix indicates which strategic options are risky or not and which are high reward or not. In this example, Strategic Option 1 has high reward if Scenario A occurs but downside risk if Scenario D occurs. Strategic Option 4, in contrast, has considerable upside potential with little downside risk. This would be a robust strategic option and would seem to be worth pursuing. Which strategic options chosen for further analysis and implementation may include some that are high risk and high reward? The size of the prize may make a given strategy worth the risk. In that case an important question becomes: How can we implement this strategy to create additional leverage or mitigate the risk? A large project, for example, may be implemented in stages over time rather than making a large commitment at the outset. As events unfold over time, the risk at each stage can be assessed.

Wind tunnelling is a valuable tool in surfacing strategic risks. It is a relatively straightforward process and generates a robust strategic conversation on the risks and rewards of the strategic options.

Example 3: Affordable Housing for Seniors

In 2010, a major foundation in Alberta that provided affordable housing accommodation for over 2000 senior citizens was concerned about planning for the future needs and expectations for seniors housing. The foundation had a range of facilities providing housing for two levels of care. One was income-regulated housing with a minimal level of additional services. The other was assisted care housing in a lodge setting. The latter included daily meals, weekly housekeeping, and staff-run recreation and other services. Neither offered medical services on site. Residents needed to be able to take care of their personal needs such as dressing, washing, and eating independently. Long-term care facilities providing a higher level of personal care, including medical care, were not part of the foundation's mandate.

Demographic projections indicated an aging population and increased demand for subsidized housing and assisted care for seniors in the future. What would be the demand for affordable housing for low-income groups? What level of care would be required? What financing would be available? What form of accommodation and service would be needed? In the face of these questions, the foundation decided to undertake a scenario-planning project to explore a range of future outcomes, review the foundation's vision and mission, and develop goals and strategies to fulfill its vision and mission.

Scenarios were developed involving approximately thirty participants from management, the board, and a number of external stakeholders. Given the board's role as guardians of the vision and mission and overall responsibility for strategic direction, their inclusion in the scenario and subsequent strategy development process was extremely valuable. This endorsed the project and created shared ownership from the beginning.

The focal question was: Looking out to 2030, how does the foundation respond to demands and expectations for affordable seniors housing? The scenarios focused on two critical uncertainties. One focused on whether public funding for affordable seniors housing would be high or low. The other focused on the form of delivery. Would health-care policy and services focus on integrated delivery or separate delivery? The latter might include a range of facilities with a range of service offerings at a range of prices. The former would entail a more coordinated range of facilities, including cooperation across health care, housing, and communities.

The scenarios provided the springboard to two strategic planning paths. One path used the scenarios to review and refresh the vision and mission of the organization. As with the NAIT example, this is a common and valuable use of scenarios. In Figure 23, showing the strategic management model, the connection of the vision, mission, and values is shown as strategic intent (bottom line of diagram), ensuring that the final strategic plan supports the vision and mission of the organization. The second path focused directly on strategy development. The process followed our workshop approach with minor variations.

Scenario Implications

Consistent with the road map in Figure 24, the first step in the process was to identify implications of the scenarios for the organization. Breakout groups in a scenarios-to-implications workshop identified challenges, opportunities, and risks for each scenario. These varied by scenario but included issues ranging from partnerships and alliances to demands on volunteers, increased diversity of new housing needs and expectations, community outreach, quality of care, relationships with the health care system, competition for revenue, and the role of government. These issues generated a range of potential strategic responses across the scenarios. Examples included flexible design of facilities for multiple use, increased outreach programs to involve the community, expanded partnerships with other senior-care organizations, private sector providers, and various professions, creating new revenue models, and expanding sales and marketing and increased training for staff and volunteers. A long list of potential responses across the scenarios was consolidated into a single list of nine potential strategic responses.

Figure 28—Impact—Achievability Matrix

Impact – Achievability Matrix

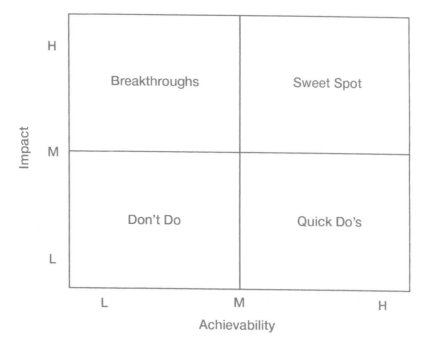

At this point we, the facilitators, introduced a slight variation in the model. We presented the concepts of impact and achievability in the form of matrix (Figure 28). For each potential strategic response, what is the size of the impact defined as high, medium, or low? Similarly, how achievable is the strategic response defined as high, medium, or low? These are obviously subjective evaluations at this stage.

The intent was to develop perspectives on the relative value of different potential responses. Some might have a high impact potential but be very difficult to implement. We labelled that combination Breakthroughs. Others might be relatively easy to achieve but have low value. We labelled those Quick Do's. A high-high combination was labelled Sweet Spot and low-low was called Don't Do.

Participants independently considered the impact and achievability of the nine consolidated strategic responses and located them on their own personal matrix template. Using consensus, each consolidated strategic response was located on the matrix. All were considered high impact with four assigned to HH (Sweet Spot) and five identified as HL (Breakthroughs). This conversation created the foundation for a discussion of strategic-focus areas. In this example, the impact-achievability analysis of the consolidated strategic responses replaced the identification of strategic issues as step 2 in the standard strategic-process model (Figure 23). This alternative path, however, was very effective in setting the stage for defining strategic focus areas.

Strategic Focus Areas

From the impact-achievability analysis, five strategic focus areas were defined. In this case there was a blending of the ideas from the impact-achievement discussions and an integrated service delivery model developed separately. As a result, the four Sweet Spot strategic responses that included consolidation, outreach, marketing, and innovative staffing and human resources were embedded in the broader elements of the integrated-service delivery model. The five strategic focus areas were: services, facilities and technology, people and culture, partnerships, and outreach.

Strategic Options

These five strategic focus areas formed the basis for a strategic goals and options workshop. In that workshop, participants developed goals and strategies for each strategic focus area, often with multiple strategic actions for each goal. For example, for the strategic focus area Outreach, goals included build integration with local seniors and community and accelerate marketing. Strategies included community integration, build awareness, and create marketing plan. Specific actions involved staging open houses, local home-based services, outreach articles in local media, resident testimonials, an advertising campaign with donors and local community, arrange charitable events, and many other ideas. The result was an array of ideas that clarified goals, strategies, and actions—essentially strategic options—that the management and board could use to structure a strategic plan for the foundation.

In this Affordable Housing for Seniors example, the scenarios-to-strategy process was modified by using strategic responses and the impact-achievability analysis to connect to strategic focus areas. The subsequent development of goals, strategies, and actions was fleshed out through a workshop, which included both management and board participation. This participation immediately ensured the validity of the work and the foundation was able to move effectively to formalizing a strategic plan.

CONCLUSIONS FROM EXAMPLES

Each of the examples offers different insights on the scenarios-to-strategy process. Two conclusions stand out. First, the basic process is adaptable to different circumstances and organizations. NAIT represents the challenge of integrating a large, multi-departmental or multi-divisional organization.[37] ABC Coal represents a large company with strong management and planning capabilities. The Foundation represents a not-for-profit charitable organization able to directly engage the board in the process.

Second, the key element in each case is the implicit or explicit development of strategic focus areas. Like the focal question that defines the key strategic issue facing the organization, the strategic focus areas define the key areas needing strategic direction, goals, and strategies. They provide the focus that is the essence of strategic planning.

ELEMENTS OF A STRATEGIC PLAN

The culmination of the strategy development process is a strategic plan. This includes strategic focus areas, goals, and strategies, which are the heart of the strategic plan. The plan summarizes the strategic intentions of the organization. As well as goals and strategies, the plan includes statements of the organization's vision, mission, and values—strategic intent—as well as financial information on the size and allocation of resources needed to implement the plan. Ultimately, strategy involves the allocation of resources primarily through capital investment.

The basic elements of a strategic plan are shown in Figure 29. The strategic focus areas, goals, strategies, and actions are generated from the strategy development process. Vision, mission, and values are declarations of aspiration and intent designed to provide direction and inspiration. Symbolically, they are at the top of the pyramid reflecting the aspirations of the organizations. Alternatively, the vision and mission are supported by a broad and deep structure of focus areas, strategies, and actions creating an integrated whole.

Vision

Vision is what an organization wants to be. This differs from strategy, which is what an organization wants to do. Specifically, a vision answers two questions. What is the future desired end state we wish to achieve? And what type of organization do we aspire to? The former focuses on the external position, and the latter focuses

---

37 Interestingly, Royal Dutch Shell had a similar problem as NAIT. Shell in the late 1980s had operations in over 90 countries with 125,000 employees. How do you build alignment and commitment in this huge and diverse organization? One approach involved the annual letter from the Committee of Managing Directors setting guidelines for the annual planning cycle. One year they had a simple request: please include a list of all pipelines crossing water and describe what plans you have to ensure there are no spills. Wow. This single question set off a torrent of requests to Group Planning. What did this mean? Like NAIT, this was subtle way of both directing strategic focus and soliciting plans created by the operating companies. Clever and powerful.

on the internal state of the organization. The comprehensive vision may be several paragraphs long. Such descriptions are powerful because the strategic conversation leading to the vision builds shared understanding—a common vision—of what the organization does or does not aspire to.

This is in contrast to a vision statement intended to capture the thrust of the vision in a single phrase. Such statements are often trite or excessively grandiose bordering on meaningless. For example, many companies have used phrases such as "world class" or "company of choice." Such phrases are meaningless unless further elucidated. For example, does world class mean beating competitors? Then this has meaning as it focuses on performance measures rated against competitors. Similarly, "company of choice" would seem to focus on customers and their requirements. These more detailed descriptions give meaning and depth to the vision. The key point is that single vision statements are often trivial and should not be mistaken for a well described vision. Plus, as you work to define your vision, you often end up with a different vision than what you originally thought.

Figure 29–Elements of a Strategic Plan

Basic Strategic Planning Model

Vision	What an organization wants to **become** and desired future **end state**.
Mission	Why an organization exists. Its unique, long-term **purpose**.
Values	What an organization **believes** (integrity, competence, safety, etc.).
Strategic Focus	Broad areas of **strategic focus or direction** needing defined strategies.
Goals & Strategies	**Goals** to be achieved within strategic focus areas. **Strategies** defined in some detail to achieve the goals and support the vision, mission & goals.
Actions	**Specific actions** to be taken to implement the strategy, including allocation of responsibilities and resources

Source: Scenarios to Strategy Inc.

Mission

A mission describes the organization's purpose for being. Why do we exist? What are we trying to accomplish? An organization may have a vision to end homelessness. Its mission might be to create affordable housing. Unlike a vision, the mission is often quite short and often meaningful. This is especially true of not-for-profit charitable organizations. These are typically founded to address a pressing social or community need that people embrace with passion. The mission espouses a passion for good. This is less the case for businesses, although some tech companies have strong commitments to expanding knowledge or doing good in a variety of ways. More recently the mission statements for business have expanded to embrace sustainability and social responsibility as part of their purpose. All of this should be applauded and emulated.

Values

Values serve to define appropriate behaviour both for individuals within the organization and the organization itself. These can be binding and powerful in helping employees and management hold each other to account. The values expressed can be rather run of the mill but nevertheless they create expectations of behaviour. Familiar expressions of values might include statements on trust or integrity or honesty. These are vague but can lead to deeper questions, such as what does integrity mean? What are examples of integrity? What does honesty mean to a customer?

As a consistent theme in this book, the process of developing vision, mission, and values statements is as valuable as the final product. In each case, such discussions encourage the exchange of ideas and deeper understanding of the organization's direction, aspirations, purpose, and codes of conduct. The depth of discussion can be remarkable. Box 13 provides an example of the deep and extensive discussion that can occur in reviewing an organization's vision and mission.

Box 13—Discussions of Vision and Mission—A University Example

In the early 2000s, the Ontario College of Art and Design, led by its new president, Sara Diamond, undertook a scenarios-to-strategy project. Part of the project included a review and update of OCAD's vision, mission, and more broadly, its strategic intent. The current vision and mission were used to generate a strategic conversation using a set of questions that challenged deep thinking on the purpose and future of the institution. A partial set of questions used in regenerating the vision and mission are provided below. Many of these questions would be appropriate for any learning institution. As a follow-up and in part because of this work, OCAD subsequently met the requirements to move from a college to university.

Vision: To become one of the world's leading art and design universities.

Mission: OCAD challenges each student to find a unique voice within a vibrant and creative environment; prepares graduates to excel as cultural contributors in Canada and beyond; and champions the vital role of art and design in society.

What Questions Do We Need to Discuss in Creating a New Vision, Mission and Strategic Intent?

- What is the unique role of art and design in society?

- Are we only graduating "cultural contributors"? Is our job larger? Should we be educators? Engineers? Inventors?

- How does undergraduate and graduate learning fit in the strategic intent?

- What are the core qualities of undergraduate experience at OCAD?

  - Discipline based or multidisciplinary approach?

  - What do we mean by studio-based learning? By practice-based research?

  - What do we mean by "unique voice," and where does collaboration and individuality fit?

- Where does research fit in the strategic intent? How do we understand research?

- Where does research intersect with undergraduate, graduate knowledge?

- Where are we art & design specific and where do we need to partner with other disciplines—in the arts, cultural industries, and beyond?

- Where does innovation/technology/policy/cultural and knowledge transfer fit into strategic intent?

- What is the role of continuing studies in OCAD's future?

- Diversity—What does diversity mean—students, faculty, courses, approaches, cultures?

- Where should our students come from? Ontario, Canada, International?

- What is the role of technology—does OCAD want to be leading edge in technology for A&D and for teaching & learning? What is the relationship between analog technology and digital?

- Size—growth in enrolment? How big? Space needs? One or multiple campuses? Where?

- International role versus local, regional, national role?

- Reputation and identity—What is our brand?

- Funding—public versus private—what is the right mix? Donor versus corporate?

Strategic Intent

Strategic Intent is an important refinement of the vision, mission, and values. The vision focuses on what we want to become. The mission focuses on what we are trying to do. The values focus on how we want to behave. The concept of strategic intent captures these ideas but also conveys a focus and intent that is grounded in reality—visionary but achievable—not only what we want to become but an indication of how to achieve it in the short term, i.e., strategic direction.

The meaning of strategic intent was developed by Gary Hamel and C. K. Prahalad (1996) in their book *Competing for the Future*. Unlike a vision, strategic intent provides direction on moving toward the vision. For example, from the questions facing OCAD in Box 13, the vision embraced the idea of becoming one of the world's leading art and design universities. What does "leading" mean? How would you measure success in achieving that vision? Clearly this involves comparing OCAD with other universities on some metric or benchmark. Without a benchmark how would OCAD leaders know if they were achieving their goal to be one of the world's leading art and design universities?

One metric might be graduates' endorsements focusing on student evaluations. Another might be the faculty's published research or the range of disciplines across university departments. Focusing on endorsements would provide strategic intent to ensure a high-quality student experience. The direction would function somewhat like a strategic focus area in narrowing the attention of the institution on a specific measure for a period of time. With success in this area the strategic intent might shift to another factor defining a leading art and design university. In short, strategic intent is the short-term path to a long-term vision. It is a powerful concept that reinforces the focus and direction of the strategic plan.

In Chapter 7 a complementary tool—The Business Idea—to developing strategy is introduced. In Chapter 8 the challenge of implementing strategy and monitoring performance is discussed.

CHAPTER SUMMARY

- The scenario to strategy development process involves five steps: scenario implications, strategic issues, strategic focus areas, strategic options, and strategic options evaluation.

- The process emphasizes a workshop-based approach to engage participants in building shared understanding, alignment, and commitment.

- The process can be modified to fit different organizational structures and cultures.

- Three examples highlight modifications to the basic process. The common critical step was the identification of strategic focus areas creating a direct path to goals, strategies, and actions.

- A process of strategy development may be undertaken without first developing scenarios. Scenarios enhance the process by providing a shared understanding of how a range of potential futures could unfold as a basis for generating strategic options and evaluating strategic risk using wind tunnelling.

- Risky strategies that have the potential for high rewards may be undertaken if the risks are understood. The worst decisions are those made in ignorance of the risks.

- The culmination of the strategy development process is a strategic plan, including the organization's vision, mission, and values as well as strategic focus areas, goals, strategies, and actions

- Vision, mission, and values are aspiration statements providing direction, inspiration, and alignment. The process of updating these aspirations is as valuable as the final statements.

- Strategic intent defines the short-term direction or priorities in moving toward the long-term vision.

CHAPTER 7
THE BUSINESS IDEA

Whenever you see a successful business,
someone once made a courageous decision.
—Peter Drucker

SEARCHING FOR SUCCESS

Strategic planning has evolved since its inception in the 1960s. A dominant question has always been: What creates success? An initial tool was SWOT analysis—strengths, weaknesses, opportunities, and threats. This approach was widely used and valuable in generating strategic conversations on both internal strengths and weaknesses, and external opportunities and threats. All too often the discussion stopped there without much follow-up action. It was difficult to focus on one element—how did you leverage strengths—and create success? Did a strength become a weakness depending on how the external business environment changed? When was a threat an opportunity? SWOT analysis was useful in gaining insights but offered no clear path to follow-up the insights. Planners needed something better.

The next evolution in this strategic thinking was to identify critical success factors. In implementing a plan, what was the critical factor for success? This was often a fruitful discussion and blended well into issue management. What was the essence of the issue? What was critical in managing the issue? This was good thinking but limited when thinking about an organization as a whole. It remained overly focused on a single factor for success.

An addition to the question of what was needed for success was the idea of a core competency. This was some inherent capability that gave an organization a competitive advantage. At one time in Shell Canada, executives viewed the company's ability to find deep natural gas as a core competency. How this became a core competency or how it could be preserved and nourished was a complete mystery. The idea that a single core competency could drive success was the silver bullet of strategy. This was not to say this was not a valuable discussion; it was just naive.

A more comprehensive perspective emerged with Michael Porter's focus on activities (1996). For him, strategy was the activities of the company, not what you say but what you do. It was also what you didn't do. The key shift in thinking with this approach was the idea that success emerged from the interlinkage of activities within the corporation. How did the activities fit together to create a whole? This approach embraces systems thinking by considering how the activities of an organization interact and complement each other. The description, however, did not include a well-defined methodology for defining and understanding the connections across activities.

A related idea that emerged in the late 1990s was the business model. Gary Hamel (2002), in his book *Leading the Revolution*, described in some detail the key elements of a business model (core strategy, customer interface, strategic resources, and value network) but they were largely disconnected components. How they were interrelated to create an integrated and sustainable business model was not well defined.

THE BUSINESS IDEA—AN INTEGRATING CONCEPT

Extending this evolution of thinking, Kees van der Heijden (1996) developed The Business Idea (BI). He asked: How does an organization create value? What are the interrelated components that work together to create value and hence success? The Business Idea is a similar concept to the business model, but it provides an integrated description of how key ingredients come together to create value. The BI focuses on the reinforcing linkages that create value and generate growth.

All organizations, whether for profit, not-for-profit, or government departments, have a central Business Idea underlying their operations. But few are able to articulate it explicitly. Some key elements—brand or technology or marketing capabilities—may be identified but they are seldom linked together into a coherent integrated model. The Business Idea unpacks the key elements contributing to a successful organization. The basic elements are shown in Figure 30 in the form of a systems diagram.

Figure 30—Elements of The Business Idea

The "Business Idea"

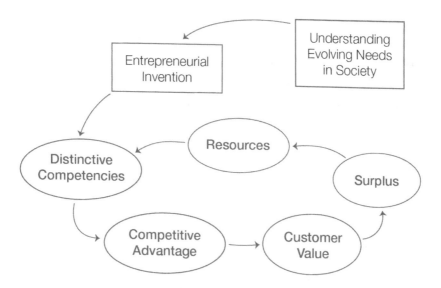

The central question is: How do the resources of the organization create distinct competencies that generate competitive advantages that provide value for customers? Providing value for customers generates cash flow (surplus) for reinvestment in resources to enhance competencies that strengthen competitive advantages and generate more value for customers.[38] In this way a virtuous cycle of growth is created.

All Business Ideas begin by satisfying a societal need. This is true of a business entrepreneur identifying a market niche, a group of citizens forming a non-profit charity to meet a community need, or a government civil servant designing a program for citizens. To be successful the nascent organization needs to fulfill a need in society. Google recognized a need to systematically access information on the web. St. John's Ambulance recognized a need for training and providing emergency medical care. Governments recognized a need to support workers who lost their jobs. The list is endless. Each created an organization or program to meet a societal need. Each was an entrepreneurial invention, since at its onset it was a novel idea. Meeting the need is the mission or purpose of every organization. If it does not meet that need or others do it better, the organization fails.

The strategic significance of the Business Idea emerges in three ways. First, developing the Business Idea is a vehicle for strategic conversation that enhances understanding of the key elements creating success. Second, it creates understanding

---

38   For a non-profit or charitable organization "buying" may be donations or financial support from a government. A government department needs to compete for funding with other departments. The key point is that creating value is necessary to generate financial support.

of the linkages critical for the organization. Identifying elements that are leverage points in the Business Idea provides a focus for strategy similar to strategic focus areas described in the basic model. Third, the Business Idea is strategic in describing the current formula for success but not necessarily future success. This is how the Business Idea links to scenario thinking. The reality is that as external conditions change, all Business Ideas erode over time. The changing external condition might be the nature of competition, regulations, technology, or societal expectations. Foresight supports examination of the Business Idea to see how it could adapt to future changes.

The impact of changes can happen quickly. Notice that the system creates growth when all the connections are positive. It is a positive feedback loop; each component reinforces the next. If one of the connections becomes negative, however, the feedback destroys value. A decline in resources, for example, perhaps due to a market change, may undermine the ability to maintain core competencies, competitive advantage, and ultimately customer value.

An Example—Nokia

In the early 2000s, Nokia was riding high as the world leader in mobile phones. Global demand was accelerating and Nokia was the uncontested leader. A representation of Nokia's Business Idea is shown in Figure 31. This was not developed by Nokia or with any direct input from them. The Business Idea shown here was based on statements by the CFO of Nokia, Olli-Pekka Kallasvuo (*The Economist*, 2000): We have the design, the branding and the technology. We also have the biggest volumes in a business where volume really helps, and the best supply chain management in the business.

To interpret Figure 31, begin by focusing on the money signified by $$. Investment in technological innovation and product design creates leading-edge products. A flow of new leading-edge products, combined with efficient supply chain management, creates an efficient global marketing capability. Combined with low-cost production, this generates volume sales and high levels of customer satisfaction. (Value proposition focuses on design and price.) The global brand is enhanced and profits are generated. Money can then be invested in new designs and technology development, as well as brand advertising and supply-chain management, improvements to leverage the global marketing capability generating more sales to customers.

The boxed elements in the diagram signify elements that are unique to the organization and thus cannot be easily duplicated by competitors. This is always true for an organization's brand. In this case, however, leading product design proved not to be unique for Nokia. Competitors were able to match and ultimately improve on Nokia's innovative product designs.

Notice how vital new products are in this Business Idea. A stream of new products feeds the global marketing capabilities. It was vital that Nokia's management understood this for ongoing success. But did they? Ultimately Blackberry, with the introduction of smart phones, and Apple, with brilliant design, usurped the dominance of Nokia. Nokia lost its advantage in leading-edge products, which made their competencies in marketing and supply chain management irrelevant.

Figure 31—Nokia Business Model—An Example

Nokia Business Idea

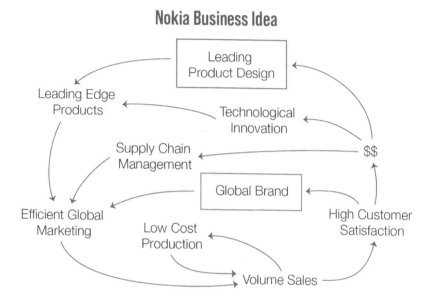

This example highlights the value of the Business Idea in surfacing a key leverage point necessary in sustaining the system that created success for Nokia in mobile phones. If Nokia's management had realized the critical importance of product design, would they have invested more in that area and remained competitive with new competitors like Blackberry and ultimately Apple? This example also highlights the reality that all BI's erode over time. As change occurs, the Business Idea must adapt. This is the connection with scenarios. They provide perspective on the future. They allow an organization to wind tunnel their BI. If scenario A occurs, how will it impact the ability of the organization to create customer value? Marrying scenarios and the Business Idea represents another vehicle for strategic conversation and shared understanding.

An Example—Fort Calgary

Fort Calgary is a major visitor attraction and event centre. It is the historic site of the original Fort Calgary dating from the 1870s. In 2011, the executive director of Fort Calgary asked me to assist in developing a strategic plan. Part of the exercise included developing the Business Idea for Fort Calgary. The result is shown in Figure 32.

Figure 32—Fort Calgary Business Idea

Fort Calgary Business Idea

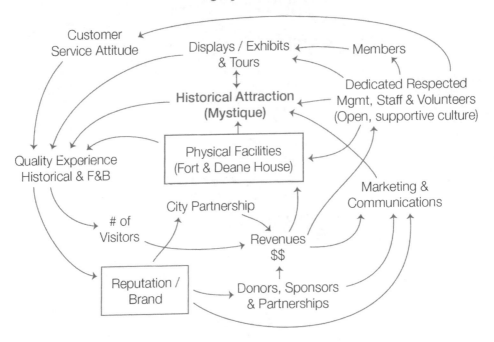

Initially, the diagram appears complicated. To understand it, start with the revenues ($$). This comes from visitors to the historic site, grants from the city, and donors, sponsors, and other partnerships. These funds support marketing and communication, ongoing maintenance and investment in the physical facilities, and go to pay management and staff and support volunteers.

These resources come together, with historical displays, exhibits, and tours to create the historical attraction that is Fort Calgary. An intangible in this system was the role of dedicated staff and volunteers supporting a customer-service attitude. Maintaining this dedicated, caring service was seen as a key ingredient in generating a quality experience for both visitors who came for the historical experience and those who came for the food and beverage (F&B) experience. A high-quality experience reinforced the reputation and brand and generated paying visitors. Maintaining the reputation was important in sustaining both city and donor support.

The Business Idea for Fort Calgary was valuable in integrating the key elements generating customer value. But there was more. Up until this exercise there was no common connection between the operation of the historical site and the food and beverage service that had emerged. One was a tourist attraction. The other provided banquet and meeting services to local organizations that was in direct competition with hotels and restaurants. What did Fort Calgary offer that was different?

Developing the Business Idea surfaced an understanding that an attraction of Fort Calgary was its unique historical experience or mystique that no competitor could duplicate. The insight was that Fort Calgary could lever its mystique to create a unique food and beverage experience. Not only the setting but the service could be tailored to reinforce the historical context, by designing and adapting the menu to enhance the historical experience. For example, create historical food offerings with unique names. Develop a list of historical drinks. Attach descriptions of period foods and what life was like in the 1880s. Redesign staff uniforms. In this way, build an aura of history to enhance and create a unique food and beverage experience. At the same time, reinforce to all staff that enhancing the historical mystique to all visitors is vital to a quality visitor experience, reputation, customer value, and the success of Fort Calgary. This mystique became a central component of Fort Calgary's strategy with great success in generating increased food and beverage sales and creating a common focus for staff.

This example demonstrates the value of unpacking an organization's Business Idea. It deepens understanding of how key elements are interrelated in creating customer value, opportunities for growth, and direction in formulating strategies that enhance the success of the organization.

VALUE OF THE BUSINESS IDEA

The Business Idea is a valuable approach to understanding strategically how an organization's resources and competencies create distinct advantages and generate customer value. In any organization, success comes from creating value for customers.

The Business Idea is valuable for large and established organizations needing to focus direction, as well as start-ups trying to clarify the critical resources and competencies needed for success in a competitive world. It is valuable for organizations facing rapidly changing operating environments as well as companies seeking insight on mature markets. It follows and reinforces the emphasis on customers in other strategic planning approaches. Understanding their needs and what they value in your organization's offering or value proposition is central to the Business Idea. But the BI also emphasizes an understanding of the constellation of activities, resources, and competencies that produce that value and make the organization unique in the operating environment. Understanding the linkages gives an organization tremendous focus and leverage in developing strategies for growth and sustainability.

Specifically, the value to an organization from developing a Business Idea includes:

1. understanding: new insight and understanding of the forces driving the business;

2. connections: shared understanding of the key elements and their connections in creating success;

3. leverage points: clarification of key strategic leverage points for growth (also points of vulnerability);

4. strategy: creation of a simple, powerful model focusing strategic priorities and supporting clear communication through the one-page systems diagram;

5. alignment supports: alignment and cohesion by engaging senior management in a strategic conversation that enhances common understanding of the business, supports shared leadership, builds team cohesion, and reinforces commitment to action.

DEVELOPING THE BUSINESS IDEA

The process for developing the Business Idea involves three basic steps.

1. Building the Business Idea. A half-day workshop is used to explore the key components and their connections. Ideally, the workshop includes from six to twelve participants. The questions used in the workshop are outlined in Box 14. The output is a summary of key elements within the major components of the Business Idea, namely resources, competencies (or capabilities), competitive advantages, and customer value. These, at best, form a rough draft of the Business Idea but need more in-depth thinking and refinement.

2. Refining the Business Idea. Following the workshop, further reflection and discussion, including feedback from the original participants, leads to a refinement of the draft BI.

3. Business Idea to Strategies. Depending on the project, the BI can serve as a framework for developing strategies directly, or in conjunction with scenario planning, can be used in another workshop to test the robustness of the current Business Idea against the range of future worlds described by the scenarios.

Box 14—Questions for Developing the Business Idea

How do you flesh out the ideas for the Business Idea? A workshop setting works well in allowing individuals to share ideas and build a description of the Business Idea. As with other vehicles, it creates an opportunity for strategic conversation. In the end, the business idea is valuable in articulating the organization's mental model of the distinct capabilities that create current and future success.

The questions follow the framework of the Business Idea. In this case, the questions start with the customer and work back toward resources. The questions are mostly focused on a for-profit organization but can easily be adapted to non-profit and government organizations.

Value for Customer

• Who is the customer?

• What is the product or service?

• What is the value for the customer in the product or service?

Competitive Advantage

• Why does the customer buy from you?

• Is there a distinct value that we bring to the transaction?

• Does that distinctiveness allow us to charge a premium price?

Competencies and Resources

• What resources (funding, people, technology) do we need to produce the product and make the transaction?

• What specific capabilities (processes which bring technology and skills together to produce a product) do we need?

• Are these capabilities distinct or easily imitated by competitors?

Growth

• How big is the potential market (size of the prize)?

• How does the company grow? What strategic investments are needed to penetrate the market and grow the business over time?

Generating and discussing ideas in each grouping allows the facilitator, on reflection, to create an initial system diagram of the Business Idea. This outlines how the organization creates a system that generates value to customers. The diagram, with accompanying explanation, is presented back to the original participants for feedback and refinement. Ultimately, the participants have to own the result to make the exercise valuable.

CHAPTER SUMMARY

- Strategic planning tools focused on what creates success have evolved since the 1960s.

- The evolution from SWOT analysis to critical success factors to core competencies to business models culminated in the Business Idea.

- All organizations have a Business Idea that satisfies a societal need, but few are able to explicitly articulate their BI.

- The Business Idea emphasizes the connection of components to create customer value and hence success.

- The central question is: How do the resources of an organization create distinctive competencies that generate competitive advantage, provide value for customers, and generate cash flow for reinvestment? In this way the model is a description of how growth occurs.

- The model is shown as a systems diagram on a single page.

- Two examples demonstrate the power in developing a BI in deepening shared understanding of the organization and identifying strategic leverage points.

- All BIs erode over time as external conditions change.

- The BI may be combined with scenarios to test the robustness of the BI against future change.

PART 4
STRATEGY
IMPLEMENTATION

Developing strategies is not enough. They must be implemented. This involves follow-through in implementing the actions identified in the strategic plan, monitoring progress over time, and adjusting as success emerges or not and as the external business environment evolves.

CHAPTER 8
IMPLEMENTATION AND PERFORMANCE

Success is never an accident. It is always the result of high intention,
sincere effort, intelligent direction and skilful execution.
—Anonymous

T he strategic management model reproduced in Figure 33, emphasizes the ongoing development and implementation of strategy in an organization. This chapter outlines a mechanism for implementing strategies, conditions for success, and thoughts on performance management in implementing strategies.

Figure 33—Strategic Management Model

Integrated Strategic Management

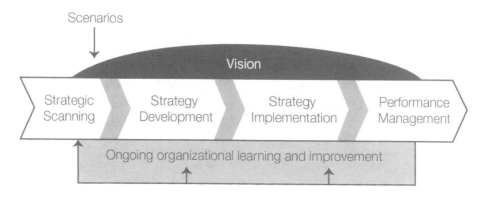

STRATEGY IMPLEMENTATION—THE PLANNING CYCLE

Strategic planning is part of an annual planning cycle. Typically, there are three planning documents: the budget, business plan, and strategic plan. The differences are shown in Figure 34. The budget is a detailed, one-year plan describing specific actions with attached budgets. The business plan is a longer time frame, typically three to five years, describing plans for a range of operations from production to marketing, sales, communications, et cetera, along with human resource requirements and financial projections. The budget and business plan are renewed each year.

Figure 34—The Planning Process

Strategic Planning Framework

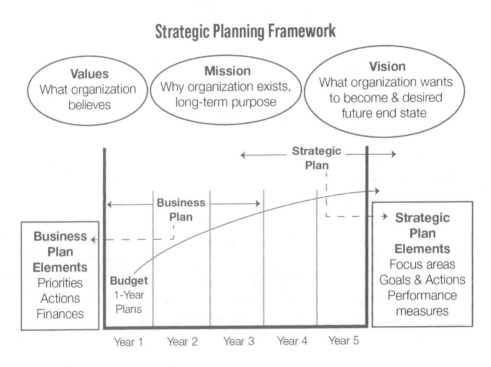

Source: Calgary Centre for Non-Profit Management

The budget and business plan should be consistent with the longer-term strategic plan as well as the organization's strategic intent. The budget, in effect, is the first year of the strategic plan. The allocation of resources should be consistent with the strategic plan. If a strategic focus area of the strategic plan was, say, customer service, then the budget should include an allocation of funding to enhance customer service. The business plan is also effectively the first few years of the strategic plan. It should allocate resources to implement the strategic plan. Not all strategies may be pursued at once. The business plan, therefore, sets the priorities. Some strategies may be pursued in the short term while others are planned for later years.

The strategic plan should be updated each year as plans are implemented, and the future unfolds. This does not mean a full scenarios-to-strategy process. The signposts are designed to monitor changes in the external environment. The organization should undertake a review of the scenarios each year. What has changed in the external business environment? Do recent events indicate that one scenario or another is emerging? Are there changes that do not fit in any of the scenarios? This last question is vital in determining if the scenarios need to be updated. When the scenarios cease to explain major changes that are occurring, then it is time to develop a new set of scenarios. Usually, this happens after a number of years in light of a major external change. In Royal Dutch Shell, for example, the relatively sudden emergence of global warming in the late 1980s triggered a need to develop new scenarios. The threat to the oil and gas industry was immediately apparent, and management correctly requested a scenario look at the potential changes this could create.

Reviewing the strategic plan entails not only monitoring the external environment but internal performance. The feedback loop in the strategic management model should monitor performance in implementing the strategic plan regularly with a major review as part of the annual cycle. The annual cycle should also monitor the overall performance of the organization.

The strategic plan is the overall planning guide for the organization. The budget and business plans implement the strategic plan as well as operations. They should form an integrated whole. The annual planning cycle creates the one-year budget as the first year in the business plan leading to fulfillment of the strategic plan. The path is updated and corrected with each annual cycle.

Box 15—The Role of Planners

An interesting question emerges frequently in large organizations. Who is responsible for planning? The process is usually the responsibility of planners in the planning department, but the plans should be the responsibility of managers. Managers must create and own their own plans. Planners help managers create plans but should never plan. When planners think they can run the company, disaster awaits.

Don Michael (1973) was the first to propose that planning is learning. This theme permeates the work of Peter Senge (1980) and was the dominant theme in Arie de Geus's book *The Living Company* (1997), which was based on research in Shell. From this perspective the role of a planner is to foster learning. Kees van der Heijden (1996; 2005) crystalized this with the concept of strategic conversation. The role of the planner is to create venues for strategic conversation so that managers can plan for

> the organization, department, division, or whatever level is required. This means that planning is both learning and facilitation. Good planners create and lead strategic conversations so that managers make good decisions and well-thought-out plans. [39]

In Royal Dutch Shell, the planning cycle was initiated by planners with the distribution of the planning premises. These were projections of a number of key variables needed by departments to estimate revenues, costs, and ultimately cash flows both for operations and investment options. These included, in the oil and gas example, projections of oil, gas, and other commodities, inflation, interest rates, and economic growth. Issuing the premises initiated the annual planning cycle. These assumptions were used by all departments to build their budgets and business plans. After considerable consultation and discussion, each department (or country in the case of Shell International) submitted its plans, based on the premises, back to the planning department. These were aggregated for the company as a whole. For Royal Dutch Shell this was a critical step in ensuring that all the plans, when aggregated, could be fully funded and implemented. In short, did the sum of the parts make sense as a whole?

Developing the premises was the responsibility of the planning department, but Shell's approach added a subtle twist to the process. The planning department would send out a survey to the top twenty to thirty managers in the company requesting them to graph their expectations of the key variables. For example, each manager would be asked to draw a line showing their expectation of the price of oil for the next five years. This was a powerful way to tap managers' insights and expectations and build a common perspective on key business parameters. This was an inclusive approach that revealed differences that could be discussed and shared, creating understanding, promoting alignment, and building commitment. It was a relatively simple exercise with huge benefits. Managers were keen to find out the results and learn what their colleagues' expectations were. To my knowledge, few organizations use this approach. Many would benefit.

Another subtle step in the Royal Dutch Shell process was the Planning Letter sent by the Committee of Managing Directors (effectively the CEO in other organizations) to operating companies. The letter highlighted key strategic issues that needed to be addressed in their company plans. In 1986, it asked each operating company to prepare a contingency plan for a steep fall in oil prices. Another, as noted previously, was for companies to document all pipelines crossing water and include in their plans what they planned to do in monitoring these pipelines to prevent

---

39 The idea that planners help managers plan is similar to the role of human resource specialists. HR experts are responsible for setting rules and guidelines, but ultimately it is managers who manage people. HR experts provide guidance but do not manage human resources.

spills. This was an effective way of allowing companies to create their own local or regional plans in response to an issue at the global level. More generally, this allows a department in a company to create their own plans reflecting their specific situation and priorities while ensuring alignment with the strategic direction of the larger organization. In Shell, this gave country management greater control in developing relevant plans within the larger global company.

CRITERIA FOR SUCCESSFUL IMPLEMENTATION

Developing strategies does not mean they are implemented. There is a widely quoted statistic that 80 percent of strategic plans fail because of faulty execution. It is not that the strategies are necessarily faulty, but the organization does not successfully implement them. Whether accurate or not, the message is clear. Successfully implementing a strategic plan is as critical as the quality of the strategies developed. The Shell example provides insight into some of the criteria for successful implementation.

Leadership

Leadership is critical for success. Leadership embraces two concepts. One is distributed leadership in which a wide swath of managers and influential employees exercise leadership. This includes the willingness to take initiative and work independently. Ken Low (2001), who developed the concept of pioneer leadership for Leadership Calgary, a community-business leadership training program, described in simple terms the concept of wisdom: Wisdom is the ability to see that something needs to be done, to know what to do, and to do it without being asked.

This is the essence of leadership. A key element in Ken's thinking is the importance of self-authorization. Others might call it initiative. Yet others might call it risk-taking. The important point is that distributed leadership, as part of an organization's culture, is extremely valuable in supporting strategy implementation (as well as a plethora of decisions and actions across an organization).

A second type of leadership is the functional leadership of senior executives. These are leaders with power imbued by their position in the organization. Most important is the CEO who, regardless of the size of the organization, sets the conditions for the culture of the entire organization. The CEO's decisions and actions send resonating signals throughout the organization. Their influence cannot be underestimated.

The Shell culture provides an interesting example. Shell was the marriage of two companies in 1907, Shell Transport and Trading and Royal Dutch Petroleum. The marriage—more marriage than merger—required cooperation in building consensus. Royal Dutch, with 60 percent of the equity, could exercise control. But if it unilaterally began making decisions, the marriage would fail. This reality created a need for an inclusive culture based on building consensus in making decisions. The top-down, bottom-up planning process in Shell, in which broad requests from the top allowed operating-companies flexibility in how they responded was an example of building consensus rather than imposing controls.

This type of culture, emphasizing consensus, is unusual. More common is a top-down command and control structure dominated by the CEO. In the mid-1990s I experienced a fascinating cultural transition as two cultures collided. A major energy company for which I was doing consulting work changed CEOs. The retiring CEO was a dominant figure in control of every major decision. No vice-president ever made a decision without consulting the CEO. The incoming CEO was entirely different. He delegated authority and encouraged his VPs to take responsibility, make decisions, and exercise their leadership. For vice-presidents who always checked every decision with their boss, this was a dramatic change. Some were able to adjust, but most felt the rug had been pulled out from under them. They lacked leadership experience. For many VPs, the new CEO was not a leader because he could not make decisions. The irony escaped them.

The key point is that leadership is important in implementing plans. Leadership sets the culture. The process of implementation must complement the existing culture whether that is top-down and directive or bottom-up and inclusive. If the process is not well led or is inconsistent with the culture, the implementation will fail.

Shared Understanding

Over the past fifty years the level of education among all employees in companies has increased remarkably. In Canada and the US upwards of 50 percent of the population aged twenty to forty has some post-secondary education. What does this mean?

One thing this means is that there has been a dramatic increase in critical thinking capabilities in organizations. The effect is that old command and control management approaches do not work. Individuals are no longer willing to blindly obey orders. They want to understand why they are undertaking a task or the purpose of the assignment. The military adage, "Ours not to question why, ours but to do and die" is not appropriate in today's organizations. Even in the military this maxim is open to question (see Box 16). More relevant is creating conditions for initiative, innovation, and creativity.

Box 16—The Value of Shared Understanding—The Battle of Vimy Ridge

In 1917, the German army commanded a strategic position on Vimy Ridge in France. Allied assaults by British and French troops had failed to capture this strategic high point of land. In the major battle of Arras, the task was assigned to the Canada Corp. For the first time in history the Canada Corp brought soldiers from all parts of the country to fight together.

The unique aspect of this battle was a number of innovations first used in warfare. One example was the first use of a "creeping barrage" leading an advancing wave of infantry into battle. More important was preparation and training. Battle plans were laid out using information from aerial photos, and these were mapped out to create a practice area for training the troops. These were major innovations in planning battles.

Perhaps most important was a major change in the command structure. "Command on the battlefield was decentralized to the platoon and lower. Soldiers, especially non-commissioned officers, were encouraged to think for themselves, show leadership, and use initiative. Keep moving, the troops were told. Follow your lieutenant—and if he goes down, follow your corporal" (*The Canadian Encyclopedia)*. The critical change was that private soldiers were informed of their objectives. Prior to this, need-to-know did not include privates. One reason was that up until that time common soldiers were largely illiterate. This was one of the first armies in which all soldiers could read and write.

Shared understanding of tactics and objectives proved to be an important factor in the outcome. Casualties were horrendous on both sides. In many instances corporals and privates were the final leaders in capturing important positions. The new decentralized command structure in which all soldiers knew their objectives proved a major factor in the battle.

The battle was the largest advance by the Allies up to that point in the war. Ultimately the battle was not significant in the final outcome. Nevertheless, it was widely acclaimed in Canada and achieved mythic status of as being the first moment Canada stood alone as an independent nation. The battle of Vimy Ridge is remembered as the birth of a nation.

In the context of strategic management, the lesson of Vimy Ridge is the importance of shared understanding in creating initiative, leadership, and commitment in successful implementation of strategy.

Modern employees want to know why as well as what. They want to understand why the task they are assigned is important. They want to know what they are trying to accomplish. And they want to be able to contribute to how the task is undertaken. If they understand, they will commit. If they do not understand, they will obfuscate, delay, or perform at a minimal level. Government bureaucracies are famous for undermining ministerial decisions. "Yes Minister" is a possible response in all organizations[40].

In our language, a key to successful implementation is shared understanding. Creating opportunities for strategic conversation engages all participants in developing shared understanding of what is required by whom in accomplishing the task, achieving the objective, or implementing a strategy. Sounds simple but it requires work and managerial time. The effort is worth it. It builds commitment and engages all participants to explore better ideas for accomplishing the task. Engagement and commitment are vital to getting things done well. This is true for all decisions, including implementing strategies.

Focus, Alignment, and Momentum

My long-time friend and colleague, Lee van Horn, had the penetrating ability to simplify complex issues into their critical essentials. In strategic management he emphasized three elements: focus, alignment, and momentum.

Focus is the essence of strategic management. What are you going to focus on? What are you not going to focus on? Strategy development is all about clarifying strategic focus. Implementation is about maintaining that focus. The cost of losing focus is often underestimated. Resisting temptations to do what you are not doing can be difficult. Losing focus is a challenge that can completely undermine the implementation of a strategic plan.

Alignment is critical for successful implementation. It means harnessing the team to pull in the same direction. Everyone needs to know what the strategies are, what the objectives are, and how those fit together into the overall path to achieve the goals.

At least two factors are important in creating alignment. First, shared understanding is a powerful instrument in promoting alignment. Shared understanding is not a one-off. It is an ongoing process involving periodic renewal of the process, the barriers, and the accomplishments. This is part of monitoring performance, the next component in the strategic management process.

Second, integration is critical in promoting alignment. In the Shell example, operating companies developed their own plans in alignment with the larger global organization's strategic direction whether managing inventory or responding to environmental issues. This encouraged operating companies to respond innovatively to their local situation while aligning with the global direction. The Northern Alberta Institute of Technology example, (Chapter 6), used a similar approach to

---

40   *Yes, Minister* was a famous British sitcom in the 1970s portraying the relationship between a minister and his undersecretary who reported to him. The term "Yes, Minister" was how the undersecretary agreed to all requests but found excuses not to carry them out.

integrate department responses to institutional objectives. The same phenomenon occurs when prime ministers or presidents assign mandates to different government departments.

These examples highlight an ongoing management challenge: to balance alignment and innovation. Excessive alignment can lead to rigidity. Excessive innovation can lead to anarchy. Everyone pulling in the same direction is powerful in accomplishing an objective, but it can be a disaster if there is a need to alter direction. Similarly, unfettered innovation can lead to a wealth of ideas and experiments vital in stimulating change and adaptation. But if they are pulling in different directions, the result can be chaos. Perhaps the one competency every company fears most is creative accounting.

Momentum is the need to maintain progress over time. Progress in implementing a strategy may be fast or slow but must never come to a halt. A stoppage can be extremely destructive as energy is dissipated and focus lost. This is an element in monitoring performance that management needs to understand. It is a challenge in the scenarios-to-strategy process, as high levels of enthusiasm in the creative scenario development process lose momentum when the group turns to the development of strategy. The group runs out of gas (or joules).

The simple message is that focus, alignment, and momentum are key factors in implementing strategies. They require balancing strategic direction for the organization and innovation for individual departments. Leadership and shared understanding are valuable approaches to sustaining focus, managing alignment, and maintaining momentum as these components interact to make implementation successful.

Ownership

Focus, alignment, momentum, shared understanding, and leadership require a final element critical for successful implementation: ownership. Individuals and groups required to act and implement the plan need to take ownership and responsibility and commit to the strategy. Ownership or lack thereof can be traced to two different situations.

First, have individuals and groups been part of the strategy development process? If so, they are highly likely to feel ownership and commit to implementing the strategy. This is especially true if they feel they have contributed to the strategies developed. It may not be that their specific ideas have been embraced, but that they have been heard. Participation and engagement foster ownership.

Second, what if individuals and groups have not been involved in developing the strategies? How do you build ownership in those who have not participated? This is more difficult; there is no formula. Nevertheless, leaders who can communicate the significance of the plans, build shared understanding, and rally support can instill ownership and commitment. More crudely, performance goals that ultimately affect promotion and compensation are visible tools to build commitment. If an individual manager's performance rating is tied to achieving a strategic goal, that goal will get attention. The point is not to use crude tools to force compliance, but to recognize the need to set performance criteria linked to strategic goals in the annual discussions that set performance goals generally. Setting performance goals from CEOs downward is an important part of successful implementation and generally associated with well managed organizations.

Performance Management

How do you measure performance in implementing strategies and achieving strategic goals? The objective in monitoring the implementation process is to provide feedback information so the process can be adjusted to meet ongoing developments. A famous quote attributed to General Dwight Eisenhower was "Plans are great until you meet the enemy."

Monitoring performance has two objectives. One is to track the organization's progress in implementing its strategies. The other is to monitor the performance of the organization overall. The two are closely linked because the indicators for strategy and organization performance often overlap.

Strategy

The approach to monitoring strategy implementation is to identify key variables in each strategic focus area linked to specific strategies and goals. For example, if a strategic focus area included a strategy to increase your share of a customer's spending across different services (e.g., brakes and mufflers, groceries, and pharmacy), then a key indicator might be the extent customers are buying two or more services or products from the company. The strategy might involve extensive advertising focused on cross buying (e.g., not just mufflers, we do brakes or check out our pharmacy in our grocery store). To implement the strategy, the company needs to monitor total sales, information on cross sales for each customer, and any relationship with advertising. You need to know whether the advertising strategy is working to achieve an increase in share of customer (share of a customer's total purchases). If not, the strategy needs to be revised.

Developing performance indicators needs to be tailored to the strategic focus area and specific strategies. It is not easy to develop nor easy to sustain. In working with a company providing rapid oil changes, the strategy adopted was to focus on customer service. The aim was not to be the lowest cost but to provide an inviting customer experience. Within a month the manager of the division operating the rapid lube stores suggested that the company could increase profits by removing the free coffee and lowering costs by $1 per customer, which was in direct opposition to the long-term strategy. Repeatedly, a major challenge in implementing strategy is to sustain the integrity of the strategy at least until it is shown to be performing or not. Few organizations are able to successfully develop a set of strategy performance indicators and follow them for an extended period of time. This does not mean strategies necessarily fail, but it means systematic implementation is rare.

In my experience, two examples of companies that were able to implement strategies successfully following the scenarios-to-strategy process were Ralston Purina and Emera (the company was created with the privatization of Nova Scotia Power). Ralston Purina used scenarios to identify strategic focus areas, including a need to expand internationally and enhance their capability in developing nutraceuticals. The company followed up by assigning a senior VP to expand international markets. The VP increased investment in marketing and production capacity in Europe. Further, within two years, Ralston Purina had purchased a biotech firm to expand their capability in developing pet nutraceuticals. (More on Ralston Purina in Chapter 9.)

Similarly, Emera used scenarios to generate a number of strategies to expand in the US and Caribbean. They subsequently followed up with investments in gas generation and electricity marketing in the US northeast and acquired an electric utility in the Caribbean. These enhanced the footprint and diversified the portfolio of the company.

Performance

There is much broader experience developing performance indicators for the overall performance of the organization. The most widely used tool is the balanced scorecard. Originally, the balanced scorecard was designed to be a framework to monitor how the organization was performing so that managers could adjust plans as required. The balanced scorecard, however, quickly became much more than a passive tool for monitoring performance. It has evolved into a highly strategic tool for both developing strategy and managing performance.

The balanced scorecard focuses on four perspectives (Kaplan and Norton, 1992):

1. A learning and growth perspective focused on employees, technology, and culture;

2. An internal processes perspective focused on a range of business and management processes;

3. A customer perspective focused on customer value; and

4. A financial perspective focused on revenue, costs, return on capital, et cetera.

These are generic descriptions. Each should develop customized variables to monitor performance relevant to that organization.

Two elements became obvious. First, the balanced scorecard is strategic. Adopting the four perspectives was strategic in focusing management on four strategic focus areas. Unlike the strategic management model, these are four generic strategic-focus areas predesignated rather than developed through the strategic planning process. Further, with the dictum "what's measured gets managed," the development of a balanced scorecard is explicitly strategic. You need to be strategic in selecting the variables to monitor because those are the ones used to manage the organization.

Second, use of the balanced scorecard quickly identified that the framework was valuable in understanding how the organization created value for customers and shareholders. The framework raised the question of how different perspectives were linked. How did learning and growth connect with internal processes to create value for customers leading to financial results? Many managers and organizations have excessively focused on financial results as the most important measures of performance. This is particularly true for publicly traded firms. What the balanced scorecard did was connect the financial results to the resources and capabilities of the organization in generating customer value. Does this sound familiar? There is clearly a close connection to understanding the causal relationships between learning, processes, customers, and financial results to the Business Idea connecting resources, competencies, competitive advantages, and customer value.

The emphasis on the balanced scorecard as an integrated strategy tool was highlighted by Kaplan and Norton (2000), who introduced the term "strategy mapping." This explicitly links elements across perspectives to enhance understanding of how learning elements contributed or were connected to processes to create customer value and drive financial results. Unlike the Business Idea, it did not explicitly identify a feedback loop in which cash flow is reinvested to create growth. Nevertheless, the two frameworks bear much in common.

What can we learn from the use of the balanced scorecard in our efforts to create performance measures for strategy implementation?

First, the balanced scorecard specifically focused on strategy implementation is valuable both as a process and product. The process of thinking through the key indicators to be monitored builds deeper understanding of the organization's strategy and its implementation. It is likely to surface barriers to implementation as well as alternative paths of action in achieving the strategic goal. It is another opportunity for strategic conversation in a learning organization.

As a product, the set of indicators creates a dashboard for management to monitor and a data set for analysis. One benefit of designing a strategy dashboard to monitor performance is that it may generate data you do not currently collect, which might be critical for both the strategy and the organization (See Box 17)

Box 17—Data Gaps

Information may be assumed but not exist. In the early 1990s, Shell Canada took an industry lead in creating an annual environmental sustainability report. I was assigned to manage the project. It was an honest attempt to document how the company was doing in reducing emissions and effluents and protecting areas of the environment. Senior management authorized the report thinking that it would be a relatively simple matter to collate the data that was already available to create a comprehensive report. They were wrong. While Shell collected swaths of data on almost any variable of interest, there was no consistent time series of any significance and, more importantly, across operating sites. Individual sites either did not collect similar data or did not do it in a consistent, comparable way. Shell's three refineries, for example, collected data on water effluents using different measures. In part, regulations in different provincial jurisdictions required different reporting information and formats. Creating valid and comprehensive reports was virtually impossible. The first report ended up being a largely anecdotal account from individual projects with no quantitative time-series information. This initial fiasco, however, stimulated change, and there was a rapid convergence of methods in data and information collection consistent across the organization. The lesson: developing a system to measure strategy implementation may identify information gaps that are important both for strategy and the organization.

Second, using the balanced scorecard disclosed a number of lessons for developing strategy dashboards.

1.   Avoid excessive detail that creates complexity: ruthlessly purge the number of indicators to the very basics; detail is the enemy of strategy.

2.   Ensure appropriate data are available, or can be generated from existing operating information systems.

3.   Ensure clear accountability for generating, collating, and monitoring the dashboard; create joint accountability where possible.

4.   Ensure CEO and senior management buy-in; CEOs who ignore or undermine the process effectively sabotage the value of the balanced scorecard.

The biggest obstacle in creating a balanced scorecard is excessive detail. A strategic map, for example, should be producible on a single page. This should not require using eight-point fonts to cram in more and more detail. Excessive detail destroys the purpose of the exercise: to clarify important connections and surface key indicators to be monitored in implementing strategy.

The thrust of performance management is to provide focused feedback information to manage the implementation of strategy. This is part of the difference between strategic planning and strategic management. Management is an active process in adapting the implementation of the plan through time.

There are three feedback loops in the strategic management model:

1. To manage the implementation of strategy,

2. To manage the overall performance of the organization,

3. To monitor and adapt to changes in the external environment, like that provided by scenario signposts.

These feedback loops have different time frames. Updating signposts may be an annual affair, unless something critical emerges in the short term. Strategy and organization monitoring are likely more frequent, especially companies reporting quarterly. Long-range planning has a dramatically different time horizon for high tech companies as opposed to power utilities. As with so much else, strategy implementation needs to be tailored to the organization, its internal culture, and changing external situation.

CHAPTER SUMMARY

• This chapter focuses on two components of the strategic management process: strategy implementation and performance management.

• Strategy implementation is part of the annual planning cycle, which includes the one-year budget, three- to five-year business plan, and longer-term strategic plan.

• The budget and business plan represent the first years of implementation of the strategic plan. They should be integrated.

• Successful strategy implementation involves leadership, shared understanding, alignment, and ownership.

• Leadership includes both distributed and positional leadership.

• Shared understanding builds alignment and ownership in creating the commitment necessary to implement strategies.

- Performance management emphasizes the need for information feedback to monitor and adjust the implementation of strategies and overall performance of the organization.

- The balanced scorecard is a valuable and widely applied approach to monitor performance. It is strategic in pre-assigning four focus areas and encouraging shared understanding of how learning and growth contribute to internal processes that contribute to consumer value and generate financial results.

- The strategic management model emphasizes three feedback loops: feedback to strategy implementation, feedback to organization performance, and feedback to changing external business environment.

PART 5
REFLECTIONS
AND LEARNINGS

Part 5 shifts from a focus on methodology to content. Chapter 10 is a narrative of my personal learning journey with scenarios and scenario planning, as a planner with Shell Canada and Royal Dutch Shell, and as a consultant with a variety of organizations. Chapter 11 focuses on common themes that emerged across a range of scenario projects.

CHAPTER 9
PERSONAL JOURNEY

SHELL CANADA

My introduction to Shell and scenario planning came through connections with two former colleagues. Liz Harman and Val Preston were colleagues during graduate studies. We worked in the broad area of behavioural geography and published a number of papers together. Liz, when she graduated, went to work with the federal government in Ottawa where she worked for Liz Parr-Johnston. Liz P-J. was impressed with the scope and expertise of Liz H. as a geographer. As a result, a couple of years later, Liz Parr-Johnston, who had left the government and was creating a new department within Shell Canada, decided she wanted a geographer in one of the positions. This is when the old-girl network kicked in. Liz Parr-Johnston contacted Liz Harman, who had also left the government and moved to Australia, to recommend a candidate. Liz H. recommended our old colleague Val Preston, who was a professor at the University of Kansas. Val came to Toronto for an interview and stopped in to visit us in Hamilton where I was teaching at McMaster University. When she decided she did not want the job, I said, "Pick me." Teaching prospects were dim and I was looking for a change. A few weeks later, Liz Parr-Johnston phoned, we set up an interview, and shortly thereafter I was hired by Shell Canada in the Macro Environment Division of Corporate Strategies. I was the social part of STEP—social, technological, economic, and political. The date was 1981. Unknowingly, I was headed for a future in futures.

Two dramatic changes hit me quite quickly in moving from an academic to a corporate world. First, there were no limits or accountability for photocopying or long-distance telephone calls. What a luxury. Second, instant results were required. Shortly after settling in, my boss's boss, a powerful and demanding executive named Lynn Hall, came into my office and requested a list and description of the five top social issues in Canada, and she needed them the next morning. I knew I was no longer in Kansas. There was no theoretical framework and no previous work to draw on. It was seat-of-the-pants time. I learned two things: first, corporate requirements were for results without details; second, unlike academia where the content was 95 percent and presentation 5 percent, in the corporate world presentation was at least 50 percent of the requirement, if not more. The power of persuasion and influence was as much in the presentation—short, clear, and pointed—as the content and logic. The theme keeps reverberating: communication, communication, communication.

First Contact

My role in Macro Environment was to monitor social trends, primarily in Canada but also in the US. My work complemented similar analyses by colleagues on economic, political, and technological trends. This work provided input on external trends affecting the business as part of the strategic planning process. As the expertise in this area, we had our first exposure to scenarios when SRI was hired to develop scenarios for Shell Canada.

The Shell Group had been developing and using scenarios for over a decade but Shell Canada had not made any effort to emulate that work. Lynn Hall, with a background using scenarios with General Electric, and encouraged by Royal Dutch Shell—known as The Group —Shell Canada hired SRI to develop scenarios. The SRI team included Peter Schwartz, Jay Ogilvy, and Tom Mandell. They provided the process and we, the Macro Team, provided most of the content. I have little recollection of the scenarios created, but I did come away with one overriding directive: this was great work and great fun. The future was exciting.

In 1983, the scenario bug was reinforced when there was another initiative to develop scenarios. This time internally. I was fortunate to have a lead role. We lacked a clear grasp of process or logic, but undeterred we forged ahead. The context was that Canada was just emerging from the deep recessions of 1980 and 1982; inflation in the 1970s had been rampant but was falling sharply; oil prices were in the mid $20s and had not spiked after the 1979 Iranian revolution, as one might have expected; and the first signs of decoupling of oil and economic growth were emerging. Canada was on a protectionist trend. The National Energy Program (NEP) was introduced and the Foreign Investment Review Agency (FIRA) was created to scrutinize foreign investment. The NEP was creating a huge backlash politically in Alberta, and FIRA (as well as the NEP) was causing consternation within Shell and probably other multinationals.

In this environment, we developed two scenarios: Protected Nationalism and Cooperative Restructuring. The former described a future of protectionism, low investment, and slow growth. The latter focused on a future open to trade with high investment and a dynamic economy.

First Experience

The critical uncertainties were political—cooperation or conflict—and structure of energy demand. The latter emerged from the growing disconnect between economic growth and the demand for oil. This was new. The sharp increase in oil prices in the 1970s, from $3 per barrel to $30 per barrel, led to a gradual restructuring of the energy market. While demand for light products such as gasoline, aviation, and diesel were maintained, there was a rapid decline in the demand for heavy oil products used as under-boiler fuel.

For the first time we were actively looking at inter-fuel competition and striving to understand how price changes in one fuel could affect another. Inter-fuel competition meant that economic growth, albeit modest, could occur without growth in oil demand. Our scenario challenge was to project whether and how these new relationships would persist. The concept of decoupling demand and growth and the importance of inter-fuel competition have re-emerged many times over the subsequent forty years and remain important today as natural gas displaces coal and renewables displace natural gas in electricity generation.

The other critical uncertainty was political relationships both international and interprovincial. The NEP drove home the importance of political factors influencing the energy industry. This theme had dominated the Shell Group scenarios in the 1970s with the emphasis on political instability in the Middle East. Now it was playing out in Canada but with different impacts. The scenario, Protected Nationalism, was characterized by political conflict leading to trade barriers and provincial-federal fights over windfall profits and slow growth. Cooperative Restructuring was characterized by provincial-federal cooperation, open borders, increased investment, and strong growth.[41]

First Insights

These two scenarios, which followed the Shell approach of only having two scenarios proved to be amazingly resilient. They remained in the planning process and Shell consciousness for at least five years. One question that emerged was: What is the life span of scenarios? Not the time horizon of the scenarios but the length of time the scenarios would remain relevant and useful. New events will occur but do they fit or not within the existing scenarios? If not, something new is emerging and new scenarios may be required. The practical rule we adopted for renewal of scenarios was that when significant events begin to occur that do not fit within

---

41 Disappointingly, the uncertainties expressed in these scenarios from the 1980s would still seem to be relevant in the divided political landscape in Canada today (2022). Conflict versus cooperation in Federal - Provincial relations and across other dimensions of society, is often a critical uncertainty in scenario studies.

the framework of the scenarios, then new scenario thinking is needed. The rise of concern about global warming in the late 1980s, after an extremely hot summer in the US, was an emergent trend that was outside the existing Shell scenarios at the time. This triggered a new round of scenarios. More on this later.

A second observation from these long-life scenarios was the power of scenarios as a vehicle for communication. The scenarios became so widely known in the company that managers and executives simply referred to the scenarios as PN and CR. One only needed to mention PN to immediately convey slow growth, political conflict, low exchange rate, and sluggish demand growth. This was a powerful aspect of creating shared understanding across the company.

Structural not Evolutionary

At this time, we began to understand another aspect of scenarios: they were particularly suited and valuable for exploring structural changes. While some scenarios explore evolutionary changes with large cumulative effects over time, a real power of scenarios was in understanding discontinuities or structural change in a system. A structural change doesn't necessarily focus on a single large event, e.g., the terrorist attack on the US in 2001 known as 911, but it may involve a series of direct and indirect changes over time.

A key scenario question is: How could the structure of the system change? We saw this with the restructuring of the oil market as heavy fuel oil demand collapsed in the early 1980s. Similarly, the rising tide of nationalism in the countries of the Middle East and North Africa led to the nationalization of oil resources in the late 1960s and resulted in the oil embargo of 1973, which quadrupled prices. The shift in control of oil reserves from the international majors to national producers was a radical change with repercussions today.

In Canada, the lifting of the National Energy Program by the Western Accord in 1985 had a hidden seed of change that few anticipated. The Accord lifted a restriction that producers could only export gas surplus to twenty-five years of production. This meant that only large companies had the financial capacity to accumulate such a large reserve that they met the export test. Typically, producers around the world operated on a reserve to production ratio of 9:1 instead of 25:1 as required by Canadian regulation. The unexpected structural change was that in lifting the twenty-five-year restriction, the door opened for the majors to begin selling surplus gas reserves. Suddenly a bonanza of gas reserves was for sale and junior producers (small, independent companies) who could now access the export market were at the front of the line in buying these reserves. A very active junior oil and gas market bloomed. As juniors were started, developed, grew, sold, and merged, not only was the oil and gas market transformed but an increasingly important financial market for investment in oil and gas was created. Long story, key result: scenarios are an extremely valuable tool in exploring structural change.

Scenarios, Modelling, and Learning

The next insight was that scenarios as well as modelling and forecasting, are vehicles for learning. The idea that scenarios are a powerful vehicle for opening and changing minds was well known in Shell[42]. For me the vital moment came when we began to quantify the Shell Canada scenarios in the mid 1980s. We had developed the stories, but within Shell, the demand for numbers was overpowering. So, we decided to quantify the scenarios. What would be a reasonable set of numbers to reflect the thrust of the scenarios' stories? For example, if the scenarios projected 3 percent GDP growth, what would be a reasonable projection for oil demand? This would depend on how the scenario characterized the relationship between economic growth and oil demand.

We could do this using our judgement but we decided to engage an economic consulting firm with a sophisticated econometric model of the Canadian economy. The intent was a more comprehensive and rigorous projection of key variables. From the logic of the scenarios, we provided a number of initial parameters such as GDP growth as input to the modelling. Two things happened. First, the model, calibrated on historical relationships, quickly veered into unknown territory. For example, in Protective Nationalism, the Canada-US exchange rate went to $.60 (US). This had never happened and sent the modellers into convulsions. But it raised an important question. Was the result a limitation of the model or a flaw in our scenario logic? Was the model based on history inadequate in defining the range of future possible outcomes? A key learning was that the modelling and the scenario building could be complementary, increasing learning and reinforcing a more disciplined approach to the scenarios. In the end we adjusted our logic in the scenarios although we were not too far from reality: the Canadian dollar fell to a low of $.62 (US) in the late 1990s.

The learning from this experience was not over. As touched on in an earlier chapter, a critical event happened in the quantification process. Having undertaken the modelling work, we were meeting with a number of the consultants in their offices to discuss the results. We were moving back and forth playing the logic of the scenarios against the numbers from the model, raising questions about specific results, and in general having a fruitful discussion prior to a second run of the model. Finally, in exasperation, one of the younger consultants burst out that these results were all wrong. He had done the analysis and developed the forecast for the next five years. It was a telling moment. He had worked so closely in fine-tuning the model that he had come to see it as the truth. The model was a true reflection of reality and

---

42 See Pierre Wack (1985a; 1985b)

able to predict the future. There was no uncertainty in his mind. This drove home to me that modelling and forecasting are as much a learning process as scenario building. While extensive modelling and forecasting are intended to predict, the model is also a learning vehicle. But once you believe its results, the questioning stops and the learning stops. Scenarios and modelling are complementary as long as they both focus on learning. Once you believe you have the truth about the future, arrogance makes you blind and you are likely to fail.

Scenario Follies

The Shell Canada experience led to other insights. One folly occurred when the company experimented with using the scenarios in budgeting. Scenarios are about the long-term future, not generally the next couple of years (although that can be the case is some specific examples). Nevertheless, we brought in a process for departments to develop two five-year plans based on the two scenarios. While this was intended to identify risks, the organization could not function on two plans. It was a disaster. Scenarios can be powerful in understanding the range of future possible paths and outcomes, but at some point, the scenarios need to be set aside and firm plans developed. This movement from scenarios to strategy to action is one of the key challenges in scenario planning.

Another folly occurred when we tried to bring the scenarios alive by describing specific events in the scenario stories. For example, to be more dramatic, we named the new prime minister in one story. In another we referred to a specific time frame for development to occur. These were not taken as examples of the kind of person who would be prime minister or the approximate date of an event. Instead, they were taken literally. The specifics became the focus of discussion at the exclusion of the broader logic and outcomes. Scepticism of these details threatened to undermine the credibility of the individual scenario and the project overall. We learned to be careful in using specific events to describe the scenarios. If that event did not occur or if that event was seen as improbable, the credibility of the entire scenario was at risk.

A similar insight on the limitations of scenario descriptions occurred when we got too close to the locus of control. What do we mean? We had developed scenarios in which one of the scenarios projected accelerated development of oil resources in the Canadian Arctic, as opposed to extended delays in the other scenario. In a meeting of approximately sixty upstream managers responsible for exploration and development, we presented these two scenarios. We were met with considerable scepticism, specifically on the question of the timing of Arctic development. As one participant expressed it, "That won't happen because we won't let it happen." Shell Canada had large holdings in the Arctic and was one of the largest players in that development. They felt, perhaps rightly, that they had control over the development of Arctic oil and gas resources. In short, there was no uncertainty as this development was within the locus of their control. Scenarios are designed to explore uncertainty. If the scope of the scenarios is limited by the power or influence of a single company or organization, then the scenarios become more descriptions of the strategies of the company than of the range of external possibilities. The scenarios should explore what is beyond the control of the organization.

Minds and Culture

The Shell Canada experience was a wonderful learning journey in developing and using scenarios within a corporation. The intellectual interplay within the department of Corporate Strategies was exciting. Our challenge was both to create the scenarios and enhance the strategic planning process. This required gaining acceptance and support from senior management and across divisions. This was not easy. Although we barely recognized it at the time, what we were trying to do was embed scenario thinking—strategic and future-focused thinking—in a project-and-operations-driven organization. For scenarios to impact strategy, we needed to engage and open minds and connect the scenarios to strategic management issues. In short, we needed to be insightful and relevant.

SHELL INTERNATIONAL

My first stint in Group Planning was in 1984. I had the opportunity to experience an entirely new world and become an integral player in developing and writing new global scenarios. The revelation for me was how limited my experience in Canada had been. I was amazingly naive. I thought being an expat in Britain was an exceptional event. It was not. I was nothing special.

I also quickly realized that Shell International (officially the name is Royal Dutch Shell), was not Shell Canada. For example, the rules provided us with a chauffeur for one day a week during transition to a permanent residence. But they would not pay for a car rental. Similarly, when I submitted my first expense form, I discovered that alcohol was not included and even small expenditures needed receipts. Shell Group bureaucrats had seen it all and had rules for everything. Their car-rental policy reflected experience in relocating a range of people from around the world, some of whom had little experience driving in a city like London. This patronizing attitude was a feature of Shell both globally and in Canada. It would not last, of course, but it reflected the vestiges of a military-designed organization that had existed for almost a hundred years. This in no way dented my enthusiasm and respect for Shell and Group Planning.

Group Planning

Group Planning consisted of three main divisions at the time. PL 2 (PL is short for planning) was responsible for compiling five-year financial and resource planning for the Group. With premises and guidelines provided by PL 2, individual countries would develop their business and financial plans to be aggregated for the Group as a whole. A key challenge was to ensure that all the individual plans when aggregated were feasible. For example, were there enough resources to accomplish all the plans? What were the major risks to the Group as a whole? This was a vital role in managing close to one hundred operating companies and 125,000 employees.

PL 3 acted as an internal consulting arm within the Shell Group. The members of PL 3 were highly experienced managers able to assist operating companies and divisions across a range of management requirements. One important activity that PL 3 orchestrated was the sharing of information and experience across Group companies. A key advantage of a global company was to learn from the varied experience of companies in different countries. One explicit vehicle for this learning experience was a planning conference to which the top planners from all operating companies and sectors were invited. This created a fruitful interchange as individuals from, say, Shell Canada, heard about new marketing initiatives in Sweden. The result was not only an exchange of ideas but a creation of relationships. I came to learn that the way the Shell Group sustained itself globally was in creating a veneer of personal relationships separate from management. After my return from Group Planning, I would often get a call from a Shell Canada colleague seeking a contact at Group to make a specific request. When I could use a personal relationship—say a phone call to Wim in Holland—the flow of information was much easier and occurred naturally without requiring formal requests or management approval. It was a form of self-organization that allowed the Group to operate differently from other international companies.

New Wave on Old Breakwater

PL 1 was responsible for the scenarios. When I arrived in 1984, the new head of PL 1 was Peter Schwartz. Peter was a dynamic and enthusiastic supporter of scenarios and an avid consumer of new information and ideas. He was particularly enamoured with new technology and the potential for technology to drive change. He was not only an observer but active early adopter. He wanted Shell to embrace new technology, notably the rapidly emerging information technology, and walk the talk. It is perhaps no surprise that one of the scenarios became Next Wave, symbolizing the tidal wave of change that new technology could bring to the world.

Group planning had a strong history in scenarios. Pierre Wack and Ted Newland had fostered the scenarios through the 1970s. They were legends in Shell. Scenarios at Shell had achieved mythic proportion by the early 1980s. The refinery story, presented in the introduction, made a simple projection of oil demand growth continuing at the historical rate and led to the conclusion that the world would be building a refinery a day in ten years. The capital and resources required were unimaginable. Something had to give. The candidate was price. The rest is history. Shell did not forecast the oil embargo and price hike, but they were not surprised and were more prepared to act than most other companies.

The refinery-a-day insight with the subsequent price increase gave the scenarios huge credibility. Wack and Newland built on this platform to create and explore a range of scenarios throughout the 1970s. Most of the scenarios focused on oil supply and the motivation and actions of the major producers in the Middle East. Studying and understanding the dynamics of OPEC, both as a single cartel and as a diverse group of actors with different interests, was central to much of the effort. Through this work, a powerful understanding emerged that Wack (1985b) captured and articulated in his *Harvard Business Review* article "Shooting the Rapids." The key understanding was that the purpose of scenarios was not to predict but to open minds. Even though much of the credibility of scenarios within Shell occurred because of the prediction of the imminent price rise that occurred, the real power was the story that opened the thinking of senior management that the future could be dramatically different than the past. That was the art of reperceiving that needs to remain central to scenario work to this day[43].

Peter Schwartz's enthusiasm for change had an interesting, unintended consequence for me. He was mesmerized by the potential for technology to drive change. In developing and communicating the new scenarios, he wanted to break from the past. The tradition was to focus on writing the scenarios with the basic communication form being a magnificently produced book. Developing presentations then followed. Peter wanted to signal change. He concentrated on developing a dynamic presentation with minimal written support. Not surprising in retrospect, the conservative Shell system fought back. Like an inevitable surprise, at the last minute, we needed to put together a book capturing the logic, stories, and insights of the scenarios as well as the array of ideas behind the scenarios.

In this rush, I was assigned to write the energy and economic side of the stories. Tim Kenny was assigned the social and political side and the overall coordination of the assembly and production of the scenario documents. It was a marvellous experience, challenging intellectually and professionally in coordinating, negotiating, and writing the scenarios.

43 This focus on opening minds or reframing is the major thrust of *Strategic Reframing: The Oxford Scenario Planning Approach* by Ramirez and Wilkinson, 2016.

The denouement of the story was that the push for change met the wall in the Committee of Managing Directors (CMD) board room. The push for new thinking was interpreted as criticism of existing management. The scenarios were rejected, scenario planning was dismissed, and the influence of Group Planning, at least for PL 1, collapsed. While not the most telling of examples, other experiences support the reality that the power of scenarios, and foresight generally, can be dangerous to one's career. Opening new thinking, if not carefully prepared as in the Pierre Wack refining story, can be seen as challenging the traditional power structure. The lesson is clear. Access to senior management is critical for strategic foresight but they need to be engaged and challenged in their thinking, not their position.

Staying Calm

The purpose of foresight re-emerged with the oil price collapse of 1986. I had a unique view of events in Shell. Having returned to Canada I led a project to develop scenarios for Shell Canada (described earlier). Interested in sharing our thinking and building relationships, I arranged a trip to London with my boss in January 1986. The timing proved priceless!

In the fall of 1985, Royal Dutch Shell intelligence picked up signals from the Middle East that there was growing discontent within OPEC and particularly Saudi Arabia. The Kingdom had adopted the role of swing producer, which involved managing output to support prices. Effectively, this meant reducing OPEC supply to prop up prices. The burden fell on Saudi Arabia. With a capacity of over eight million barrels per day (b/d) production had been successively ratcheted down to two million b/d. Frustration was growing. The condition could not last.

Recognizing this—good foresight—Shell realized a price collapse was imminent. If Saudi Arabia opened the spigots, the price of oil would fall. Shell senior management issued an alert to all Shell companies in the fall of 1985 and asked every operating company, including Shell Canada, to prepare contingency plans to minimize the effect of a sudden collapse in crude prices. A key element in all plans was to minimize inventory. Shell companies around the world adopted this strategy. One back-of-the-envelope estimate was that Royal Dutch Shell saved $2 billion by minimizing inventory prior to the price collapse. Unfortunately, belief in the price collapse scenario was not embraced by Shell Canada management. The company did not minimize inventory and wrote down hundreds of millions of dollars after the collapse. This demonstrated one of the weaknesses of a decentralized structure: you were allowed to ignore directions from the centre.

My unique perspective comes from being in London in January 1986, trying to present our Shell Canada scenarios, when the price collapsed. This happened in days. We were able to watch the internal dynamics at Shell Centre as interested spectators.

It was remarkably calm. In anticipation of the collapse months before, Shell had issued a directive that if the price fell, management should take no action for at least two weeks. Both in foresight and hindsight this was a powerful insight. Scenario thinking had allowed the company's leadership to prepare for a fall in oil prices and develop appropriate responses.

Even when we returned to Shell Canada, there was calmness within the organization that was in sharp contrast to the chaos evident in other companies in the oil patch. Being able to pause and reflect before acting proved valuable. Shell companies did not act in haste and managed the crisis with minimal impacts.

Group Planning Again

My Shell International experience was not over. Seconded for a second shift at Group Planning, the family arrived New Year's Eve, 1987, was invited to a party, and emerged on New Year's Day like everyone else—with a hangover. Ours, however, was more from jet lag than alcohol.

The world had changed, Shell had changed, and Group Planning had changed. The new leader of PL 1 was Kees van der Heijden. He combined a deep intelligence with long experience in Shell. He was quiet and reflective. You knew he was listening. He loved ideas. He was slow to verbalize but you listened when he spoke. This intellectual approach was combined with a deep understanding of how Shell was structured and operated. It was a rare, insightful combination.

When I arrived, Group Planning, specifically PL 1, was still recovering from the management team rejection of 1984. With limited access to senior management, Group Planning had cultivated a number of relationships with individual operating companies and regions. Again, luck was on my side. Group Planning had committed to a number of regional scenario projects when the first signals of climate change spattered the radar. Senior management immediately recognized that climate change was a critical issue challenging the legitimacy—social licence—of the oil and gas business.[44] They turned to group planning. Starved of attention, the request from the CMD to develop scenarios exploring global warming, then the common name, was like steak to a starving mongrel. It was all-hands-on-deck. Except, wait a minute, what about the commitment to do regional scenarios?

Sun and Rain Down in Africa

This is when I hit the jackpot. I was assigned to lead the regional scenarios while everyone else focused on the new global scenarios. My first assignment was Africa.

---

44   The concept of social license was first used by Jim Cooney, a personal friend, in the mid 1990s in relation to the mining industry. It was not used in Shell but reflects the challenge recognized by senior management at the time.

The regional coordinator was Bob Taylor from Canada. I had worked indirectly for Bob in Canada where he had been senior vice-president. In fact, it was due to his insistence that Group Planning honour their commitment to develop scenarios for Africa that I got the assignment. It was a wonderful experience. I was on my own in developing the scenarios but had considerable resources. This included a trip to Kenya for research with a side trip to Uganda. The experiences included walking alone in a game reserve (there is nothing dangerous in this park!); a trip to a school in Uganda, where I had organized a load of books from the private school my children attended in England (the science labs were completely stripped from the time of Idi Amin); staying with the Dutch Consul in Kampala, who was a Brit named Goldsmith (the Shell rep in Uganda usually became the Dutch consul); and being shunned and forced to be the last to board a plane from Kampala because I refused to make a contribution to my friends in Uganda (a bribe).

Intellectually, the challenge was to find the positives. Every headline about Africa at that time was war and famine. Was that the only future? No.

Going beyond the international news, local accounts of micro businesses, new agricultural practices, emerging entrepreneurs, and growing cooperatives raised another possible future. It was one of hope generated from below. It was not widely endorsed. The stories emerged and I presented them to numerous groups, mostly in London (unfortunately). Nevertheless, they gained traction and generated interest. Perhaps the most memorable event occurred when I made the presentation to an outside group of about sixty people of which about half were Europeans and half were Africans. A conversation I had had in Africa remained in my mind. While in conversation with a senior bureaucrat in Kenya, the question of debt emerged. The heavy debts and debt payments that many African companies were faced with was seen as a huge burden stifling public investment and growth. There was a push afoot for debt relief. If only you would remove the debt, we would be able to grow and prosper. Our fate is in your hands. In this context I asked what would happen if all the country's debt was forgiven. The immediate response was "we would borrow more money." This was entirely reasonable but signalled a repeat of the cycle of debt and always present, corruption, which was the unspoken elephant in the room.

Back to the presentation with the group of Europeans and Africans. In light of the debt discussion, I had started to ask a simple question at the end of my presentation. Is the future of Africa in the hands of Africans or dependent on others? Taking a show of hands, the audience split fifty-fifty. Not surprising. What was surprising was the mix. Almost all Europeans felt the future of Africa was in the hands of Africans. The Africans, in contrast, overwhelmingly felt that the future of Africa was not in the hands of Africans. It was, in their view, heavily dependent on the international community.

Cerveza Por Favor

My next regional assignment was the future of Latin America. Not a small topic. I did not have the luxury of travelling to Latin America but pieced together thinking from a variety of sources, including many Shell employees with extensive experience in Latin America. The overwhelming insight from that work was how dependent most countries were on trade with the United States. For almost all countries, the US was their biggest trading partner. Regional country-to-country trading flows were small compared to their trade with the US. (This was also true in Africa.) New regional blocks were emerging but the dominance of trade with the US was an unanticipated insight. Much of this has changed, especially during the commodity boom in which trade with China skyrocketed. The scenarios gained little traction at the time, but the connection would serve me well when Group Planning decided to take the global scenarios on the road. I was assigned to the team travelling to Shell operating companies in Latin America.

Glasnost and Perestroika

My next opportunity was to develop scenarios on the future of the Soviet Union. Another small task! These were exciting times. Gorbachev was leading a revolution. Perestroika and Glasnost were transforming every aspect of the Soviet Union. How was I to proceed? This time I vowed to spend the budget with on-the-ground research. Not only was I able to visit a range of academics across Europe, from Birmingham to Grenoble to Cologne, I was able to arrange a trip to Moscow. With a colleague and interpreter, we set off for one of the most fascinating trips anyone could imagine.

Shell had sponsored two scientists from the Soviet Union to visit Shell in London. We hosted them at Group Planning. To reciprocate, Shell was invited to send representatives to Moscow. Since I was leading the work on the future of the Soviet Union, I was one of the fortunate recipients. With a colleague, Doug Wade, and an interpreter, we set off for Moscow. A key to the trip was our interpreter. Raised in St. Petersburg, she lived in London and did contract work for Shell. Although she no longer lived in Russia, she had connections everywhere, or so it seemed. She was able to set up some amazing interviews, both official and unofficial, including with an independent journalist from Latvia and the minister of propaganda on our last evening in Moscow.

The date was 1989. The Berlin Wall had not fallen, but glasnost and perestroika were in full bloom. The story begins at the duty-free shop at Heathrow. Cigarettes and booze were common currencies in Moscow. So, we stocked up. We used the booze as gifts. The cigarettes were used to barter, particularly for taxi rides. There was a free market in taxis: every car was a potential taxi. We just had to raise a hand and a car would pull over. Our interpreter would then negotiate a price in cigarettes and off we went. This was part of the new mood in Moscow: open, uncontrolled and chaotic.

Over the course of a week we gave several presentations and met some of the most influential people—all men—in the country. We were treated well above our pay grade, in part because we represented Shell, a major international company, and in part because we represented an opportunity to learn about the West. We, of course, were trying to understand the changes occurring in the USSR.

Several experiences stand out. I recall giving a presentation to upward of one hundred people in a large room with a single overhead projector. This was not a modern projector focusing PowerPoint slides onto a large screen, but an old-fashioned projector casting a dim image from transparencies onto a small screen of dubious quality. It was rather ghastly. The audience was enthralled. Perestroika was changing everything. Prices, production, distribution, indeed the entire economy was undergoing radical change. What was intriguing was realizing that the old economy, centrally controlled in every aspect, had no concept of market prices, competition, or private investment. The idea of opportunity costs, for example, was unknown with huge implications. (See Box 18). The audience was desperately eager to learn about markets, prices, and competition since they had no experience with these things. While they may have been eager to learn, I am sure they were more mystified than enlightened by my presentation of scenarios on the future of energy and the global economy.

Box 18—Understanding Opportunity Cost

Opportunity cost is the value foregone by choosing one option over another. For example, you could invest in repairing an old car or buy a new car. If you choose repairs you are foregoing the opportunity and value of a new car. At some point the old car will not be worth repairing. Such was not the case in the Soviet Union of the 1980s. In a fascinating interview, one of the most prominent and knowledgeable economists in the country, who understood opportunity cost, remarked that the Zil car factory was still using equipment from the 1930s on an assembly line. There was no concept of opportunity cost in replacing the ancient equipment, only repairs. It was producing cars; that was the only requirement. Efficiency was not part of the equation. He further noted that one of the important performance measures for management bonuses was not the number of cars produced, their quality, or cost, but the amount of steel used. At that time, the value of any product was measured by the raw materials included. As a result, Zil cars weighted in excess of three tonnes. This may be a product of Marx's theory of value (see footnote[45]).

A second example was the story of the factory manager faced with the problem of installing new computer equipment sent by central planners. He could install the computer, but that would lead to a short-term slow-down in production during installation and start-up. Or he could ignore the computers and maintain existing production processes. He chose the latter. Why? He was able to massage the data for eleven months claiming high levels of production, which assured his monthly bonuses. On the twelfth month, discrepancies were adjusted and he lost his bonus for that single month. The computers? They were stored in the snow behind the plant. True or false, it demonstrates the distortions that plagued the economic system. Whether a system with markets, prices, and competition would solve those issues is open to debate. Without the concept of opportunity cost, however, decisions can be severely distorted.

We did a number of interviews, varying from an interview with a dissident Latvian journalist (held in the suburbs, which were off-limit to foreigners) to the Minister of Propaganda (yes, that was his official title at least in English). In between we had a memorable meeting with senior managers from Gaz Prom, which managed all gas and electricity production in the Soviet Union. We met in a large room with a long table. With my colleague and interpreter, we occupied three chairs on one side of the table. On the other side were eight senior managers. They reminded me of eight replicas of Nikita Khrushchev. Intimidating initially but quite congenial as we began discussions. They were extremely open about their ambitious plans for the future. Most prominent was their visible enthusiasm for a huge project to convert a vast supply of brown coal to electricity. Even in those days, the environmental impacts of dirty brown coal in the form of harmful emissions such as sulfur and nitrogen oxides, particulates, and heavy metals such as mercury were well known. We were stunned at the ambition. On reflection we realized this was characteristic of the Soviet Union's

---

45 Mark Carney (2021) in reviewing the history of economic thinking on value distinguishes between objective and subjective value. Karl Marx adopted an objective view of value: the value of a good or service was defined by the labour (and materials) used to create the product. The focus was on the utility value of the good or service and not the exchange value. A shirt can be used (utility) or exchanged for another good. More recent economists have defined value in subjective or relative terms. In that thinking, the value of a good depends on demand, i.e., what a consumer would pay for it. Setting a production goal based on tonnes of steel reflects this objective view that value comes from the labour and materials. Opportunity cost reflects the subjective or relative view of value, along with the concept of marginal costs. In retrospect, my story of the car plant reflects a gulf of misunderstanding based on hidden assumptions. The need for strategic conversations and shared understanding becomes evident again.

fascination with mega-projects. To my knowledge none of this occurred in the wake of the upheaval that was to follow.

Perhaps the most fascinating interview late on the Friday before we left was that with the Minister of Propaganda. This included management of all theatres and cinemas in the country. His ministry had complete control of all shows and movies presented in every single theatre. Glasnost, however, was radically changing this. First, there was a relaxation of control so that local theatres could choose which movies they wanted to show. Second, and more onerous, was a requirement that they pay for the shows. Previously, all the expenses were absorbed by the state. Now local theatres had to make enough money to support the operations. The minister was less concerned about the loss of control, even admitting that some foreign or banned movies might be shown, than the financial impact on theatres. Many, he feared, would go broke and cease to operate. The shift to a market economy was painful.

In interviewing the Minister of Propaganda, set up by our interpreter, I did not feel it was appropriate to take notes. So, the next day on the plane as we were returning to London, I asked her what she could tell me about the interview. I was trying to organize my thoughts on the key points of the interview. Instead, she began with the first sentence and recited the entire one-hour discussion verbatim. I was stunned. It was a feat of memory that I found amazing. It revealed that the role of the interpreter was to, well, translate and not to make meaning of the content. I made my notes and thanked my lucky stars that we had such a talented interpreter. She made this perhaps the most remarkable business trip anyone has ever had.

The story of our trip is almost over, but not yet. In the following days I was faced with a dilemma. Recall the large stash of cigarettes and alcohol we bought at Heathrow. How did I expense that? Shell was meticulous at not expensing tobacco or alcohol. Could I fudge it? Not a good idea. Instead, I decided to address the problem head on. I contacted the department that scrutinized and approved all expense forms. I explained my dilemma. The answer was immediate. "Sir, the approved code for this expenditure is PK10448 (or something like that). Please use that in assigning expenses on the form you submit." I submitted the expenses as instructed and received payment. People often berate bureaucracy, but sometimes you have to marvel at its efficiency and good sense.

The Limits of Expertise

The interviews with leading academics, business leaders, and government officials in Moscow and Western Europe provided the insights to develop scenarios on the future of the Soviet Union. A description of the scenarios is provided in Box 19. In hindsight they proved prescient and insightful, although they were flawed in one important way. They failed to explore the possibility of a breakup of the Soviet Union.

It was on my radar and I explored this with numerous Soviet experts. Unanimously they declared that the USSR would not break up and I left that out. Scenarios are intended to think the unthinkable. Sometimes, you need to follow your instincts. As a rule of experience, I have found that experts who have thought deeply about a topic whether politics, economics, or technology, tend to have quite narrow and firm views. In some ways that is the nature of expertise: a clear, well-thought-out view. It just doesn't encourage the lateral thinking needed for scenarios.

Box 19–The Future of the Soviet Union (1989)

The USSR was undergoing dramatic change. It was a revolution from the top led by President Mikhail Gorbachev. The overriding theme was perestroika, which means restructuring. Its scope and scale were breathtaking: to restructure the entire economic and political system of the USSR. A long period of economic stagnation had created a growing realization that economic reform was necessary and urgent. Fundamental changes in the economic system, however, would drastically alter the distribution of power. The future of the Soviet Union would depend on sustaining the momentum for economic reform in the face of powerful political barriers. The challenge was that reform was always associated with a breakdown of order. In the history of Russia, order always had a higher value than democracy.

The focus of reform was to restructure the economy: 1, from extensive growth (more inputs) to intensive growth (more efficient use of inputs); 2, from centralized decision-making to decentralized; and 3, from administered planning to markets. Political barriers involved, 1, individuals facing more risks and less security (e.g., job dislocations); 2, bureaucracy losing power as a market system would replace a centrally controlled system; 3, the party losing power as a market system would separate economic decisions from political decisions thereby undermining the power of the party to control the economy through political appointments; and 4, nationalists losing power as weakened central and party controls would allow the rise of pluralism.

The scenarios reflect these colliding forces. The dilemma is to encourage economic reform but lose centralized political control or maintain central control but truncate economic reform. In a top-down system this was a political choice. Complicating this struggle was the realization that quantum changes were needed. In moving to a market economy evolutionary change is inadequate; radical reforms are required. Similarly, de-nationalizing major industries and breaking up central ministries cannot be done incrementally. These require quantum leaps. This was called the reform gap.

Figure 35—Future of the Soviet Union—1989

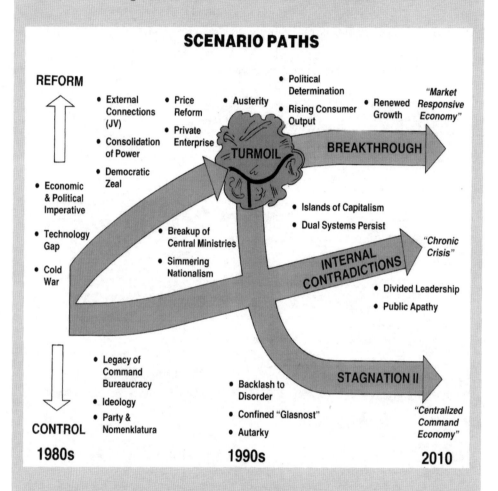

The logic of three scenarios developed to explore the future of the Soviet Union is shown in Figure 35 In Breakthrough, consolidation of power at the top drives economic reform. Initial reforms erode the central power of the bureaucracy, glasnost encourages individual freedoms, private enterprises are encouraged, foreign joint ventures are set up, and market pricing occurs in some markets. The seeds of reform are in place but there is no critical mass. Price reform, in particular, is problematic, creating winners and losers. The system is disjointed. The dual economy is not sustainable. The inconsistencies lead to turmoil and crisis.

In Breakthrough, the need to accelerate major reforms is recognized. Price reforms, strengthened market institutions, financial reforms and government reforms are steps forward but create turmoil. This lasts for an extended period. In Breakthrough, however, the momentum for reform overcomes the political barriers leading to a market-responsive economy and a decentralized political system. The system bridges the reform gap in this scenario.

In Stagnation II, efforts to implement economic reforms are increasingly interpreted as threats to established power. As more radical reforms are imposed, resistance increases. As the reform agenda pushes for the quantum leap, the turmoil created leads to panic responses. There is a reflex action to reassert control and restore order. Troops are called. The use of force effectively ends perestroika. Non-Russian nationalism is suppressed and reformers lose power. A period of consolidation leads to rescinding some reforms but primarily to a focus on rationalizing the existing system with a push back to a command economy. Reform has not so much failed but been contained and controlled by the political interests.

In Internal Contradictions, the process of reform progresses but it is tentative and insecure. The political structure remains in place and the Party is still in control with central ministries intact. Reforms are initiated but poorly implemented. The names change but not the system. Efforts to undertake price reforms are too extreme. Perestroika cannot gain critical mass. Barriers prevent and subvert reform efforts. The system is trapped in transition as two systems exist in conflict. Private enterprises, including foreign joint ventures, exist as islands of capitalism in a sea of confusion. Increasingly, reform is seen as ineffective as well as threatening. There is a fear of losing control. Pluralism is rejected and Russian nationalist sentiments prevail. The need for reform is further undermined by rising oil prices, which cover underlying economic problems. Higher oil prices are a poison chalice for reform and economic integration. The result is a system caught in permanent transition with some rationalization and many reform contradictions.

In retrospect, the scenarios were wonderfully prescient. They did not anticipate the breakup of the Soviet Union, although they recognized the dividing forces of nationalism in autonomous regions. While there was a crisis and potentially violent moment, the reality of the past three decades seems to be more of an Internal Contradictions scenario than either Breakthrough or Stagnation. The rise of nationalism was not a major factor in the scenarios but has been a major aspect of the new Russia.

I am reminded of three points highlighted in my interviews. First, there are dark forces in Russia. This was a direct reference to nationalism. Second, communism was a continuation of the feudal system that existed up to the overthrow of the Czar. The system of peasant and elites continued with communism. Even in 1989, the elites in Moscow were openly dismissive of the peasants in the provinces. Citizens, for example, were not allowed to move and live in Moscow without government approval. When I asked why this restriction was in place, I was told that everyone would move to Moscow! Third, in the history of Eastern Europe, including Russia, democracy has always been treated with scepticism. Democracy was related to anarchy and chaos. Inevitably, when there had been a choice between order and security and democracy, order and security have prevailed.

On the Road

My adventures in Group Planning were not over. As referred to earlier, Kees van der Heijden brought a new perspective on the role and the use of scenarios to Group Planning in the late 1980s. He recognized that the scenarios needed to be relevant to management if they were to be useful. In this respect he initiated two innovations.

First, he developed the 7-question interview to engage senior management in the process at the outset. This generated interest, commitment, and perspective. The perspective of management on the key issues facing the company provided the basis for developing the focal issue and focal question. This ensured the scenarios focused on a major issue relevant to management.

Second, he developed the first scenarios-to-implications workshop design. He realized that creating scenarios alone was insufficient in stimulating strategic action. You could not present the scenarios and walk away expecting managers to draw implications on their own. There was a gap that needed to be bridged between the insight of the scenarios and strategic responses. In short, a process was needed to engage management in actively thinking about the implications of the scenarios for the future of their business. This void was filled by the development of the scenarios-to-strategy workshop. A one-day workshop was developed to present the global scenarios, explore specific local variations, and then, through a series of questions, engage a management team in systematically identifying implications for their business and potential responses. Not a full step to strategies but a major step in management teams internalizing the implications for their business that hopefully they would act on.

The next step was to implement the engagement process. Kees van der Heijden again came up with a novel approach. He got permission to present the global scenarios to the top thirty decision management teams in the Group. This included almost all operating companies and major division and functional groups. We were off and running.

Back to Africa

My experience in developing scenarios for Africa and Latin America meant I was assigned to the teams presenting the scenarios-and-implications workshop in Africa and Latin America. My Africa experience focused on a trip to Nigeria. Our three-man team was disrupted when our executive facilitator was delayed by a visa hiccup. My colleague and I were faced with a CEO who was sceptical of our ability, without our senior colleague, to conduct the workshop. We finally convinced him and proceeded (after a bout of stomach disorder, to put it nicely), to conduct the workshop. It was held in the board room. Being young and presumptuous, we rearranged the furniture to suit our needs. This involved dismantling the board table. Unbeknown to us this was the CEO's pride and joy. As participants entered, they exchanged nervous glances at our expense. Eventually we found out that we had trodden on sacred ground. But when the CEO entered, he did not bat an eyelid. All went well. We did another workshop in Eastern Nigeria focused on field staff. I was offered an opportunity to tag along with a crew doing seismic work in the mangrove swamps the next day. I was flying home and declined. I will always regret that.

An interesting aside from the Nigerian experience was the challenge of maintaining relationships between the company and the government. There were two tensions that complicated the relationship. One was the inherent distrust of a multinational oil company. From the country's perspective, the global oil company was powerful. It was feared that the oil company was "ripping us off" and country leaders needed to be vigilant. The oil company saw it differently. The result was often friction.

To control this relationship, the company banned all but the most senior managers from interacting with government officials. This denied low-level relationships that could have smoothed over many difficulties. Instead, any misunderstanding required communication at the top, making every issue a major issue. A further complication was the open competition between different ethnic groups. A promotion to one group often required a promotion to another group to maintain harmony. This internal challenge complicated external communication. You needed to make sure the right ethnic group was representing the company at any given meeting. All told, it was major challenge to maintain a strong working relationship with government without affecting internal balances.

Lost in Transit

The bulk of my scenarios-to-implications workshops were conducted in Latin America. One trip in particular was memorable and insightful. The trip included workshops in Brazil, Chile, Mexico, and Puerto Rico. Brazil and especially Chile had strong management teams and the work went well. The locations were delightful and the teams were enthusiastic and engaged. Then things got interesting. We discovered when travelling from Chile to Mexico City that all travel to and from Latin America went through Miami. More cities in Latin America were connected directly to Miami than to each other. At least that's what it seemed like. The difficulty on this connection was they lost our luggage in Miami.

We ended up in Mexico but all our materials were resting in Miami. In those days our presentations were done using transparencies. Power Point was still in its inception. Further, we used magnetic erasable hexagons in recording and grouping ideas during the implications workshop. All these tools were in transit in Miami. What could we do? Our hosts suggested that since all the management team was going to be assembled, perhaps we could develop scenarios on the future of Mexico. Whoa! We had never done that before. We had no process that we could use in a workshop setting. But we decided to try it anyway. We blundered through and developed scenarios in a single day. Our hosts were pleased, both with the quality of discussion and the insights from the final products. I was enthralled with the power of the workshop process. The key learning was that by engaging senior management directly in developing scenarios the scenarios were unquestionably relevant. Since they created them, they owned them.

Power of Workshops

Kees van der Heijden had recognized that for scenarios to be truly valuable they needed to be relevant to management. He initiated the 7-question interviews and the scenarios-to-implications workshop to bridge that gap. A third initiative, for me, emerged from the realization that engaging the management team directly in developing the scenarios through a workshop guaranteed relevance. Developing the scenarios themselves meant they owned them. I have embraced the workshop approach ever since.

There are two further insights to complete this journey. First, the initial workshop design was flawed. When developing implications, the focus ended up almost entirely on internal issues and capabilities. It was very difficult to generate discussions of external developments. Discussions of relationships with governments sometimes emerged, but discussions of competition, for example, were non-existent. Why? Was it a design problem—not asking the right questions—or a product of Shell's culture?

Except in retail marketing, and perhaps trading, the industry is not intensely competitive. The focus is on access to production and minimizing costs. Joint ventures are common. It is not Pepsi versus Coke. It is much more an internal game of efficiency. In any case, this was an important flaw to be corrected.

Second, the workshop approach reinforced a realization that scenarios were disposable. What does that mean? Within Shell the scenarios books were magnificent productions carefully crafted. I, for one, was in love with the glossy books produced in the 1984 scenarios. We began to realize, however, that what we needed was not a cut-glass Waterford crystal masterpiece but a plastic water pitcher. We needed to use it, modify it, scuff it up, and discard it when it was no longer relevant. The workshop approach lends itself to that perspective more than the expert intensive approach used in Shell up to that time. We needed more of the internet philosophy of try it, break it, fix it instead of perfection only. More on that in the next section.

CONSULTANT TALES

Leaving Shell in the mid 1990s, I had two choices. Find another corporate planning job or become a consultant. I decided to see if I could use my experience in scenarios to develop a consulting business. My experiences over forty years include almost one hundred engagements. This section highlights a few of the more memorable projects that were either interesting personally or involved insights in scenario planning.

A Fortunate Connection

Shortly after parting with Shell I had the opportunity to attend a seminar presented by Peter Schwartz, (whom I knew from Shell Group Planning days). He was one of the founders of Global Business Network, which periodically did presentations with key clients in various locations around the world. This one was in Calgary. One of their Calgary clients was TransCanada Pipelines. A consultant for them was Lee van Horn. He was a long-time consultant with numerous major companies in Canada, US, and the Middle East. He was also a former Shell employee in both London and Toronto. We connected at the seminar. Lee was brilliant in identifying corporate needs and developing ways to address those needs. Further, he was able to relate to CEOs both as a consultant and confidant. CEOs often have few people inside their organizations with whom they can be completely frank and open in discussing major problems. Lee was able to build trust and confidence in supporting CEOs. This is not a common ability, and I certainly did not have it.

Bridging the Gap using Web-based Scenarios

Lee van Horn saw an opportunity to use scenario building within TransCanada. A new CEO had taken charge and the new style was more open and less command and control. Managers were being given more freedom and encouragement to make their own decisions and not look to the CEO to solve every problem. This was causing confusion and specifically, a perception gap between senior management—CEO and vice-presidents—and the next level of managers. Reporting managers felt they did not know where the company was going or what the strategies were. They felt rudderless. Senior management, in contrast, felt they had communicated direction and strategies clearly and were perplexed by the perception gap. Lee had the brilliant idea of using scenarios to bridge the alignment gap. How could scenarios do that?

First was a decision to combine the process of scenario development with the emerging capabilities of the internet. How did it work? We assembled a small team in corporate planning at TransCanada to manage the project. We used the questions that we would use in a workshop to engage participants from across the company through the internet. Recall this is 1995. A consulting company from Washington was hired to handle the internet interface. In this case it was similar to a chat room in which each individual response was captured and all participants could see it. We would pose questions such as, what changes have occurred over the past ten years that have affected the industry? We would allow input and discussion for three weeks then close that off, summarize the results, and introduce a new question, e.g., what changes could occur over the next ten years that would affect the industry? The process took several months.

Over two hundred people participated. This included participants from locations around the globe at any time of the day. For example, an entry from a manager in Regina might be followed by an entry from an employee on business in Colombia or Britain. Participation also included active contributions from the CEO and most vice-presidents. Visible support from the top was a key element in stimulating participation. The project was both a major success and disappointing failure. First, an aside on culture.

Suits versus Jeans

An interesting dynamic emerged in this web-based scenario project. Two cultures met head on. One culture was the traditional corporate IT culture, which focused on technical perfection. In that approach, the IT department was meticulous in testing software to ensure there were zero bugs or problems. The standard was that even the least tech-literate employee could use it without a problem. In contrast, the emerging web-based culture was free-wheeling. Try it. If it doesn't work, try something else.

These cultures collided on this project. For example, the interface for accessing and inputting comments was an ongoing work in progress. At one point, the developers included a button to click to access a new function. The function, however, had not yet been developed, so the button was inoperable. They would sort that out later. The corporate IT folks were appalled. This was just not done! There were numerous other examples. Frictions ran high. My intermediation skills were taxed to the limit. Whether things have changed, the philosophy of break it and fix it did not apply in the corporate world, at least not then.

The project was a great success in engaging a very large number of participants—two hundred in this case—across the company. The web-based approach worked well. Two key lessons emerged. One was to have strict deadlines for participants to make comments. This clarified the time frame for participants and a timeline for managing the project. The other was to have a strong supporting team to monitor the process, intervene when necessary to direct the discussion away from dead ends, and develop summaries at the end of each stage in the process.

There were two disappointments. First, the project developed insightful scenarios that could have been useful for the company in developing strategies. The project, however, lost energy and the planning team was never able to present the final results to the senior management team. Their impact, therefore, was successful in engaging a wide range of managers and closing the perception gap, but not in directly influencing direction and strategy. Second, the scenarios were global. We had not developed a focal question and this was a major weakness. Why? As the scenarios emerged in their final form, comments began to raise the question of relevance. What did the fall of the Berlin Wall have to do with TransCanada's business? Although the company was pursuing opportunities around the world, the major upheaval that had recently occurred did not resonate with company executives. This was a failure of the process. My resolution was to never do global scenarios again. All scenarios needed focus to be relevant. And I have kept that resolution.

Pets and Power

A fascinating project was one with Ralston Purina on the future of pet foods. The history of pet foods in the US was dominated by two developments. In the late 1950s, a researcher was experimenting with extrusion technology—like pushing pasta through a mold to make spaghetti—and accidently dropped some product on the floor. His dog gobbled it up. Dry pet food was created. Dry pet food provided a complete balanced diet, was easy to package and easy to use. Sales grew rapidly and Ralston Purina became the largest pet food company in the US.

The second development emerged in the early 1970s when the industry realized there was no limit to what pet owners would spend on their pets. The premium, super premium, and extra super premium blends, each increasingly expensive, entered the market. This was a boon to margins but allowed new competition to enter the market through new channels. Purina had focused on grocery stores and supermarkets to distribute their popular Dog Chow. Now specialty brands using veterinarians to distribute high-end pet food penetrated the market. Specialty pet stores would follow.

By the late 1990s the market had evolved with numerous competitors, both domestic and international, competing across a range of channels and brands. Two aspects of the business were important. First, it was an interesting marketing challenge when the consumer and customer are different. The consumer—the dog or cat—was critical. But the pet owner was the customer. For dry pet food the consumer was king. It was the taste not the look that mattered. For wet food, however, the look of the food was important regardless of how much the dog or cat liked it. It had to appeal to the pet owner, not the pet. Baby food producers face the same difficulty.

Second was the relationship between the branded manufacturer and the supermarket distributor. Power in that relationship was evolving toward the big supermarket chains. They not only controlled shelf space, they were increasingly encroaching on the brand itself by introducing their own private-label brands. This was a dilemma for branded package goods manufacturers that remains today.

The scenarios were highly successful in developing strategies for the company. A key insight was that new technology was emerging in the nutrition area. New formulas for big dogs, little dogs, young dogs, old dog, pregnant dogs, et cetera proliferated. A major challenge was to secure a cheap supply of protein to meet these varying demands. As well, the prospect of nutraceuticals in pet foods was on the horizon. Genetically modified foods were the forerunner of more advanced biological research to enhance the nutritional value of foods. Nutritionally enhanced ingredients would likely be used in pet diets before human diets. Ralston Purina needed an enhanced capability in biotechnology. Not long after our work on scenarios, they bought a company with strong biotechnology capabilities.

Similarly, Purina faced increased competition from global competitors who were using their strong position on Europe and Asia to support aggressive pricing strategies in the US. (This was similar to the Japanese car industry strategy in penetrating the US market in the 1970s.) Purina realized they needed to strengthen their operations in overseas markets to be more effective as a global company. That became a major strategy. They were a first-class company, progressive in their thinking, and able to act on the insights from the scenarios. Ralston Purina was purchased by Nestlé some years after these scenario studies were completed.

News without Paper

My work with Lee van Horn continued with a major project with the *Los Angeles Times* on the future of newspapers. It was a challenging and intriguing project. The *LA Times* was facing a major decision. The *Times'* printing presses were old and needed replacing. Should they invest literally hundreds of millions of dollars on new presses or not? A major factor in considering this decision was the rapidly expanding internet and new web-based competitors who threatened their traditional business. In that context, the *Times'* management decided to undertake a scenarios-to-strategy project to explore the future of newspapers.

Technically, the project was challenging, primarily because management wanted to engage a large number of people in the process. This started with the pre-workshop interviews. Typically, ten to twelve interviews are sufficient to exhaust almost all ideas and perspectives. In an effort to be inclusive rather than efficient, over twenty interviews were conducted.

In the next step of the process, the scenario-development workshop involved fifty-five participants. The scenario development process is not designed to accommodate large numbers. Breakout groups, for example, are usually facilitated by a consultant experienced in the process. In this case, the solution was to alternate large plenary sessions with self-directed breakout sessions. The breakout groups made up of four groups with approximately fifteen participants each, worked through a set of questions, recorded answers, and reported back to the plenary. At the beginning of each breakout session, one person would take the role of facilitator, another the recorder, and a third the timer. They would be given a series of questions to answer.

Groups were exposed to the ideas of advocacy and enquiry to improve the quality of conversation and the process of writing down ideas before sharing ideas. These were well educated and enthusiastic participants, a majority trained as reporters and journalists. Lee and I supervised, rotating from group to group. The process worked brilliantly. The introduction of the concepts of advocacy and enquiry were extremely valuable both in individuals accepting and using the ideas and in legitimizing us as facilitators to intervene when conversations went off the rails as they did occasionally. [46]

The group we worked with was highly trained in assimilating ideas and writing coherently. Many were writers and editors. Understanding this, we decided to use groups of writers to write the scenarios. Usually, we as the consultants wrote the

---

46   Lee van Horn introduced the ideas of advocacy and enquiry into the scenarios workshop process to improve the quality of the dialogue. He realized that one way of improving strategic conversations was to improve the quality of the conversations. His presentation on enquiry and advocacy also emphasized the importance of leadership and challenged the group on their role as leaders. These ideas instilled the importance of strategic leadership in developing and implementing strategic management in an organization.

stories and used the inherent expertise of the client to ensure their validity with respect to content. In this case, the challenge was to create a writing template with guidelines. The scenarios were written and thus owned by the client.

The scenarios dealt with the challenge the paper faced from web-based competition. The traditional business model involved two spheres of activity. One was the collection and generation of news stories. The *LA Times* had a global network of news offices and reporters. Historically they were a major international newspaper with an impressive reputation both as a news agency and as a political influence. The long, wide corridors of the *Times* headquarters were lined with pictures of editors and presidents going back decades. It had an aura of power and influence that was both intimidating and impressive.

The other activity was the dissemination of news via newspapers. The wide distribution was a vehicle for advertisers to reach consumers. That was the basic model. Use the news to attract an audience for advertisers. The formula worked for two centuries, and then the internet came along.

Revenue was generated in three major areas. First was the advertising space. This was used by a wide range of advertisers from grocery supermarkets, fashion and clothing retailers, car dealers, real estate companies, governments, and a range of other businesses seeking to reach a wide consumer audience. These full-page and half-page ads were called display advertising. The second major source of revenue was the classified ads. They created a market for the exchange of everything from cars to houses to apartment rentals to appliances to jobs. These typically covered many pages and were extremely lucrative for the newspaper. The third source of revenue was the obituary pages. These three sources represented a major and consistent source of revenue that was used to pay for the extensive world-wide network of reporters who assembled and wrote the news.

The model survived the introduction of radio and TV as competing sources of news. Newspapers may have lost their advantage in the breaking-news category but they were still a major source of comprehensive and reliable news in the late 1990s. The internet was different. The first impact was on the classified section. Upstart web platforms were more efficient at facilitating transactions between individuals and cheaper than print media. Online sites for car sales, real estate, and any good imaginable were taking over the role of the classifieds in exchanging goods and services. This was a blow. The second impact was the loss of advertising from traditional customers. The breadth and ability to target audiences via internet companies, Google being the emerging giant, meant that advertisers were shifting to electronic channels and away from traditional newspapers. In contrast, revenue from the obituaries was holding up. It seemed people still wanted to record their passing the old way.

Our scenario work was followed by an intense process of strategy development. While ideas for change were numerous, the *Times* executive could not see how to make money using the internet. Newspapers had been virtually free for a long time and news was free on the internet. Who would pay for news? They could not see how to use the new communication channel to create revenue. By default, they remained committed to the traditional newspaper business idea. Two decades later, newspapers are still struggling to generate revenues from the news they produce. A few have created a significant paying consumer base such as the *Wall Street Journal,* the *Economist,* and the *New York Times*, but most still try to survive on diminished advertising revenues. A recent development is the push to force major international tech companies such as Google and Facebook to negotiate and pay for local news provided on their platforms. This is a significant new revenue source for news organizations—I hesitate to use the word newspaper.

Building Relationships

Over time one realizes how important relationships are both in business and personally. In this case I had the most fortunate of connections when I met Jim Cooney. He proved to be a great business colleague and personal friend. He was educated as a philosopher, spoke a number of languages, and worked in a mining company, Placer Dome. He was a leader in championing sustainable development in both Placer Dome and for the industry globally. He was a key actor in developing the World Bank sustainability criteria for investing in the mining industry. He was one of the first to realize that sustainability meant more than minimizing the environmental impacts and physically restoring a depleted mining site. There was a responsibility to ensure sustainable communities after the mine closed. This combined environmental sustainability with social and economic sustainability. He coined the phrase "social licence," a concept now universally adopted. His leadership in building consensus through relationships led him to a novel use of scenarios.

Our first exercise was in Venezuela in the late 1990s. Placer Dome was developing a mine in Venezuela and wanted to build shared understanding of the country among both country managers and corporate executives and build relationships with local leaders. Jim's idea was to use the scenarios as a vehicle to bring together influential leaders in politics, academia, business, religion, and communities, with Placer Dome managers from the country and senior executives from the company, primarily from head office.

Scenarios allowed a dialogue on the future of the country without major concerns about the past. Cooney was the key organizer in identifying influential participants and bringing them together. He was the ambassador and magician who made it happen. I was the conductor. My role was to lead the scenarios process and maximize dialogue. Ultimately, the scenarios were less important than the dialogue. Relationships were established. Senior executives gained a much deeper understanding of the country and the project and local managers gained stature with influential country leaders. A major benefit for the company was a deeper understanding of what was needed for a successful project not only politically but socially and environmentally. Placer Dome executives recognized from the start that they needed to satisfy both the national government and local community to be successful. Mining developments had often faltered in other countries when taxes and royalties paid to the national government did not provide any benefits to the community where the mine operated. This was a recipe for disaster.

The exercise was successful in Venezuela (although the mining venture ultimately failed) to the point we repeated it in Costa Rica, South Africa, Tanzania (twice)[47], Dominican Republic, and Chile. The scenario process was magic in generating frank and insightful dialogue. The open exchange built up respect and trust. Jim Cooney, as the key organizer for Placer Dome, gave the process and company great credibility, which was an important element in the success of these projects.

Over time, the scenarios gained more importance. Initially, the final stories were valuable in broadening thinking but were not part of a strategic process. This changed when Jim connected the scenarios to the risk-management process in Placer Dome. This was a highly developed and sophisticated activity in the company. Beginning with the Tanzanian project, we developed a follow-up workshop with the Placer Dome management to identify and assess strategic risks using the scenarios. It was a detailed assessment of identified risks similar to a wind-tunnelling exercise. In some cases, the process identified new risks or new perspectives on known risks. Later we would use aspects of the scenario development process to identify reputation risks for the company. Working with a gold company was a new experience. They were a first-class company open to using scenarios in a new and creative way.

Mining, Minerals and Sustainable Development

In 1999, nine chief executive officers of some of the world's major mining companies met in Davos, Switzerland, concerned about a gap between mining practices and social values undermining the social licence. They initiated a project with the World Business Council on Sustainable Development to undertake a series of regional studies titled Mining, Minerals and Sustainable Development (MMSD). In North America, the International Institute of Environment and Development (IIED) was commissioned to conduct the study. The overall objectives were to: 1, assess the current state of transition to sustainable practices; 2, identify services to meet future requirements of sustainable development; 3, propose key elements of an action plan for improvements; and 4, build a platform for ongoing analysis. Overarching was a desire to influence government policy. One task of the study was to develop scenarios

---

47 A summary of the scenarios and their use was presented in Brummell (2008).

on the future of mining in North America. A colleague, Terry Harbottle, and I were hired to conduct the scenarios development process.

From the perspective of scenarios, the project was significant in three ways. First, it was challenging to facilitate. Unlike a single company or government department, this project involved thirty participants from a wide range of interests. These included representatives from mining companies, academia, governments, and a variety of environmental non-government organizations (NGOs). Historically, these interests often clashed. Fortunately, while such groups might disagree quite vociferously about the past, the future was a different matter. With scenarios, every individual could have their voice heard and their viewpoints and insights captured. Nevertheless, with such a divergence in perspectives, facilitation was challenging and exciting. One challenge, for example, was to ensure each idea was captured in such a way as to ensure the meaning was clear for everyone in the group. Implied bias or innuendo was not helpful. One aspect that made this exciting was the range of ideas. This was not a group that needed to be encouraged to think more broadly.

One of the more unexpected and powerful outcomes in facilitating this group was the expertise demonstrated by the NGO representatives. Their grasp of the situation and detailed knowledge of chemistry, for example, was impressive. The level of mutual respect within the group was almost visible. It is astonishing how bringing together groups that had often been antagonists could lead to greater respect and understanding when simply placed in a situation requiring open dialogue and shared conversation.

Second, the scenarios themselves were insightful. The scenarios framework is shown in Figure 36. Two observations are worth noting. One is the definition of societal values. The emphasis on trust and respect was particularly important in this exercise focusing on the mining industry. These elements have repeatedly emerged in projects since then. (This is a key dimension discussed in Chapter 10). Two is the insight from specific scenarios. Money Divides is perhaps most instructive. It describes a future in which the industry does extremely well financially, at least initially, but falters because it fails to recognize its social and environmental obligations. It is a scenario of hubris. (See Box 20). This was a mind-opening experience for several mining company managers.

Figure 36—Mining, Minerals and Sustainable Development Scenario Framework

MMSD Scenario Framework

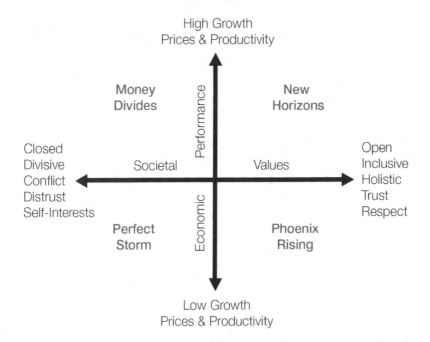

Third, the scenarios were instrumental in defining priorities in other parts of the project. For example, one task in the project was to define practical principles and criteria for design, operation, and performance. The scenarios were valuable in helping define these criteria. Another task was to create an agenda for change to meet future expectations. The scenarios provided a platform of future expectations to assess the effectiveness and timing of the agenda for change. Finally, a third task was to articulate implications for all communities of interest. Implications work from the scenarios directly contributed to that analysis.

Originally, the scenarios were seen as a distinct part of the project. As the work unfolded, the scenario work proved to be an integrating factor as the insights and priorities that emerged in the scenario discussions helped to define the requirements in other areas. An important lesson was the value of multi-interest groups to bring diverse views to the scenario process and how the scenario process could build new respect and relationships across multi-interest groups. Is that a win-win? Working with numerous associations and multi-interest groups since then, the answer is yes.

Box 20—Compelling Stories

In describing Money Divides, we used a story within a story to capture the essence of this scenario.

Imagine a small town in a remote area. A sleek business jet lands on the dirt runway. Four exquisitely dressed men exit the plane and step into a waiting car. They are whisked off to the local community centre or school gymnasium where they present their plans for a new mine in the area to a crowded room of local citizens. The Power Point presentation describes the exciting investment for the town, job opportunities and prosperity for all. A few questions of the effects of the mine on local streams, water quality, and tailing ponds are quickly answered. Then they exit, jump into their waiting car, head back to the plane, and disappear into the sky. Come and gone in two hours.

An exaggeration? Of course. But most people got it. It was particularly damning for mining executives who recognized that many mining companies had, in the past, disregarded local concerns such as the long-term environmental impacts. That, clearly, didn't work anymore. Stories within stories can be valuable in opening minds.

Sustainable Freight

The Commission for Environmental Cooperation (CEC) was established as part of the original North American Free Trade Association (NAFTA) to address environmental disputes not included in the main agreements. A second part of their mandate was to undertake research focused on environmental issues. In late 2009, they initiated a project focused on sustainable freight transportation in North America. Part of the work included developing scenarios out to 2030. My colleague Greg MacGillivray and I were engaged to facilitate the process of developing scenarios. It proved to be a fascinating experience.

The project was challenging in designing three workshops across three countries with upwards of forty-plus participants representing a range of positions and perspectives. Not all participants attended all three workshops. This necessitated flexibility in adapting the design to include review and updates for new participants. The range of experience and perspective, however, greatly enhanced the quality and diversity of discussions. The shared common purpose in exploring the prospect of sustainable freight transportation across North America and the range of perspectives generated rich discussions and insights. There is nothing like diversity and shared purpose to create insights.

The focus of the scenarios was to explore pathways to sustainable freight transportation. This put the emphasis on greenhouse gas emissions, primarily carbon dioxide (CO_2). The critical uncertainties in the scenarios were environmental impacts and technology adoption. Would the absolute level of greenhouse gas emissions from freight transportation rise or fall? Would technology be developed and adopted to reduce emissions, improve efficiency, and increase competitiveness? This meant the scenarios revolved around two key variables in a differential equation. Would the rate of economic growth increasing freight traffic demand, and hence emissions, be faster or slower than the rate of adoption of advanced technology that would increase efficiency and reduce emissions? Advances in technology should always improve energy efficiency and emission intensity, (e.g., emissions per tonne-mile), but would the improvement in efficiency be sufficient to overcome the increase in freight demand? If not, then the absolute level of emissions would increase despite the efficiency gains.

While policies focusing on climate change could impact economic growth, to a large extent this was considered an independent factor in the scenarios. Growth would either be high or low. The main focus of discussion was on the factors influencing technology adoption. This included adoption of technologies that would directly impact CO_2 emissions per tonne-mile and indirect technologies and investments that would improve the efficiency of the system. Direct technologies emphasized improvements in diesel engines as well as the potential effect of using alternative fuels such as LNG, electric, or hybrids. (Hydrogen was not on the horizon then.) LNG was a potential candidate offering significant reductions in emissions and reduced maintenance, thereby adding to competitiveness. The prospect of creating a continental supply network, however, was daunting. The prospect of electric vehicles or even electric hybrids in long haul freight was equally unattractive at the time (2009). Advances in materials and design offered more immediate opportunities for improved vehicle efficiency.

Indirect improvements focused on the system rather than the efficiency of the trucks and trains. This included infrastructure such as a new bridge between Detroit, Michigan, and Windsor, Ontario, or enhanced capacity between Laredo, Texas, and Nuevo Laredo, Mexico, two of the busiest transborder crossings in the system. The tri-country scope of this work emphasized the north–south corridors and transborder crossing as well as overall transportation flows. Beyond the physical infrastructure, a major aspect of the transportation system was the accompanying information system. Every truck, container, and train car needed documentation. This had major impacts on the efficiency of the system. Long lineups of trucks crossing at Detroit or Laredo signalled inefficiency in the system. This congestion, and subsequent excessive emissions from idling trucks, could be alleviated with improved information. Systems were being tested to shift to electronic manifests and apps to coordinate arrivals at borders. A shift to digital and enhanced information systems offered significant opportunities to reduce costs and emissions in a more sustainable system.

These insights were not particularly profound, but when articulated and explored in the context of potential future developments, they opened new thinking on what was possible. In one scenario, Destination Sustainability, which combined slow growth in freight demand and fast, integrated technology adoption supported by aggressive climate-change policies, the prospect of an absolute reduction of 25 percent in emissions was estimated as a feasible outcome.

With my background in energy, I could not see how this could occur. The great value of oil is its high energy density. In other words, the energy per volume is extremely high compared with other fuels. This is vital in transportation, particularly for heavy trucks and airplanes. To achieve anything comparable for natural gas (or hydrogen) required storing the gaseous fuel in high-pressure tanks. LNG, in contrast, depends on very low temperatures to store the liquid natural gas. Similarly, electricity is stored in heavy batteries undermining the load that a large truck could haul. I was a sceptic. Was I an expert locked into a narrow paradigm? I was even more shocked when several participants raised the prospect of achieving zero emissions by 2030. My mind did open; not to net zero emissions but to the prospect of a 25 percent reduction in freight emissions by 2030.

Time has proved the scenarios captured many of the changes that have occurred. Major advances in battery technology combined with integrated design of vehicles has led to rapidly growing adoption of electric passenger vehicles. Tesla is no longer an experiment. The era of electric vehicles seems inevitable. Will freight transport, both short and long haul, be far behind? The CEC scenarios were amazingly prescient in identifying a major issue—CO_2 emissions in transportation—and in societal changes well ahead of time. The scenarios anticipated a growing public concern about climate change, how that would include a focus on transportation, including freight, and how major policy initiatives would play out. There was considerable discussion of the effectiveness of carbon taxes versus cap-and-trade systems versus direct limits—all of which have been implemented in various forms in different jurisdictions. The scenarios heralded concerns about the environment, sustainable development, and policy proposals to address these rising public issues.

Smart Cities

These concerns about environment, sustainability, and policy to address climate change were central to another project. These were early studies on the energy transition to a low-carbon future.

In 2007 the Canadian government established a target to reduce Greenhouse Gas (GHG) emissions by 60 to 70 percent by 2050. While much of the discussion around reducing GHG emissions focused on the mechanisms such as carbon tax or cap-and-trade systems, another perspective realized that 50 percent of emissions in Canada came from urban energy uses such as heating, lighting, and transportation. To achieve the 2050 goal the end-use sector must be addressed.

In this reality, QUEST was formed—Quality Urban Energy Systems of Tomorrow. The focus was reducing emissions through integrating urban energy systems. Integrated smaller-scale distributed energy systems could reduce emissions but would require major changes in thinking, investment, and policy. This included not only the distribution of energy directly —transport fuels, natural gas, and electricity—but all the other complex systems of cities such as transportation systems, distribution of housing and population (land use), water, and sewage. How could these changes in these systems occur? The stage was set for scenarios.

S2S was contracted to facilitate a scenario-development project to open thinking on the future of urban energy systems. The scenarios provided the input to a major conference designed to engage stakeholders in understanding and identifying implications for strategies, policy, and actions.

The QUEST collaborative was a large tent. It included major national associations such as the Canadian Gas Association (CGA) and Canadian Electricity Association (CEA), numerous utilities, municipalities, and companies, as well as NGOs and academics. Scenarios were developed to build shared understanding of the range of future energy end-use patterns, systems, and markets as a basis for developing strategies and action plans. The scenario framework that emerged is shown in Figure 37.

The project had at least three major insights. First, the project was initiated through a collaborative. It involved the coming together of diverse participants representing often diverging interests. Gas and electricity associations seldom share common interests. In this case, they did. Developing scenarios that focused on a shared concern—reducing GHG emissions—brought these groups together and successfully reinforced the collaborative initiative. The collaboration strengthened the collaborative.

Second, the scenarios highlighted the differences in thinking about a low carbon future from the perspective of a top-down, large-scale approach versus a bottom-up, small scale approach. Gigawatt Kings, for example, epitomized the adoption of large-scale projects, such as large nuclear plants and wind and solar farms to drive down emissions. In contrast, Sustainable Canada and Hidden Joules focused on integrated systems and small-scale projects to reduce emissions incrementally but steadily over time. This meant designing land use to reduce car travel, using heat exchanges to take waste heat from one location to one nearby, or using geothermal energy to heat clusters of homes. The examples are endless. The exploration of these differences reinforced the strategic commitment to focus on integrated urban systems—not large-scale centralized systems—that would subsequently be married with the idea of Smart Cities.

Third, the scenarios reinforced the important role of policy in directing change. A major distinction between Hidden Joules and Sustainable Canada was the role of government in supporting change. In Hidden Joules, progress in integrating systems and reducing emissions occurs entirely from the bottom as individual municipalities, utilities, and companies take initiatives on their own. In Sustainable Canada, governments are active in supporting and coordinating the transition. Progress is much more rapid and effective. Manifesting this in the scenarios emphasized to QUEST the need to focus on building strong relationships with government to create supportive policy. Governments were important actors.

Figure 37—QUEST Scenarios Framework

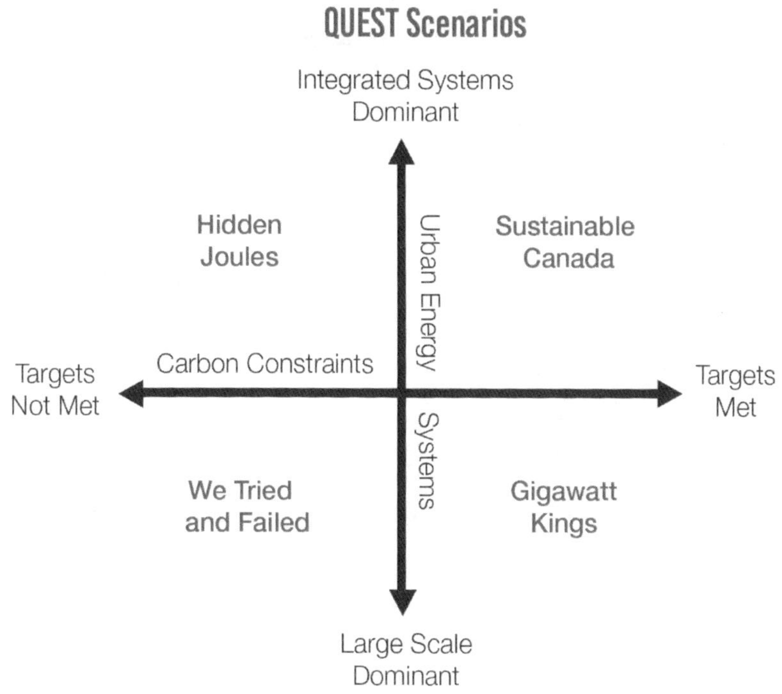

QUEST Scenarios

The project was not quite done. There was the need to design a conference to accommodate two hundred people. How could we engage everyone in understanding the scenarios and developing implications? The rhythm of plenary presentation and small breakout groups with a defined agenda and then reporting back to the plenary worked brilliantly.

A key learning emerged. The expertise in any audience is much greater than any set of presenters. Presentations followed by questions from the audience is a pale substitute for actively engaging in the discussion. This example used formal breakout groups. In many settings, however, an informal approach works. For example, after a presentation, pose one or two relevant questions and ask the audience to form small groups—four or five—and discuss the question among themselves for a few minutes. Self-organized groups seem to occur seamlessly. Then ask each group to report on their discussions. In short, engaging the minds of the audience is much more powerful than the traditional presentation followed by Q&A.

Pathogens and Systems

This tale focuses on the value of scenarios in designing a system to manage a health emergency from a mutating infectious disease. The focus in this case was animal health rather than human health, but the analogies with the COVID 19 pandemic are stark in retrospect. The project, undertaken in 2009, was commissioned by the Canadian Food and Inspection Agency (CFIA). The purpose was to identify future challenges facing animal health emergency management and to develop strategies to create a more effective, robust anticipatory system to meet those challenges. The project was unique in using two complementary foresight methodologies: 1, to identify future challenges and 2, to map the system and identify system requirements to meet the challenges.

Scenarios were developed to identify future challenges. The focal question was: Looking out to 2020, how do we build an effective, robust, anticipatory animal-health-emergency management system in Canada? Four stories were developed around two critical uncertainties (Figure 38).

One critical uncertainty distinguished between a stable array of existing pathogens at a regional scale versus an increasing array of new, mutating pathogens at a global scale. A driving force in understanding the potential of increased global pathogens in Canada was the prospect that known pathogens might be able to thrive in Canada because of the country's warming climate. In addition, new mutant pathogens were possible. Clearly both prospects were frightening.

Ensuring a robust emergency management system was a vital requirement recognized by the CFIA.

Figure 38—Animal Health Emergency Management Scenarios

Animal Health Emergency Management
Scenario Framework

The second critical uncertainty focused on societal values. One extreme emphasized a human-centric perspective with a strong focus on the economy and efficiency; animal health and welfare were secondary to human health and welfare. The other extreme emphasized a perspective in which human and animal welfare were seen as interdependent and convergent, with greater importance attached to a healthy environment rather than economics. This was insightful in understanding how different human perspectives could affect an animal health emergency.

Of the four scenarios, one is perhaps noteworthy in light of recent events. Safe Food Inc. described events in a future combining a human-centric perspective on societal values and the emergence of new classes of global pathogens. What would that world look like? Rapidly mutating pathogens lead to accelerating global outbreaks and public outrage. The focus is on human health and mitigating financial impacts. There is little concern for animal health and welfare. Relationships fail and knee-jerk government responses focus on detection and eradication of the animal disease. In short, there is considerable confusion and lack of coordinated response. Does it sound hauntingly like our COVID-19 pandemic experience? Of course, the relevance is clear in hindsight. The foresight was to recognize the need for a robust emergency-management system, to initiate a process to create that system, and to do that before an emergency occurred. Wisdom before its time.

Figure 39—Example of Systems Map from CFIA Study

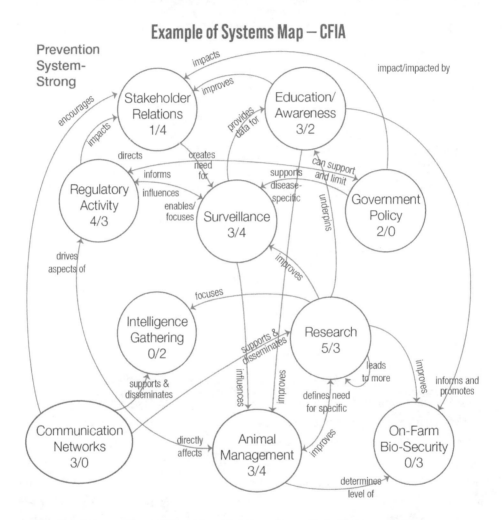

Example of Systems Map – CFIA

The scenarios were used to identify a number of challenges to the emergency management system. The next phase was to map the system. Systems mapping was a methodology developed by Brian Woodward (2009). It is a detailed process to develop cognitive maps of a system reflecting the common perspective of a group of participants on a specific problem or issue. The graphic is a systems map showing a series of elements and their connections. For example, in the prevention system, Figure 39, elements are shown as circles and connections shown as arrows. The arrows indicate influence. For example, regulatory activity influences animal management, stakeholder relations, government policy, and surveillance. In turn, regulatory activity is influenced or impacted by surveillance, government policy, and animal management.

The numbers for each element, for example 5/3, indicate first the number of other elements that are impacted by that element, in this case 5, and second how many other elements impact that node, which is 3 in this example. A connection can show impact in one direction or both. In this map, only strong relationships have been shown to simplify the map and highlight key relationships.

The visual representation of all the relationships among the key elements, shown in Figure 39, is complex. Analysis of the maps, however, allows key relationships and loops in the systems maps to be identified. For example, looking for nodes that are influential in impacting other nodes raises educational awareness, research, animal management, regulatory activities, and surveillance as important. They form a reinforcing loop of connections that are important in the prevention system. Elements that have an influence on many other elements are particularly important as they represent potential leverage points in the system. Strengthening a leverage point can have significant knock-on effects in the system. In this way, an intervention at one point, for example, improving surveillance in the prevention system, can have magnified impacts across the system. This is the nature of systems.

Figure 40—Animal Health Emergency Management System Components

The Animal Health Emergency Management System (AHEMS)

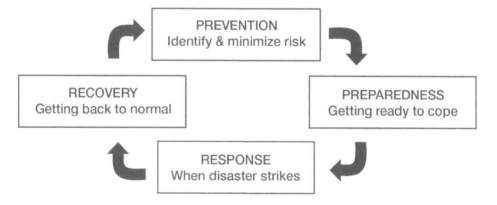

In this study, four subsystems were identified: prevention, preparedness, response, and recovery (Figure 40). These reflected participants' perspectives on how the overall system operated. The mapping process involved identifying elements in each subsystem and assessing how each element influenced all the other elements. This included direction of influence and strength. A set of visual maps were constructed for each subsystem. These were analyzed to gain insight into and understanding of the system and how it works. The result is a mapping of the current system.

The maps also highlight connections across subsystems that can be very important. The question then is: What needs to be done to enhance the system to meet future challenges? The future challenges identified from the scenarios were used to identify system requirement and design criteria. System requirements are qualities or characteristics that a system must display or contain in order to successfully address a strategic challenge. Design criteria are structural options that a system might adopt with the subsystem or across subsystems in order to meet the system requirements. For example, if a system requirement was to demonstrate the capacity to distribute information quickly, reliably, and continuously, then a design criterion would be to have strong, formal links connecting the processes of communications, intelligence gathering, surveillance, and education/awareness.

Another example, if a system requirement was to demonstrate the capacity to effectively coordinate the detection, control, and elimination processes with public stakeholder process, then the design criterion would be to create stronger communication links with primary response processes (linking preparedness and response subsystems). As these examples indicate, the systems-mapping methodology combined with scenarios is extremely valuable in representing and analyzing complex systems.

CHAPTER SUMMARY

My personal journey has covered three phases. The intent was to share my learnings and highlight the multiple uses of scenarios across a range of experiences. This varied from the perspective of an operating company to that of a global multinational linking companies across the organization to specific engagements as a consultant. These scenario-planning experiences ranged from web-based scenarios to pets to news to mining to freight to smart cities to emergencies. In all these cases, the central theme has been the use of scenarios as a vehicle for strategic conversation leading to better decisions and better strategies.

CHAPTER 10
MAJOR THEMES

What are the foundations of society? Some have argued that class is a basic dimension of Western society. Others emphasize the importance of race or income or education. If we review the dozens of scenario-planning projects over the decades, what are the major dimensions that emerged? Of course, each project identified critical uncertainties that were specific to that project. But there were a number of common themes that reappeared across projects.

In reviewing over sixty projects since the mid 1990s, three major themes emerged: social values, environment, and economy.

SOCIAL VALUES

A major dimension that emerged repeatedly was a critical uncertainty focused on social values, and more specifically on the tensions between the individual and society. This took many forms with different inflections. For example, the dimension was not always labelled as social. Often the dimension would be defined as political or economic. The descriptions of the extreme end points differed across projects, but the underlying theme was the tension between individual rights and responsibilities and the community or common good.

Examples are revealing. The individual-society dimension is evident in two studies of the future of the non-profit voluntary sector focused on social values. One, labelled societal values, contrasted the extremes of the critical uncertainty as individual responsibility for self and standard of living versus collective responsibility for others and quality of life. The other study defined a critical uncertainty as social complexity, with polar extremes labelled individual responsibility, self-interests, and linear view versus community focus, embracing social change, and system view.

A similar dimension is present in two studies of education. A project on the future of educational publishing defined one critical uncertainty as the learning model distinguishing one end point as a student-centred learning and individual focus model versus a teacher-centred learning group focus. A study on the future of advanced learning and technology identified learner expectations as a critical uncertainty. One extreme was defined as learner driven and individual choice as opposed to system driven and societal outcomes.

Two studies focusing on health care included variations on the range of individual and social values. One project on the impact of science and technology on the future of health specified one of the critical uncertainties as social values and ethics with polar extremes defined as individual values and decisions versus collective values and outcomes. Another study focused on future health care needs, defined a critical uncertainty as population health and self-care with one pole labelled engaged, self-management versus the other pole as disengaged, system focused.

A study on environmental futures listed one critical uncertainty as societal values with one pole characterized as individual focus, caring for self, and private silos, and the other pole described as concern for others and the environment with shared accountability. The Alberta Ecotrust project, described in Chapter 4, which focused on the future of environmental policy and decision-making processes, defined a critical uncertainty as stakeholder engagement with extremes labelled as polarized and private versus collaborative and public.

These examples are from social and government projects. The individual-society dimension is also a critical uncertainty in economic-focused studies. A project on the future of mining, Mining, Minerals and Sustainable Development in North America, described in Chapter 9, focused on a critical uncertainty named societal values with end points clarified as distrust, self-interest, and conflict versus trust, inclusiveness, and holistic. A study on the future of the pipeline industry defined one critical uncertainty as societal discourse with end points on the axis described as conflict, self-interest, and legalistic versus cooperative, common resolutions, and negotiated. In the same vein, a study on the future of thermal coal identified a critical uncertainty as societal and environmental values with polar extremes contrasting self-interest and internal focus with sharing and global perspective. Cohesive and collaborative versus divided and conflict is a similar description that has emerged in a number of recent scenario projects.

These examples display a number of variations on the basic individual-society dimension with different attached and implied meanings. One interpretation emphasizes responsibility: individual responsibility as opposed to collective responsibility. Individual rights, for example, also entail responsibilities. Although individual responsibility could include responsibility to others, this is seldom included. Similarly, collective responsibility could include tolerance for individual differences, but usually the interpretation is quite decisive in defining common good.

A second aspect of the dimension is the association between individual and self-interest. This is often viewed as a negative with self-interest associated with lack of trust, conflict, and exploitive behaviour. The collective, in contrast, is often viewed as positive, involving sharing, collaboration, and mutually supportive behaviour. (See Box 21 for an alternative view). When the individual-collective perspective emerges as an economic dimension, it invariably defines the individual extreme as competitive, focused on self-interest leading to conflict, and creating either efficiency on the "good" side, such as entrepreneurism and innovation, or chaos and destruction on the "bad" or undesirable side. Numerous scenarios have incorporated this thinking with revealing names like Wild West, Dog Eat Dog, Chaos, and Perfect Storm. All of these are real names in real projects. In contrast, there are few examples of the common good being viewed as negative with the system imposing constraints on individuals. The common good is, by definition, a good or desirable outcome.

Box 21–Security and Rights

An aspect of the individual-society tension emerges in concerns about the imposition of security measures at the expense of civil rights. The 911 terrorist attacks led to a clampdown on a number of activities, notably airport security. The public looked to governments to provide security and were supportive of increasingly invasive laws and regulations in the name of security. That trend has continued. How far should governments go in enforcing security measures at the expense of civil rights? This debate is ongoing. At another level is the tension between autocratic and democratic societies. Imposition of order by authoritarian regimes to ensure security and the public good is viewed negatively by those espousing democracy. In many parts of the world, notably Eastern Europe, there has been a long history of associating democracy with anarchy and disorder. As a result, authoritarian regimes have prevailed with public support. Populist politicians tap into this same theme, which often includes an anti-establishment component. Security and order versus individual rights and choices is an ongoing example of the tensions highlighted in this individual-collective dimension.

A third aspect of the dimension is the idea of choice. An individual's ability to make decisions and choose is implicit in the interpretation. In contrast, the collective aspect of the dimension emphasizes the lack of choice that individuals have. In some cases, this focuses on the perspective that individuals should not have the right to choose. For example, should an individual be allowed not to accept a vaccination during a pandemic? Or should the common good require the individual to be vaccinated for the good of the community? In other cases, the collective perspective emphasizes the limit to choices imposed by society. Is poverty, for example, a result of individual choices or the social conditions that an individual has experienced through life? Poverty is frequently viewed as a result of poverty as a child, limited access to education, living in poor neighbourhoods, being raised in a single-parent household, and generally being channelled to adult poverty by the social conditions that the child grew up in. It is not choice but the system that determines a person's future. My point is not to advocate for one or the other explanation but to emphasize the importance of the individual-collective dimension in clarifying different perspectives. Understanding these different perspectives is vital in understanding and reconciling different public policy positions. From a collective perspective, welfare is a morally right approach to supporting the disadvantaged. From an individual perspective, welfare can be supported as a means to expand an individual or household's choices.

A fourth aspect is a sense of action. A study on the future of newspaper publishing included a critical uncertainty defined simply as consumer. The extremes distinguished between active customized content versus passive general-interest information. The same element is evident in the studies focused on education and health. In both, one axis for the quadrants defining the critical uncertainties in the scenarios emphasized an active-learner or patient-driven future as opposed to a teacher or system-designed future.

The individual-collective contrast is an important dimension of society. It helps explain a range of important social tensions dividing society. At a global scale, the UN Human Rights Council is facing a challenge from China in pushing to rewrite language emphasizing state development over individual rights. Margaret Thatcher is famously quoted as saying that the basis of society is individuals and families: there is no such entity as society. This is in sharp contrast to many European thinkers emphasizing the importance of community and society and the need for individuals to restrain their personal interests for the sake of the common good.

At a somewhat different scale, another individual versus collective debate revolves around the highly emotional and sensitive example of racism. On the one hand we want all individuals to be treated equally without prejudice. This is a collective view. On the other hand, we want all individuals to be treated as distinct and unique. We want justice to be colour blind but preserve the distinct nature of Black or Indigenous or Chinese culture. These are dilemmas and tensions that reflect the ongoing trade-offs implicit in the tension of the individual-collective dimension.

ENVIRONMENT

**The 21st century will be the age of nature, when humans finally
come face to face with its limits and potential.
—Thomas Homer-Dixon**

A second major dimension that has been common across a range of scenario projects is the environment. The uncertainty has focused on public concerns for the environment rather than environmental outcomes specifically. An interesting feature of this dimension is how thinking has evolved over the decades.

Concerns about the environment can be traced back at least to the publication of *Silent Spring* by Rachel Carson in 1962. She first raised public consciousness of how the environment was being maltreated. When the Cuyahoga River caught fire in Ohio in 1969, everyone knew without question that something was wrong. Concerns about water and air pollution mounted. Mercury poisoning in Japan and Northern Ontario was part of a shift in focus from local to regional and from concerns about pollution of the environment to the impact on human health. The pollution from coal-fired power plants, cement plants, and other industrial operations, in terms of harmful air pollutants, intensified public concerns about pollution and health at a regional scale. A raft of laws and regulations designed to deal with these issues only temporarily slowed the rising tide of environmental concerns.

Increasingly, there was a recognition that piecemeal efforts to resolve single issues was insufficient. Fish dying in a river was a sign of much more than an accidental oil spill. It was a sign that the ecosystem was under stress. A much more systematic, ecological view of the environment emerged with increased understanding that this was not only regional in scope but often national or international. The Montreal Protocol of 1987 was aimed at phasing out hydrofluorocarbons and other substances destroying the ozone layer and threatening life on earth. This was the first environmental agreement on a global scale. This was the first recognition that human activities could influence the global environment. Concerns for global climate change mirrored this evolution. The interpretation is that climate change is influenced by human activity. If we have the capacity to alter the climate at a global scale, then we have the responsibility to manage the environment at that and all other scales.

Box 22—Nature: To Conserve or Conquer?

In December 1900, one of the most remarkable foresight studies was published in the *Ladies Home Journal*. The author, John Elfreth Watkins, had interviewed leading scientists and technology experts on what might happen in the next one hundred years. It was amazingly prescient. He predicted longer life (to fifty instead of thirty-five) with advances in medicine, sanitation, food, and athletics; kitchens full of electric appliances— stoves, dishwashers, coffee-grinders, and liquid-air refrigerators; fast food meals delivered by automobile wagons; trains travelling up to 150 miles per hour and automobiles making the working horse extinct; wireless telephones spanning the globe with automatic signals replacing the "hello girl," and photographs and images transmitted around the world in real time; advances in agriculture with strawberries the size of tomatoes and peas as large as beets; hydroelectricity replacing coal, which would be increasingly scarce; free university for everyone; microscopes able to see inside the body with rays of invisible light; elevated trains or subways replacing street cars; and aerial warships, forts on wheels, and guns able to fire hundreds of miles, transforming warfare. Although wrong on many details—agricultural advances in productivity were in quantity of product not size—his predictions have withstood the test of time.

One prediction, however, was remarkably wrong. His predictions on the environment reflected a view of nature as it was understood in the 19th century, not the 21st century. He predicted the extermination of all flies, mosquitoes, and cockroaches by eradicating all breeding grounds by draining all stagnant pools and swamps, and there would be no wild animals except in zoos and menageries. This was to be a triumph in technology in eradicating pests and controlling the environment. It was the triumph of man over nature.

Much has changed since 1900—or has it? The concept then was man conquering nature for the benefit of humanity. The concepts of conservation, ecological systems, and interdependence of human and ecological systems was not understood. The common understanding, today, is that all systems are impacted by human activities even to the extent of driving global climate change. It is our human responsibility and challenge to manage nature. We have more tools and different goals, but is the task today much different than that a century ago? Then it was to conquer; now it is to manage nature for the benefit of humanity.

Are these changes reflected in scenario projects over the years? My experience in the 1980s and early 1990s was that within senior management levels of corporations, the environment was viewed as a regulatory issue within the HSE silo—health, safety, and environment. This meant that responsibility for environment could be assigned to a department manager. It was seen as a compliance function within operations; it was not strategic.

By the late 1990s, environmental concerns were occupying more and more management time and becoming increasingly strategic. A scenario study on the future of nuclear energy defined one of the critical uncertainties as social acceptance. The dimension appeared in subsequent studies on the future of coal and oil sands. The uncertainty was not limited to natural resource companies. A project examining the impact of genetically modified organisms (GMOs) on pet food raised public acceptance as major uncertainty facing the industry. Would there be high acceptance of GMO foods by farmers and consumers or not? If GMOs were rejected by the public, a major change would be required to eliminate GMOs in the supply system.

The emerging reality was that social perspectives could drive political decisions, leading to constraining regulations. The risk was not in the impact of the environment but the impact of environmental regulations. Some companies viewed this as a lobbying issue. Others recognized the need to show environmental responsibility by responding to public opinion. Increasingly, the question shifted from how to respond to public concerns about the environment, to what actions would governments take that could impact the organization? The risk was in the potential actions of governments.

Concerns with government actions raised the issue of what to do and how fast to do it. This was particularly the case as climate change began to dominate the discussion in many organizations. In a 2005 study of the future of coal, a critical uncertainty was competitiveness. The most important factor affecting competitiveness was penalties imposed on greenhouse gas emissions, particularly carbon. The uncertainty for organizations was not whether penalties would be imposed but how severe penalties would be and how soon regulators would impose them. Would the penalties take the form of specific quantitative limits, e.g., tonnes of CO_2, or a cap-and-trade system allowing the buying and selling of credits, or a carbon tax? In each case there was uncertainty about how quickly and onerously such systems might be imposed. Interestingly, in all foreseeable scenarios, even quite severe penalties were not seen as undercutting the competitive advantage of coal (see discussion in Chapter 9).

A similar study in the power utility sector defined a critical uncertainty as environmental constraints. The extremes were described as low and deferred constraints versus high constraints imposed quickly. As with the 2005 coal study, there was unanimous agreement among study participants that environmental constraints would be imposed. The questions were: How? How much? When? Overall, the key perspective was that such regulations would be a cost of doing business that the company could manage.

Whether nuclear, coal, oil, or GMOs, the individual organizations viewed the environmental uncertainty as an isolated or separate challenge facing their unique situation. They recognized possible actions being imposed and developed scenarios on the impacts. In some cases, they went beyond the immediate impacts to consider how they could adapt. Technological advances were one possible response. Or simply they would find a way to adapt without being too specific. In a study of the future of agriculture, for example, a major uncertainty was economic diversification with the extremes defined as risk-averse versus risk-taking and adaptability. Climate change was a key part of the discussion. Farmers who were constantly adapting to droughts, floods, and other weather fluctuations would adapt to climate change. Or at least that was the accepted assumption among participants in the project. Details, however, were scarce.

The concept of environmental regulations continued as the key uncertainty, with problems fixed one by one as they emerged. But this began to change in the late 2000s. A study by Alberta Environment identified a critical uncertainty as societal values with one pole defined as individual focus versus the alternate pole as concern for environment and shared accountability. The concept of shared responsibility and accountability was part of a different emerging perspective.

For some time, there had been discussion of the trade-off between economy and environment. Clean air and water were not negotiable. Reducing pollution and preserving the environment could not be sacrificed for economic growth. Yet a vibrant economy producing wealth and jobs was essential. There was a push to overcome this false trade-off. People needed both. Was it simply a matter of compromise or something more fundamental?

Two studies in 2008 were instructive in how perspectives on the environment were evolving. A scenario project by QUEST—described in Chapter 9—focused on how Canada could achieve government-declared GHG emission targets for 2050. One critical uncertainty was whether carbon constraints would be met. In developing the scenarios, two broad approaches were identified in achieving the national targets. One approach involved the adoption of large-scale energy projects, such as the construction of major nuclear, wind, or solar installations. The other approach was through integrated urban systems: using waste to generate power or heat, integrating the design of transportation systems with development, sharing heat across building and upgrading the energy standards in all buildings. The key concept was integrated systems. The savings in energy and hence emissions were endless. The potential for innovation was unlimited. Or at least that is the perspective that has been reinforced with numerous examples over time.

The second study, conducted by Industry Canada, looked at the future competitiveness of Canadian industry. A critical uncertainty was perspective on the environment. One extreme emphasized the concept of compliance: the environment was a technical problem solved one problem at a time and controlled by regulation and enforcement. The other extreme described an integral perspective: environment was a societal issue requiring system changes that recognized cumulative effects in which environmental concerns needed to be internalized in all corporate, community, and government decisions. Compliance was the traditional view of many organizations. Set the rules, and we will adapt. The description of environment as integral to all decisions was different. The Industry Canada scenarios articulated a need to reject the idea of a trade-off between the economy and the environment. Society needed to incorporate environmental factors in all decisions. How to do this was more difficult. The QUEST work, however, complemented this integral view by beginning a discussion of specifics on how to implement an integral approach.

The evolution of our thinking on the dimension of the environment was not over. Two studies sponsored by Alberta Environment show a further shift in our relationship with environment. One study focused on the future of public forests. A critical uncertainty was biophysical capacity. One extreme was reduced capacity from floods, drought, and fires. The other extreme was high biophysical capacity, which could be achieved through well-managed forests. A second study on the future of energy and environment identified Alberta's environment as a critical uncertainty. The environment would either deteriorate with ineffective management or improve through effective management. Both emphasized that environmental outcomes were dependent on human management.

Over the past one hundred and twenty years, our perspective on the environment has shifted from something to be conquered (See Box 22) to something to be preserved—not polluted—to something to be conserved, to a broader ecological system to be maintained, to an integral system to be managed. In one sense we have come full cycle, from active suppression to active management. Scale has shifted from local to regional to global. We have now embarked on a journey to actively manage the global climate.

This new management ethos has challenges. A recent story from Britain is illustrative. A local region saw an increase in crows and a consequent decrease in songbirds. The crows were affecting the nesting and survival rate of the songbirds. Local authorities decided to cull the crows in the area to allow the indigenous songbirds to survive. Not all environmentalists were supportive.

One theme in the long environment story has been to preserve nature and let nature heal itself. Active management of specific species was not deemed appropriate. In Canada there are now active programs to protect caribou from the increased threat of wolves, following changes to the landscape from human activities. One program rounds up female caribou into an enclosure that is safe from wolves for birthing and protecting young when they are small. How far can this go? There are active programs across the world removing invasive species or managing indigenous plant populations. Major initiatives are underway to preserve and sustain coral reefs. This includes genetic modifications to increase existing coral's resistance to heat.

Another is focusing on the microbiomes that are integral to coral growth. Managing the survival of coral reefs around the world is on a scale similar to the ultimate challenge of managing global climate change.

The environment emerges as a major dimension of tension and uncertainty in society. It is central to the challenge of climate change and the energy transition— transformation?—from oil, gas, and coal to low-carbon renewables. Reviewing a range of scenario projects through three decades, the importance of understanding the issue of environment in strategic planning projects has increased dramatically. How we understand our relationship with the environment has progressed from an external challenge leading to regulations and the need for compliance to a much deeper, integral view of the environment and humanity and the responsibility that society has accepted in managing the environment, even at a global scale. How we do it and how well we do it is a major uncertainty for the future.

ECONOMY

Economic factors have been a dominant theme across scenarios projects. The most common critical uncertainty has been whether economic growth will be high or low. More advanced descriptions include changes in the structure of the economy. Others include some reasoning for the causes or factors determining the rate and structure of growth. Others focus in on prices, supply, and demand.

An early study on the future of Alberta defined one critical uncertainty as economic growth ranging from either low no growth to spectacular boom. The US study on the future of coal, described previously, defined global economy as simply low growth or high growth. In this example, global economy was a proxy for electricity and hence coal demand. A study on the future of pipelines defined the range of uncertainty on external growth and stability as weak economic growth and energy demand versus strong growth and stability. A scenario project on the future of airports and aviation identified an economic dimension simply as air traffic growth, either moderate or high and accelerating.

A second component of the economic dimension is the focus on structure. A study of the future of education-publishing identified industry structure as a critical uncertainty with simple extremes described as consolidated or fragmented. A study on the future of minerals and mining in North America described one critical uncertainty as economic performance with extremes detailed as low growth, prices, and productivity versus high growth, prices, and productivity. A study on the future of rural development in Alberta identified a critical uncertainty as economic diversification, with one extreme described as primary resource-based and risk averse versus diversified value-added and risk-taking and adaptable. A study on the future of higher education simply described economy as either commodity-based and cyclical or knowledge-based and stable.

As well as the rate of growth and structure of the economy, economic dimensions often include concepts of competitiveness and policy. The study on the future of coal emphasized coal's competitiveness against other fuels as a key dimension. A project on the future of public forests in Alberta included, as a critical uncertainty, the economic competitiveness of the provincial forestry industry versus other regions as uncompetitive with low prices, slow growth, and traditional products versus a competitive industry with strong growth, high levels of innovation, and new products. Not much was left unsaid in that detailed description. Yet another project, focused on the future of newspapers, identified a critical uncertainty as the competitive landscape becoming either fragmented across channels with low barriers to entry or consolidated in channels with high barriers to entry. Ironically, both developments occurred. The spread of social media created a low barrier of entry for competing sources of news while the shift to electronic channels created network effects that overwhelmed the local and regional basis of traditional newspapers. Low barriers to news sources coupled with high barriers to online tech giants meant newspapers were caught in a deadly trap.

As well as rate of growth, structure, and competitiveness, economic dimensions often include a policy or technology element. This goes beyond whether growth is high or low to a deeper probing of why growth is high or low or leads to new structures. A study on the future of innovation emphasized government policy as a critical uncertainty. The policy extremes were defined as laissez-faire with little intervention and high entrepreneurship versus active intervention with public and private sector partnerships. The underlying idea was how government economic policy was shaping innovation and economic activities.

A project on the future of resource development defined a critical uncertainty as global forces with extremes of protectionist-interventionist versus market-driven. Technology dimensions occasionally focus on the pace of development but more often focus on whether the technology is reinforcing or disruptive. This emphasizes technology's role as a major driver in economic structural change.

Economic change is a common theme across scenario projects. Economic growth is a measure of change that affects demand in many industries as well as the level of government revenues, which in turn affects funding for a range of public services. A key aspect of scenarios is to emphasize restructuring. How the economy or society could shift structure is a question that traditional forecasting methods find difficult. It is the heart of scenarios and is a frequent element of economic uncertainties. The focus on competitiveness is a specific example of concerns about how an industry could be restructured. For instance, Uber and Tesla have dramatically restructured the competitiveness of the car transportation industry. Further, some studies include the role of government policy in affecting both the rate and structure of growth. In all these cases a major dimension of society involves the economy in some form.

OTHER DIMENSIONS

As well as social, environmental, and economic dimensions of society, there are other divisions and tensions that merit discussion. One is political. Some political uncertainties are included in social, or environmental, or economic dimensions. For example, is policy focused on social and community welfare or economic growth? Policy and the role of government is central to descriptions of environmental uncertainties. And laissez-faire versus intervention is both a political and economic dimension. Political divides are undoubtedly a key dimension of society. I have largely subsumed them in the discussion of the other major dimensions.

A second major dimension is energy and the energy transition. The direction seems clear: the momentum toward a low-carbon future seems inevitable (a word never used in scenarios), but the pace of change remains uncertain. We are all likely to be driving electric vehicles by 2050 but how fast will that transition be? And the mix of energy supply and demand is uncertain. For example, what is the future role of hydrogen or nuclear? What are the limits to windmills and solar farms? How much space will be required and what are the implications to the environment from mining lithium, cobalt, nickel, and other materials? This is an important cleavage in society that is integrally connected to environmental concerns.

Finally, technology is the ultimate wildcard. We have connected technological change to economic restructuring, but that hardly does it justice. New technologies can be anticipated—like self-driving cars, artificial intelligence, block chains, or genetic engineering—but the impacts on society are difficult to anticipate. Scenarios are a vital tool in this area but are seldom used. The simple distinction most often used is between reinforcing and disruptive technologies. This is a useful starting point, but imagination and creativity are needed to explore the potential consequences of technological change. One caveat is important: anticipate unintended consequences. A contradiction perhaps, but it emphasizes the need to approach the future with an open mind.

CHAPTER 11
CONCLUSION

Recently, as we were throwing out some old *National Geographic* magazines, my wife happened to note an article from February 1992 entitled, "Smart Cars Map Route to the 21st Century.".

> Automobiles that navigate for themselves were once a staple of science fiction. But so-called smart cars are becoming a reality. . . Researchers envision dashboard computers that use data from the Pentagon's Global Positioning System in conjunction with onboard navigational aids. Digitized maps and synthesized voices would provide drivers with step-by-step guidance. Navigation systems are already available in top-of-the-line cars in Japan . . . Smart cars also will be able to receive information by radio from traffic control centers. The car's computers would then determine the best routes to avoid congestion. By decreasing idle time in gridlock, smart-car technology can reduce the volume of pollutants . . .

In retrospect, this is amazing. Its accuracy in anticipating advances in automobile navigation technology over the intervening thirty years is remarkable. What does it tell us about how we think about the future, how we understand the future, and how we plan for the future?

This example emphasizes the importance and power of foresight. Foresight is the capacity to anticipate, understand, and respond to change. Key characteristics underlying this simple definition are forward looking, intentional, and reflective to expand insight and understanding, interpretative in putting ideas into perspective, inclusive in dialogue and debate, and action-oriented in anticipating and shaping the future. Is our *National Geographic* item an example of foresight? Yes. It emphasizes our capacity to anticipate future change, to bring insight and understanding to what we observe around us and to shape the future. This example is what I call a memory of the future; it provided profound insights into how the future of automobile navigation could evolve over time.

Foresight is a broad process; scenario planning is one specific approach to foresight that has proven valuable in addressing a range of management and planning issues across a range of organizations. The value of scenarios that we have explored, derives from the product and the process.

The product is a set of scenarios, the stories describing a range of future possible paths and outcomes. These generate value in the context of the strategic-management model first presented in Chapter 1. The model incorporates the scenarios as part of a rational integrated approach to developing robust strategies for any organization, whether business, non-profit, or government. The scenarios articulate a range of different possible futures that provide a context for generating new strategies and analyzing those strategies, as well as existing strategies, to identify potential risks and rewards. In short, the scenarios allow the organization to identify the future consequences of current decisions. This is the powerful logic of scenarios that makes them valuable.

The process of developing scenarios is equally valuable. Actively engaging participants in scenario building creates shared understanding and insight. Shared understanding provides a platform for common commitment and action. Common commitment is vital in implementing any set of strategies. In today's world, it is insufficient to command action. Employees are educated and will not respond if they do not understand what the strategy or action is intended to achieve. This is the power of participation and engagement in creating shared understanding that builds commitment and alignment in implementing strategies specifically, and change more generally, in an organization. In short, the process involving the open exchange of ideas and insights in developing scenarios creates common ground and alignment.

Scenario development is a vehicle for strategic conversation, which builds shared understanding leading to better strategic decisions and actions.

The ultimate goal is not scenarios or strategy but better decision-making. The logic is clear; how to accomplish this is more difficult. How to practically and effectively implement a scenarios-to-strategy process leading to better decisions is a challenge. This goal is realized only if the scenarios are translated into strategies with clear goals and plans of action to implement the strategies and improve the performance of the organization. An important part of this book is to describe, in detail, a step-by-step path from scenarios to strategy to performance. This involves identifying strategic implications and issues and defining strategic focus areas, strategic options, and strategies with specific goals and actions. Clarifying this process from scenarios to strategy is important in ensuring the value of scenario planning is realized in supporting better decision-making by leaders in all organizations.

APPENDIX

EXAMPLE OF A SCENARIO REPORT

The purpose of this appendix is to provide an example of a written scenario report. This shows the structure and style in the template suggested. It is a template that has proven useful but it is not a formula. As with all scenario work, innovation and creativity are essential and the culture of the organization and audience are the most important factors in deciding how to present the results of the scenario exercise.

The example is Full Speed Ahead, which was one of the four scenarios (Figure A1) from the Alberta Ecotrust Foundation study described in Chapter 4.

Figure A1–Alberta Ecotrust–Scenario Frameworks

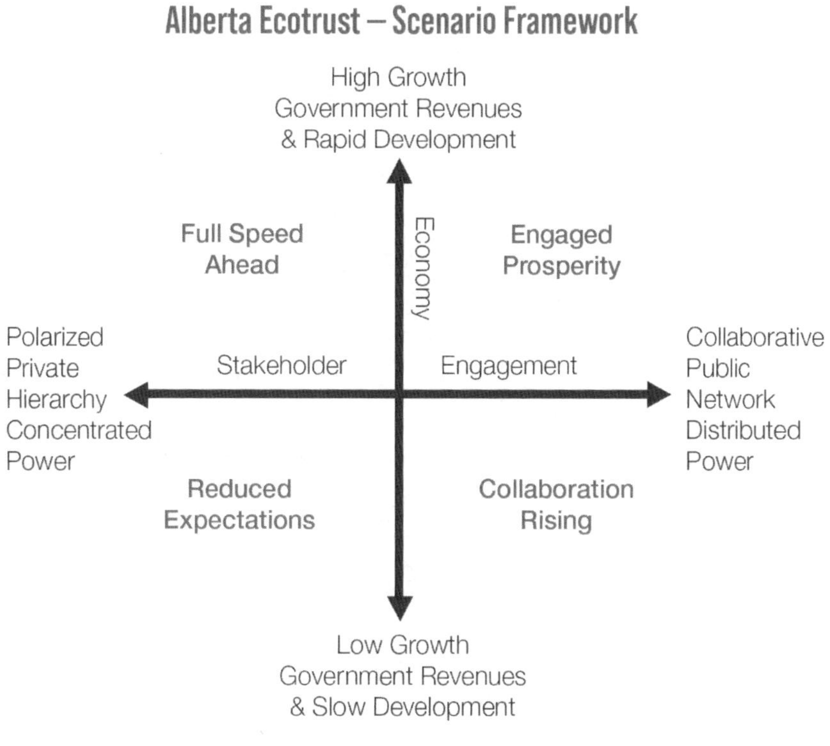

Alberta Ecotrust – Scenario Framework

High Growth
Government Revenues
& Rapid Development

Full Speed
Ahead

Economy

Engaged
Prosperity

Polarized
Private
Hierarchy
Concentrated
Power

Stakeholder   Engagement

Collaborative
Public
Network
Distributed
Power

Reduced
Expectations

Collaboration
Rising

Low Growth
Government Revenues
& Slow Development

The template for the scenario document begins with three to four pages introducing the purpose of the project and the process for developing the scenarios. This includes charts showing the driving forces (see Figure 11), and the scenario framework (Figure A1). This is valuable both as an introduction to new readers as well as a refresher for scenario participants.

The scenario descriptions begin with a one-page summary of characteristics across the four scenarios with each summary presented in its respective scenario framework quadrant. This gives the reader an overview before the individual narratives.

The narratives, as shown in Full Speed Ahead, begin with a short overview. This provides the reader with a summary of the main characteristics and thinking ahead of the more detailed story. The overview is also valuable if an executive summary is required. The introduction with the purpose and process along with the one-page summary of characteristics and four overviews provide the basis for a concise executive summary.

The overview is followed by the written scenarios. The stories are written from the perspective of an observer looking back from the future. The scenarios, written in the third person as a history of the future, are more believable and taken more seriously by the reader.

Getting started is often difficult. One useful approach is the use the first paragraph to connect the present with the future. Interpreting a known event consistent with the scenario anchors the scenario in reality. The same events from the past can be used in more than one scenario with different interpretations. For example, the Great Recession might be interpreted as a failure of regulation, and that theme would be a key part of the scenario. Alternatively, the Great Recession might be seen as a failure in risk management and overconfidence, which would be a theme in a second scenario.

A further feature in the template is the use of subheadings to break up the dialogue and provide a way for a reader to gain a quick scan of the logic. Subheadings are also useful in forcing the writer to clarify the logic of the scenario. The story provides a path over time with notional dates for each development.

The final paragraph is used to describe major outcomes for the scenario. While the scenario describes a path over time, it is important to have a clear picture of the changes or outcomes described in that scenario. This is the punctuation point for the scenarios. Make it memorable.

Finally, the template includes a summary of key characteristics at the end, the table of characteristics summarizing differences across the scenarios for all the original driving forces. It provides a detailed bullet-point description of the characteristics as a reference and as an alternative learning style for readers.

This is a well-used template that you may find helpful. Or you may incorporate variations that stimulate thinking depending on the culture of the organization or participants. The main thing is to continue stimulating strategic conversations with readers.

Summary of Key Scenario Characteristics

Full Speed Ahead	Engaged Prosperity
• High growth & resource development; rising incomes	• Steady, managed growth attracts investment; good standard of living & government revenues
• Economic values and private rights dominate	• New definition of "the commons" shares ownership of assets and problems
• Government supports markets & market instruments	• Government role to engage people constructively to develop new ideas
• Environment viewed as an externality; a technical problem solvable through technology	• Environment viewed as an integral asset and basis for all activity
• Major economic actors dominate; influence policy decisions	• Albertans / stakeholders empowered, engaged, and informed; enhanced science, social & economic knowledge
• External pressures deflected; seen as economic problem; minimum compliance	• External pressures addressed as they come but growth on Albertans' terms
• Policy development concentrated in cabinet & small elite group	• Social innovation creates high social capital and trust that modulates use of power
• Rising pressure on landscape and deteriorating environmental outcomes	• Landscape under pressure but integrated management improves outcomes
Reduced Expectations	**Collaboration Rising**
• Weak economy undermines government ability to manage conflicting stakeholder demands	• Low growth & resource development; criticism of environmental performance
• Government under siege leads to short-term reactionary decisions	• New reality leads to sense of crisis & need for new approaches
• Investment for growth dominates policy	• Recognition of interdependence of ecological systems & societal well-being
• Government conservative, risk averse & intolerant of criticism	• New approaches focus on collaborative models
• Multi-stakeholder processes seen as uncontrollable & dysfunctional	• Government commits to implement consensus decisions from multi-stakeholder processes

• Lack of resources contributes to lack of policy capacity • Industry self-regulation and streamlined approval processes using independent regulators adopted to deflect political accountability • Piecemeal environmental impacts; slower growth & development reduces environmental pressures, e.g., decline in GHG emissions & urban sprawl	• The public values environment • Virtuous cycle as stakeholders support consensus leading to government commitment and action; complementary cycle of engagement & trust • Learnings define criteria for success • New collaborative processes lead to improvements in ecosystems' health and society's sustainability

FULL SPEED AHEAD

Overview

In Full Speed Ahead, environmental policy and decision-making processes are unable to reconcile sharply divided views on environment and economic trade-offs. The attraction of jobs and rising incomes trumps environmental concerns, leading to increased polarization and conflict across stakeholders.

High levels of investment in energy resource development drive the economy and increase pressure on the landscape. The government presses ahead in implementing existing policies—Water for Life, Land-Use Framework, Clean Air Strategy 2012, Cumulative Effects Management System, and the Regulatory Enhancement Program—to manage environmental issues. Despite a range of challenges from local, regional, and international stakeholders, these initiatives are accepted as adequate. As a result, there is little investment in expanding internal government capacity in policy development or consultation processes, which leads to a breakdown of relationships and increased mistrust across environmental NGOs, Aboriginal groups, municipalities, regional groups, and other stakeholders.

A key factor is strong public support for economic growth over environmental concerns. Efforts to reconcile differences focus on economic approaches, e.g., seeing the environment as a provider of goods and services, that needs to be preserved and sustained versus the view that the environment is an economic externality and environmental challenges are one-off problems that can be solved with technology. The diversity of unresolved views creates conflict and frustration and puts pressure on the government to arbitrate differences and impose decisions that are often focused on simple, short-term technical fixes to mitigate effects, with minimal standards for compliance. Industry and private landowners are particularly influential. By 2023, the lack of collaboration and integration in environmental policy and decision-making leads to pockets of improvement but generally more sprawl, more GHG emissions, more disputes and litigation over water and air quality, more rural–urban differences, and more ecosystems at risk.

THE STORY—LOOKING BACK FROM 2023

Long Boom

The turn of the century saw the start of a long boom in Alberta driven by resource development. The rapid pace of development stimulated economic growth, jobs, and rising incomes. Immigration accelerated to meet employment needs. Prosperity, while not universal was widespread. The global recession and the sharp decline in natural gas prices with the development of shale gas, only momentarily halted the path of growth in Alberta.

Environmental Concerns

But a few dark clouds emerged. The rapid pace of development was raising environmental concerns. Locally and regionally, there were concerns about water and air and impacts on human health. Aboriginal communities in particular were increasingly mistrustful of and hostile to developments that were polluting ecosystems near their communities. The huge technical achievements of the oil sands were challenged as international ENGOs raised questions about "dirty oil" and the environmental footprint of the "tar sands."

New Perspectives—Old Thinking

Perspectives on the environment and management were also changing. Explicit recognition of ecological thresholds and limits raised the need to understand cumulative effects. This changed development project-approval from meeting standards for each project to managing the overall impacts of all development projects in that ecosystem. New thinking and new approaches were required but the process and models were unclear. Many key stakeholders active in consultation processes were often disillusioned by the lack of action and lack of influence in development decisions. By 2012, economic development and environmental protection were cast as competing adversaries in a win-lose competition. Which would win and which would lose? Were there processes and mechanisms to bridge the gap and reset the dialogue? Or would conflict persist?

2013-2015

Rooted in Development

The spirit of Alberta was pride: pride in having the fastest growing economy, strongest employment growth, highest incomes and lowest taxes, and pride in a frontier heritage that praised the entrepreneur, the landowner, and the rugged individual. Coupled with this was a deep love of the land. These were seldom in conflict. There was a strong view that economic growth and innovative technology would solve environmental problems. In short, there was wide public support for economic development and faith that environmental problems were manageable and solvable with creativity.

Centralized Decisions

Policy responses to environmental concerns were reflected in initiatives such as the provincial government's Water for Life policy and the Land Use Framework, which depended on regional councils and groups to design plans to ensure environmental integrity. Many stakeholders were disillusioned. Major development decisions, despite extensive consultation, invariably were stamped Yes and approved. Despite the seeming decentralization of decision-making, the reverse was happening. In health care, power was centralized into a super board of appointees responsible for supervising all public health-care provision in the province. In energy, power was concentrated in a single regulator.

Positions Harden

Outside of these policy platforms were Aboriginal communities and international NGOs. First Nations and Metis groups were increasingly disenchanted with the lack of consultation on projects that affected traditional lands. As development continued, the potential for reconciliation declined. Like the international groups, positions became increasingly rigid. For many groups the question was not how to do development in an environmentally responsible way, but how to stop development in any form.

Support for the Status Quo

As resource development and economic growth surged, the conditions for confrontation and conflict increased. One side emphasized the status quo. Strong public support for economic growth was reinforced by immigrants to Canada from overseas, who valued the employment and income opportunities provided with a growing economy. Alberta was a great place to work and raise a family, economically, socially, and environmentally. On the other side, activists pushing for change were appalled at this collective apathy. The reality was that the majority of the population liked the direction Alberta was headed. They were not pushing for change.

On the ground, the impact of development across energy, agriculture, transportation, recreation, and urban growth (sprawl) was accelerating. Scientific and anecdotal evidence was raising serious questions about the ecological integrity of major ecosystems. Such views were often undermined by contradictory studies and anecdotes that obscured interpretation. Among environmental groups there was a growing sense of urgency for action but this was not shared by government.

Private Rights

The provincial government was focused on implementing existing policies to manage environmental issues. As well as pressure from local, regional, and international groups, there was pressure from landowners and others who were resolved to maintain property and individual rights. There was resistance to public planning on private lands. Industry was also resistant to raising environmental standards and obligations. Protecting the environment was accepted as a responsibility but was viewed as an externality to be mitigated and not an integral part of their core business.

We Were Right

Further, the provincial government was focused on the economy and not the environment. The environment gained leverage only when economic interests were threatened, as in the case of the XL pipeline that was halted by environmental groups in the US. But eventually it was approved and the proponents of economic benefits were reinforced in their view that ultimately economic reality trumps environmental extremism.

2016-2018

Frustrations Rising

By 2016, conflicting views across stakeholders were entrenched. All parties were frustrated. Environmental NGOs were frustrated at the impact of development on the environment, the failure of environmental policies, and the intransigence of the government to face the need to change. Aboriginal groups were frustrated at the lack of meaningful consultation, rising health risks for many communities, and lack of respect by federal and provincial governments for treaty and aboriginal rights. Duty to consult remained more rhetoric than reality. Municipalities and regional planning groups were frustrated by the lack of direction, indecision, and input when decisions were made.

Lack of Capacity

The government was frustrated by the entrenched and uncompromising positions. Part of the government challenge was the lack of understanding of the need to invest in policy development and consultation, to build capacity for engagement, and to integrate policy across departments. The government was blind to these requirements and thus woefully inadequate in coordinating and facilitating the consultation requirements needed to have any effect on the escalating concerns and frustration among key stakeholders.

Economic Lenses

Government efforts to reconcile differences focused on economic approaches. Seeing the environment through economic lenses led to a focus on financial incentives and penalties. For example, viewing the environment as a provider of goods and services led to incentives for landowners to preserve environmentally-sensitive areas such as wetlands, a valued and effective, market-based approach. Similarly, discussions with Aboriginal communities focused on mitigation and economic benefits. But this did not resolve the underlying causes of the environmental problem. For many national and international environmental NGOs there was no room for economic trade-offs or compensation. Halting development entirely was the only solution.

In this political environment, traditional consultation and negotiation processes were completely ineffective. There was no agreement on the scope or scale of the problems, on the range of potential solutions, or on how to reconcile deep differences across many stakeholders. There were no process solutions to resolve these difficulties. And there was no basis of trust to try.

The result was that government, under pressure, was increasingly autocratic in imposing policy. The focus was on resolving immediate issues with direct solution, emphasizing technical approaches, mitigation, and compliance. Consultation efforts were frequently designed to approve, not question, solutions or raise wider system effects. Some policies set provincial standards; others allowed regional variation. Some were highly effective; others created unintended and often negative environmental consequences. All raised frustration with key stakeholders.

2019-2023

Despite the conflict among stakeholders and frustration with government, political support for government policy remained strong. The government followed public opinion. Resource development sustained the trajectory of economic growth, jobs, and rising incomes. Alberta was prosperous. With infrastructure in place to access markets east, west, and south, international challenges to Alberta's reputation were a hollow threat.

For most people, overworked and time-starved, environmental issues were under the radar or unimportant. Even with growing evidence of environmental degradation and signs that some ecosystems were beyond carrying capacity, there was little sense of urgency or action. Frustrated stakeholders resorted to litigation, campaigns, and protests but to little avail.

2023

Alberta has experienced a long economic boom based on rapid resource development. Deep concerns by many stakeholders about the environmental impacts have had little effect on the pace or form of development. With strong public support, governments have favoured economics over environment in almost all situations. Policy and decision-making became concentrated and centralized, less open to criticism, and focused on short-term solutions emphasizing economic compensation and mitigation to resolve differences. There has been limited investment in government policy development and consultation capacity. Without a robust environmental policy and decision-making process and without broad-based input or perspectives, systemic ecosystem-based strategies have not emerged. For environmentalists, crises loom. For the population, however, it is full speed ahead.

Environmental Outcomes

In Full Speed Ahead economic development dominates environmental concerns. Environmental outcomes reflect these priorities. Implementation of the Land-Use Framework and Water for Life continue, but outcomes are affected by centralized decisions and jurisdictional conflicts. The focus is on regulation, compliance, and mitigation whenever conflicts arise. GHG emissions increase, water supplies fall, and quality declines as agricultural run-off increases in many watersheds. Species extinction is a major issue as habitat encroachment affects a range of species, notably caribou in Northern Alberta. Urban sprawl takes over large tracks of agricultural land and urban air quality declines.

The following summary table allows the reader to compare the scenarios across key dimensions. These should include all the original driving forces that were defined as the key elements in any description of the future. Some dimensions have not been reproduced for brevity.)

Summary Comparison of Characteristics

Characteristics	Collaboration Rising	Reduced Expectations	Full Speed Ahead	Engaged Prosperity
Economic Growth & Development	• Low growth • Slowdown of resource development • New realism on future prospects	• Low growth • Slowdown from low energy prices & discounts on Alberta commodities • Frustration & denial of new reality	• High growth • Rapid resource development	• High growth • Managed/integrated resource development • Economy & environment interdependent
Public Engagement	• Increasing public participation • High interest in environment	• Active stakeholder groups • Frustration declining to apathy in general public	• Indifference and apathy to environmental issues	• High public engagement & demand for change

Characteristics	Collaboration Rising	Reduced Expectations	Full Speed Ahead	Engaged Prosperity
Role of Stakeholders	• Very active • Search for consensus • Motivated by government commitment to act on consensus	• Active participation; unwilling to compromise; high conflict	• High levels of conflict across stakeholders • Increasingly rigid positions • High frustration with government	• Constant tension of positions but willing to engage and change • NGOs challenged to stay ahead of public opinion
Social Values	• Environment highly valued • Environment & economy interdependent • Integrity and sustainability of ecosystems understood • Public goods valued	• Strong economic values; growth, jobs, and incomes over environment	• Strong economic values; growth, jobs, and incomes over environment • Private rights paramount	• New definition of growth and broad ownership of assets & problems • New expectations of individuals and their lifestyles

Characteristics	Collaboration Rising	Reduced Expectations	Full Speed Ahead	Engaged Prosperity
System Management	• New models incorporated into existing structure (e.g., Land Use Framework) • Limits, thresholds, cumulative effects endorsed & implemented	• Existing policy structures • Lack of commitment to environmental issues • Limits, thresholds & cumulative effects not implemented	• Existing policies seen as adequate • Limits, thresholds, and cumulative effects endorsed but not implemented	• Upgrading of CEM, LUF, Water 4 Life • Limits, thresholds, targets set, regulated & enforced • Limits based on science & community input
Role and Capacity of Government	• Limited capacity • Risk-taking leadership role in committing to listen and act on stakeholder recommendations	• Limited capacity • Siege mentality: conservative, risk averse, intolerant of criticism • Not open to risk	• No need seen to invest in policy and consultation capacity	• Create space for ideas and solutions • Open policy development support of local initiatives • Provide funding

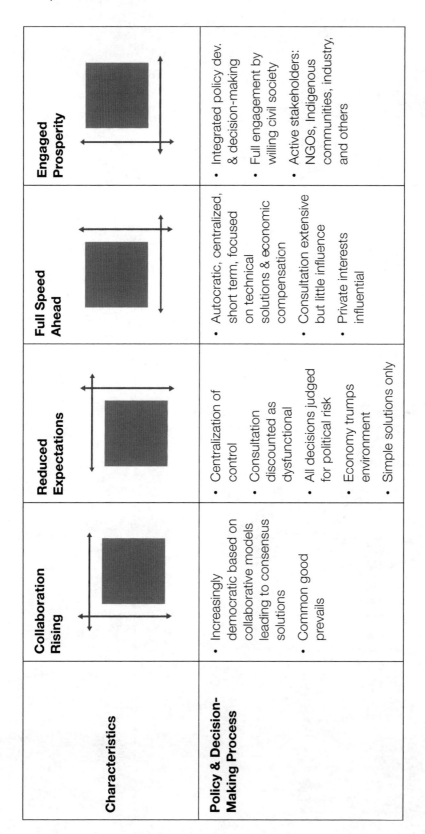

Characteristics	Collaboration Rising	Reduced Expectations	Full Speed Ahead	Engaged Prosperity
Policy & Decision-Making Process	• Increasingly democratic based on collaborative models leading to consensus solutions • Common good prevails	• Centralization of control • Consultation discounted as dysfunctional • All decisions judged for political risk • Economy trumps environment • Simple solutions only	• Autocratic, centralized, short term, focused on technical solutions & economic compensation • Consultation extensive but little influence • Private interests influential	• Integrated policy dev. & decision-making • Full engagement by willing civil society • Active stakeholders: NGOs, Indigenous communities, industry, and others

Characteristics	Collaboration Rising	Reduced Expectations	Full Speed Ahead	Engaged Prosperity
	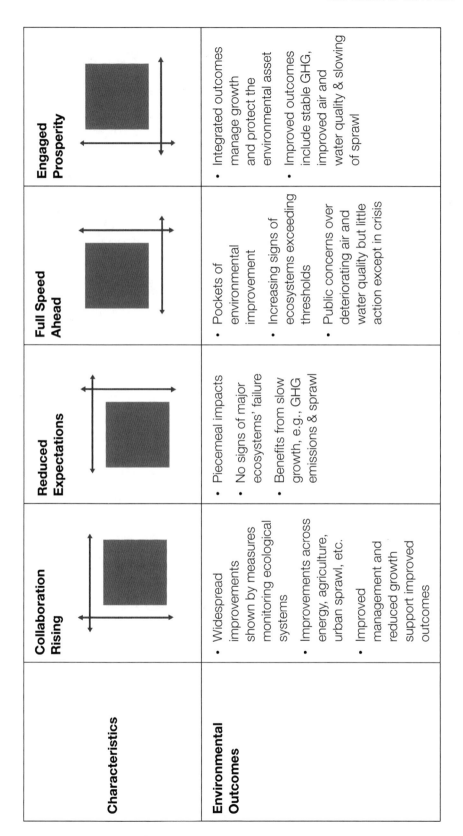			
Environmental Outcomes	• Widespread improvements shown by measures monitoring ecological systems • Improvements across energy, agriculture, urban sprawl, etc. • Improved management and reduced growth support improved outcomes	• Piecemeal impacts • No signs of major ecosystems' failure • Benefits from slow growth, e.g., GHG emissions & sprawl	• Pockets of environmental improvement • Increasing signs of ecosystems exceeding thresholds • Public concerns over deteriorating air and water quality but little action except in crisis	• Integrated outcomes manage growth and protect the environmental asset • Improved outcomes include stable GHG, improved air and water quality & slowing of sprawl

REFERENCES

Alberta Ecotrust Foundation, 2013. *Taking Stock: A Scenarios and Systems Approach to Understanding Alberta's Environmental Policy Development and Decision Making*, Calgary: Alberta Ecotrust Foundation.

Brummell, Arden C., Shaw, Sam and Hoy, Dave, 1999. "Strategic Dialogue: Building Scenarios at NAIT," *NAIT News,* Edmonton: Northern Alberta Institute of Technology.

Brummell, Arden C. and MacGillivray, Greg, 2009. "Introduction to Scenarios," Unpublished paper, Calgary: Scenarios to Strategy Inc.

Brummell, Arden C. and MacGillivray, Greg, 2007. *Scenario Planning: A Tool to Navigate Strategic Risks*, Edmonton: Alberta Oil and Energy.

Brummell, Arden C., 2008. "Case Study: Mining in Tanzania," *The Africa Journal*: 17-18.

Carney, Mark, 2021. *Value(s)*. Toronto: Penguin Random House Canada.

Carson, Rachel, 1962. *Silent Spring*. New York: Houghton-Mifflin.

Chermack, Thomas J., 2011. *Scenario Planning in Organizations*, San Francisco, CA: Berret-Koehler Publishers Inc.

Cooney, Jim, 2017. "Reflections on the 20th Anniversary of the Term Social Licence," *Journal of Energy and Natural Resources Law*: Issue 2, 97-100.

de Geus, Arie, 1997. *The Living Company*, Boston: Harvard Business School Press.

Gregorian, Hrach, Olson, Lara and Woodward, Brian, 2019. "Understanding Peacebuilding Coordination and Impact Using Complex Adaptive Systems Method," *Journal of Peacebuilding & Development*.

Hamel, Gary, 2002. *Leading the Revolution*, Boston : Harvard Business School Press.

Hamel, Gary and Prahalad, C.K., 1994. *Competing for the Future,* Boston: Harvard Business School Press.

Homer-Dixon, Thomas, 2010. "How the World is Changing: Complex Adaptation in a World of Turbulence and Surprise," Presentation at Science and Technology Innovation Workshop, Health Canada, Ottawa, August 2010.

Kahane, Adam, 2004. *Solving Tough Problems*, 3rd ed., San Francisco, CA: Berrett-Koehler Publishers Inc.

Kahane, Adam, 2001. "The Mont Fleur Scenarios," *Deeper News*. Emergyville CA: Global Business Network.

Kahane, Adam, 2012. *Transformative Scenario Planning*. San Francisco, CA: Berret-Koehler Publishers Inc.

Kaplan, Robert S. and Norton, David P., 2000. "Having Trouble with your Strategy? Then Map It," *Harvard Business Review*, September-October.

Kaplan, Robert S. and Norton, David P., 1992. "The Balanced Scorecard—Measures that Drive Performance," *Harvard Business Review*, Jan–Feb: 71-79.

Low, Ken, 2000. *Pioneer Leadership Journey*, Calgary, AB: Action Studies Institute.

Macklin, Lois, 2010. "Case Study Analysis of the Efficacy of Scenario-based Planning as a Public Policy Formulation Tool," PhD diss., University of Calgary.

Michael, Don, 1973. *Planning to Learn and Learning to Plan*, San Francisco: Jossey-Bass.

Mining, Minerals and Sustainable Development North America (2002). *MMSD North America final Report: Towards Change: The Work and Results of MMSD North America*, International Insititute for Environment and Development (IIED).

Mintzberg, H., Ahistrand, B. & Lampel, J., 1998. "A Guided Tour through the Wilds of Strategic Management," New York: The Free Press.

National Geographic, 1992. "Smart Cars Map Route to 21st Century," February 2.

Nelson, Ruben, 1993. "Four Quadrant Leadership," Presentation to Strategic Leadership Forum, Dallas, Texas.

Porter, Michael, 1980. *Competitive Strategy*, New York: The Free Press.

Porter, Michael, 1996. "What is Strategy?" *Harvard Business Review*, Nov-Dec.: 61-78.

Ramirez, Rafae, and Wilkinson, Angela, 2016. *Strategic Reframing: The Oxford Scenario Planning Approach*. Oxford: Oxford University Press.

Senge, Peter, 1990. *The Fifth Discipline*, New York: Doubleday.

Schoemaker, Paul, 1995. "Scenario Planning: A Tool for Strategic Thinking", *Sloan Management Review*, 36: 25-40.

Schwartz, Peter, 1991. *The Art of the Long View*, New York: Doubleday.

Schwartz, Peter, 2000. "The Official Future, Self-Delusion, and the Value of Scenarios," The *Financial Times*, May 2, 2000.

Taleb, Nassim Nicholas, 2007. *The Black Swan*. New York: Random House

The Canadian Encylopedia, 2006, 2022. "The Battle of Vimy Ridge."

The *Economist*, 2000. "A Finnish Fable." October 13.

van der Heijden, Kees, 1996. "Scenarios, Strategy and the Strategy Process" *Presearch* 1, No. 1. Emeryville, CA: Global Business Network.

van der Heijden, Kees, 2005. *Scenarios: The Art of Strategic Conversation* 2nd ed., Chichester, England: John Wiley & Sons.

van Horn, Lee, 1999. "The Challenge of Strategic Change." Presentation to Valvoline.

Wack, Pierre, 1985b. "Scenarios: Shooting the Rapids." Harvard Business Review 63, No 6: 139-150.

Wack, Pierre, 1985a. "Scenarios: Uncharted Waters Ahead," *Harvard Business Review* 63, No. 5: 72-79.

Watkins, John Elfreth, 1900. "What May Happen in the Next Hundred Years," *Ladies Home Journal*, December.

Wilkenson, Angela & Kupers, Roland, 2013. "Living in the Futures," *Harvard Business Review*, May.

Wilson, Ian, 2000. "From Scenario Thinking to Strategic Action," unpublished paper.

Woodward, Brian, 2009. "Systems Mapping: Purpose, Process and Analysis," personal communication.

ACKNOWLEDGEMENTS

At the outset, I want to acknowledge the tradition that this book is based on. First, I want to recognize Peter Schwartz and Jay Ogilvy from *Global Business Network,* who initially developed the scenario workshop process that I have used throughout my work and popularized the concept of strategic scenarios. Second, I want to emphasize the intellectual contribution of Kees van der Heijden at Shell, who understood the power of strategic conversation and need for scenarios to be relevant to decision-makers if they were to have an impact.

The origin of this book starts with the founding of *Scenarios to Strategy* with my colleague, Greg MacGillivray. He urged me to document the scenario and strategy-development processes we were using with our clients. He assembled the pieces into a coherent and consistent account. That initiative laid the groundwork for the book. Thanks Greg.

My early consulting work depended on two key people. Lee van Horn was instrumental in securing assignments and in refining important aspects of the work. His thinking initiated the scenarios-to-strategy process and the importance of advocacy and enquiry in strengthening conversations. Thanks Lee. The other client, colleague, and friend instrumental to my early work was Jim Cooney. His innovation in using scenarios to bring corporate and external groups together and create a basis of understanding was a valuable learning. His thinking enriches everything he touches. Thanks Jim.

Special thanks to Pat Letizia, President and CEO of Alberta Ecotrust Foundation for allowing me to use the scenarios on the future of environmental policy and decision-making processes in Alberta.

Drafts of the manuscript were reviewed by a number of friends and colleagues. Special thanks to Alan Blue, Lois Macklin, and Brian Woodward. Your comments and encouragement were welcome and valuable in improving the work. Special thanks to Marc Zwelling for his detailed editing and ongoing encouragement and insight. His patience never wavered as we created and discarded dozens of titles. Thanks Marc.

Finally, I want to thank my wife, Susan, for being there for everything in life.

Arden Brummell
September 2022